Feelbad Britain

Feelbad Britain

HOW TO MAKE IT BETTER

EDITED BY

*Pat Devine, Andrew Pearmain
and David Purdy*

Lawrence & Wishart
LONDON 2009

Lawrence and Wishart Limited
99a Wallis Road
London
E9 5LN

First published 2009

British Library Cataloguing in Publication Data.
A catalogue record for this book is available from the British Library

ISBN 9781905007936

Text setting E-type, Liverpool
Printed by the MPG Books Group in the UK

Contents

Introduction

The four authors of the first chapter of this book, a preliminary version of which was published online in February 2007, have all been involved in left-wing politics for upwards of forty years.[1] That chapter, and this book, were written as an attempt to apply the insights and experience of our political lifetimes to the history of the past thirty years – an era characterised, above all, by the ascendancy of neoliberalism, both as a general world-view and as an approach to public policy.

The period that more than any other shaped our political outlook was the 1970s, a turbulent decade that began with such high hopes for the left and ended with the triumph of Mrs Thatcher. As we struggled to understand the unfolding drama of these years and to respond with creative intelligence, we drew heavily on the ideas of Antonio Gramsci, whose *Prison Notebooks* became more accessible in the English-speaking world with the publication of a must-read new translation in 1971.[2] Gramsci's efforts to explain the ebbing of the revolutionary tide that swept across Europe after 1917, the rise of fascism in Italy and the resilience of capitalism in its heartlands, resonated powerfully with our predicament and preoccupations.

The editors of this volume still believe that the 1970s were a watershed in British history, and that our Gramscian heritage remains indispensable for understanding what went wrong then and what needs to be done today to tackle the besetting weaknesses of the British left: its ambivalent attitude to democracy, its workerism, its economism, and its failure to appreciate the role of moral and intellectual leadership in defending or challenging the prevailing social order and in winning or retaining political power.

This is a suitable moment to take stock. The New Labour project has reached the end of the road. Neoliberalism, on the other hand, lives on. It has, to be sure, been severely shaken by the

near collapse of the global banking system and the onset of what
is shaping up to be a deep and prolonged global recession. And
beyond these classic manifestations of capitalism in crisis loom the
longer-term challenges of climate change and the shift in the
balance of global economic power from West to East.
Nevertheless, the return of boom and bust and the end of light-
touch financial regulation do not in themselves portend an
impending change of regime. The struggle to replace neoliberalism, at national and global levels, is what the politics of the next
ten years will be about, just as the Great Crash of 1929 and the
Great Depression that followed it prompted an urgent search for
workable alternatives to the discredited economics of laissez faire,
leading, eventually, to a new international order – though only
after ten years of world-wide economic carnage and six years of
total war.

In Britain, it looks as if the baton of government may pass from
New Labour to a revamped Conservative Party, which has redis-
covered 'society', but remains hostile to 'the state' and continues
to idolise 'the market'. Conceivably, the Labour government
could tackle the recession by repudiating neoliberalism and
forging ahead with a green new deal. Thus re-invigorated and
perhaps inspired by the example of Barack Obama, Labour could
reconnect with Britain's own progressive past, rally the broad-
based popular coalition required to sustain a radical shift in course
and proceed, against the odds, to win a fourth term. But if the
pattern of the 1930s repeats itself, as Obama's election victory
suggests is more probable, the voters will eject a government
which has presided over a major crash. The further consequences
of a change of government at Westminster are hard to foresee, for
with nationalist parties in office for the first time in Scotland and
Wales, the future of the UK as a union state and the whole pattern
of British party politics are in a state of flux.

NEW LABOUR, NEOLIBERALISM AND THE
DEMOCRATIC LEFT

The central thesis of *Feelbad Britain* is that contemporary British
society is troubled and dysfunctional. Three decades of neoliberalism, extended by New Labour into the heart of the welfare
state, have undermined the institutions and social relations on

which solidarity, trust and citizenship depend and in which they were once embedded. Our sense of social membership and our shared identity as citizens have been effaced by individualist consumerism, the dominant culture and common sense of the age.

Structurally, the source of the problem is the social and environmental damage caused by the incorrigibly expansionist dynamic of capitalism. Historically, the malaise goes back to the organic crisis of the 1970s, when the post-war political settlement imploded and the radical right seized the chance to launch a neoliberal counter-revolution. In the absence of a countervailing hegemonic project of the left, the New Labour government elected in 1997 embraced the new order and, indeed, set out to complete Mrs Thatcher's unfinished business by placing public services on a quasi-commercial footing and driving market forces deep into the welfare state. As a result, after thirty years of neoliberal social engineering, there is now a gaping hole in British politics where the democratic left ought to be.

The British left today is a shadow of its former self, a diffuse and amorphous body of opinion with almost no presence in mainstream politics and little impact on public affairs. Not only this: there is also a marked gap in experience and outlook between the remnants and survivors of the old left and the new generation of green activists and counter-cultural campaigners. Of course, intergenerational misunderstanding and conflict is a feature of the human condition. But as long as the past is remembered, young and old remain connected by a common culture. By the same token, if historical memory fails, radical traditions are lost and radical politics flounders. If we are to fill the vacuum on the left, we need to retrieve our own history and reconnect the generations.

TIMESCALES

Clearly, a long road lies ahead for those who aspire to turn the democratic left into a serious political force. But the longest journey starts with a single step, and if this book turns out to be that step, other steps might reasonably be expected to follow. Before discussing these, however, it is worth outlining what kind of journey we have in mind and how long it is likely to take.

In a world where questions of economic and social organisation impinge on the very future of our planet, we need to distinguish four timescales:

- *the short run*: roughly speaking, anything up to twelve months from the current moment;
- *the medium run*: more than a year and up to about four years ahead, the length of a 'normal' parliament;
- *the long run*: extending over several parliaments up to, say, a generation or between twenty-five and thirty years; and
- *the very long run*: subdivided into the *human lifespan*, as measured by the expected lifetime of a child born in the West today; and *eco-time*, the timescale appropriate for thinking about eco-systems and the impact of human activity on the biosphere, which would normally be measured in centuries and millennia.

Our project spans all these timescales. Conventional politics deals only with the short and medium run. This is what preoccupies the political class and the media, their eyes fixed firmly on the next election. Inevitably, if this is your time horizon, you will be mainly concerned with trying to cope with the issues that are thrown up by the ongoing development of capitalism and the exigencies of party political conflict. It is the timescale natural to anyone who is primarily concerned with *managing* the existing social order. Of course, managing the system is difficult enough and may be done well or badly. But ever since the French Revolution, the left has aspired to *transform* society, an even harder task. And for socialists – once the core of the left, but now in the West almost an endangered political species – this meant working towards a post-capitalist civilisation.

Some of us believe that this should still be our aim. It will not, of course, be achieved any time soon, but this does not mean that the *idea* of post-capitalism has no relevance to the problems we face today. The reason we need to look beyond the short and medium run and think about life after capitalism is that if we do not, we shall simply be buffeted about and carried along by the prevailing winds and tides, rather than steering towards a goal of our own choosing. In other words, the left needs not only *policies* for the short and medium run, but also a *project* oriented towards the long run and the very long run.

Naturally, policies and project must connect. It's no use proclaiming long-term goals as the solution to today's problems, because that gives you no purchase on the current situation and simply means that other political forces will take charge and decide what actually happens. But neither can we afford to ignore the long run and respond to today's problems on a purely pragmatic basis – 'doing what works' in the current vogue phrase – because that does nothing to change prevailing social institutions, cultural patterns and power relations.

The distinction between the long run and the very long run turns on the difference between *transforming* capitalism and *transcending* it. At a time when US global supremacy is coming to an end and the neoliberal paradigm is being seriously tested, transforming capitalism involves, above all, a concerted effort to dethrone neoliberalism and install a new regulated 'social market' policy regime. Transcending capitalism means, quite literally, building a post-capitalist society. Undeniably, a wider range forces can currently be mobilised in support of a change in policy regime than will be prepared to work for the end of capitalism. But just as the left in general needs to look beyond the short and medium run, so serious opponents of capitalism need to convince their allies in the struggle against neoliberalism that if the beast is merely caged and not killed, pressure will eventually grow for the bars to be removed and the cycle of crisis, regulation and deregulation will repeat itself.

THE STRUCTURE OF THE BOOK

Chapter 1 below is a thoroughly updated and revised version of the original, on-line, stand-alone text. The argument falls into three parts. The first describes the main symptoms of Britain's contemporary social malaise, citing evidence relating to subjective well-being and the prevalence of mental disorders, and identifying those changes in the framework of social life which have damaged social cohesion over the past thirty years. The second part, having set out a theoretical framework to guide the subsequent argument, traces the roots of the malaise to the organic crisis of the 1970s and the neoliberal counter-revolution by which the crisis was resolved. New Labour, it argues, confirmed and deepened this regime change, introducing market forces and business norms into areas of social provision from which they had hitherto – with good reason – been largely excluded. The third part considers what is to be done and outlines proposals for revitalising the British left, challenging neoliberal hegemony and developing a political project aimed at creating a greener, fairer, happier, more democratic and less divided Britain in a greener, fairer, happier, more democratic and less divided world

Subsequent chapters expand on central themes and issues raised in the long opening essay. Five of these are written by the editors and six by invited contributors, whose enthusiasm for the project and whose discipline in sticking to strict word-limits and tight deadlines we gratefully acknowledge. We should also point out that neither the editors nor additional contributors necessarily agree with everything that follows, though all share a common commitment to stimulating debate about the future of the British left.

These eleven chapters fall into three groups. Chapters 2, 3 and 4, headed 'Directions', examine the distinctive values and ideas of the democratic left: the analytical framework we employ in thinking about the economy; our commitment to developing forms of social ownership as distinct from private- or state-ownership; and the arguments and prospects for moving towards a post-consumerist civilisation.

The next four chapters focus on Policies. Chapter 6 on the health service and Chapter 7 on education offer detailed critiques of New Labour's approach to public sector reform, illustrating the general case argued in Chapter 1. Chapter 5 on democratic renewal and Chapter 8 on climate change deal with areas in which New Labour's record is at best patchy and, in many respects, lamentable, but which are central concerns for the democratic left.

Chapters 9-12, grouped together under the heading of 'Politics', tackle what is usually known as the problem of agency. Three questions need to be distinguished here. What social forces have an interest in dethroning neoliberalism and transforming or transcending capitalism? What kind of organisation is required to weld these forces into a stable historic bloc? And what are the sources from which such an organisation, a new 'Modern Prince', might emerge? Since these questions precisely parallel those investigated by Gramsci in *The Prison Notebooks*, Chapter 9 assesses Gramsci's theoretical legacy and considers its relevance to our world. Chapters 10 and 11 focus on gender and the environment, respectively, as central sites on which the struggle for hegemony is waged. And Chapter 12 asks what we mean by left and right, whether this distinction is outmoded, in what sense the British left still exists, where it can be found, and how it can be brought together.

NEXT STEPS

None of the contributors to this book would claim to have produced definitive answers to the questions it addresses. The problem of agency, in particular, remains a conundrum in Britain, which for most of the twentieth century was a centralised, two-party state; even though this political system is now dying, if not dead, it continues to be very difficult for the British left to achieve even a modicum of organisational coherence. Nor is there any guarantee that any new formation of the left would make an immediate or substantial political impact. The point is to keep on trying, repeatedly probing the weak points in the neoliberal edifice in a bid to change the terms of debate and shape the course of events.

This brings us, finally, to next steps. If it is to develop the capacity for flexible, timely and creative political intervention, while at the same time elaborating and disseminating the various elements of its long-term project – convergent global development, Citizen's Income, social ownership, stakeholder democracy, post-consumerism and the rest – the Gramscian democratic left will need to develop a variety of networks, organisations and publications to articulate, defend and promote the values, visions and policy directions that we have sketched in this book. To begin with, the necessary work will have to be done on a shoestring and the results disseminated via the internet and occasional conferences. But once a series of further, more narrowly focused, publications has been produced by these means, we might hope to establish a permanent institutional presence and solicit regular financial support in the form of membership subscriptions, donations and grants. This in turn would lead naturally to the forging of links with other organisations, including political parties, both in Britain and overseas.

It will be hard work. But it will also be good work – in its aims, in the satisfaction it brings to those involved and, we hope, in its practical achievements. Worthy work, as William Morris argued, is inseparable from hope: '... hope of rest, hope of product and hope of pleasure in the work itself ... All other work than this is slaves' work – mere toiling to live, that we may live to toil.'[3]

Pat Devine   Andrew Pearmain   David Purdy

REFERENCES

1. Pat Devine, Andrew Pearmain, Michael Prior and David Purdy, *Feelbad Britain*, available on www.hegemonics.co.uk, 2007.
2. Antonio Gramsci, *Selections from the Prison Notebooks*, edited and translated by Q. Hoare and G. Nowell-Smith, Lawrence and Wishart, London 1971.
3. William Morris, 'Useful Work Versus Useless Toil' (1885), in A.L. Morton (ed), *The Political Writings of William Morris*, Lawrence & Wishart, London 1979, pp87-88.

1. Feelbad Britain

Pat Devine, Andrew Pearmain, Michael Prior
and David Purdy

The financial crisis of 2008 ushered in what could well be the most severe economic slump since the 1930s. The crisis had been maturing for years, though no one could have predicted exactly when it would break. Despite Chancellor Brown's claim that he had abolished boom and bust, both the global economy as a whole and the British and American economies in particular were seriously unbalanced. The long period of expansion that began in the early 1990s was based on a credit-fuelled consumer boom and ballooning house prices. Britain and the US ran up record balance of payments deficits as consumer spending sucked in imports that could no longer be produced in their de-industrialised economies. The ratio of consumer debt to national income reached unprecedented levels, while the deregulated financial sector invented more and more arcane and risky financial instruments – from sub-prime mortgages, through collateralised debt obligations to credit default swaps – which no one, not even their inventors, fully understood. In the end, most of the banking system went bankrupt and had to be partially nationalised. This in turn prompted growing acceptance of the need to re-regulate the financial sector, to take active steps to counter the recession, and to reform the international monetary system. It remains to be seen whether these measures will be temporary or whether the neoliberal era that has prevailed since the 1980s will now give way to a new era of more regulated capitalism.

Even before the crash, there was abundant evidence that rising material prosperity had failed to improve people's sense of wellbeing. On average, people felt no better off than thirty years earlier and some indicators suggested they felt worse off. With the end of the boom, what had previously been a general sense of unease turned into a high state of anxiety as people worried about their ability to maintain mortgage payments and to service debts in the face of rising unemployment and falling real incomes. The feelbad factor affected us all in different ways and to different degrees, but there was enough of it about to suggest a general trend across society as a whole, amounting to what we would characterise as a crisis in social relations and others have called a 'social recession'.[1] We were and remain a society of people who don't appear to like themselves or each other very much. Twenty-first century Britain, our country, is afflicted with a deep-seated and widespread social malaise. If we are to form a realistic assessment of the prospects for a progressive democratic response to the current financial and economic crisis, we need to understand the social crisis on which it is overlaid.

SOCIAL CRISIS? WHAT CRISIS?

As the twenty-first century began, a serious reappraisal of British society was also beginning, based upon the realisation that there was something fundamentally amiss. One example is Richard (now Lord) Layard's popular book, Happiness.[2] Its main assertion, supported by substantial and authoritative research, is that despite increasing material prosperity people are on average no happier now than they were twenty or thirty years ago. Sociologist Richard Sennett has written several books on the increasing strains of modern life, whilst there is mounting concern about the widespread incidence of clinical depression and anxiety amongst both adults and children. Little of this should surprise any normally perceptive person. Britain today is a divided and sour country. It can quite reasonably and properly be described as unhappy with itself.

Layard's group at the London School of Economics observed that 'crippling depression and chronic anxiety are the biggest causes of misery in Britain today', with one in six so suffering.[3] And this is a view held not only by this one group. There is also substantial evidence of high rates of depression and anxiety among young people – and you can tell a lot about a society from the health of its children. According to another appraisal, there are:

sharply rising rates of depression and behavioural problems among under-17s. The British Medical Association reported that more than 10% of 11- to 16-year-olds have a mental disorder sufficiently serious to affect their daily lives. At any one time, a million children are experiencing problems ranging from depression to violence and self-harm. What is truly sobering is how abruptly these problems have arisen. The incidence of depression in children was almost flat from the 1950s until the '70s. A steep rise began in that decade, doubling by the mid-80s, and doubling again since. The rises have affected both sexes and all classes, although children in the poorest households are three times as likely as wealthy ones to be affected.[4]

In a survey of twenty-one rich countries based on forty indicators, ranging from babies' birth-weight to how often children talk to their parents, UNICEF placed Britain in bottom place, just below the US. Young Britons fared badly in each of the six broad categories into which the data were grouped – material prosperity, family and peer relationships, health and safety, behaviour and risks, education, and subjective well-being – and fared worst of all in the sections on their social lives. Only 43 per cent were willing to describe their peers as 'kind and helpful'. Conversely, by the age of fifteen, 31 per cent admitted being drunk on two or more occasions and 38 per cent had had sex.[5]

There are other indications of serious social crisis. Under New Labour, the steep rise in inequality that distinguished the Thatcher years was checked but not halted, let alone reversed. The most recent figures show that Britain is now more unequal in terms of income than any year since 1961 when statistics were first published, whilst the number of those in poverty is actually increasing. Every index – income, property, health and longevity, educational and occupational achievement – reveals a less equal society than at any other point in modern times, creating a new super-rich elite, casting the lower orders into lumpen drudgery, and leaving everyone in between anxiously insecure. British society is made up of an overclass, an underclass and what we might call a 'de-class', unsure where they belong.

This is what Will Hutton some time ago characterised as the 'thirty/forty/thirty' society, split three ways between the securely prosperous, the anxiously aspirational, and the permanently poor.[6] Growing inequality damages everyone, not just the worst off. In his cross-national study of health in the 1990s, Richard Wilkinson showed how the health of a whole society and of every group within it suffers when income gaps widen.[7] This is a new, modern take on the old collectivist insight that an injury to one is an injury to all.

More recent research in Britain indicates a stalling of social mobility, so that people are less able to rise up our social hierarchies through personal talent and application. This ossification of social relations also seems to have set in at some point in the mid-1970s. Prior to that, there had been considerable movement both up and down the social scales of wealth and income, status and occupation, primarily because of new, wider educational opportunity. This was one of the undoubted benefits of the post-war social-democratic consensus, even if it also had the side effects of detaching bright young people from their families and communities, consigning the rest to eleven-plus failure and a secondary-modern education and, arguably, deepening the cultural impoverishment of the British working class.

Even the old social-democratic ideal of equal opportunity within a classless meritocracy has fallen away. Nowadays, wealth and status and the power they confer are being steadily accumulated by the already wealthy and powerful, and transferred between generations in a way not seen since Victorian times. Inequality in Britain is growing, entrenched and multifaceted. There is a rising clamour about this throughout British society, even extending to the newly cuddly Conservative Party. But the Labour government, under the supposedly socially conscious Gordon Brown, retains an almost religious faith in the benevolence of the super-rich.

This damages us all. The rich use their wealth to purchase privacy and separation, another markedly recent development. The retreat of our ruling classes from any serious notion of social engagement and responsibility means that Bill Gates-style philanthropy stands out as an exception that proves the rule. We still enjoy the legacy of public works commissioned by the morally conscious elements of the Victorian ruling class in sanitation and public health, decent housing, libraries and the beginnings of mass education and transport. But it is hard to identify any comparable legacy to wider British society bequeathed by our contemporary elite, unless we include such follies as the Millennium Dome and the National Lottery.

Consumer capitalism splits the rest of us into self-contained niche-markets and discrete, like-minded enclaves. We all have less to do with those 'others' who are 'not like us'. Conviviality, surprise and delight give way to suspicion, fear and gloom. The closing-down of meeting points between differences (of all kinds, not just ethnicity) – such an important ingredient in the vitality of any modern society – leads to the decline of the public realm and, more visibly, cultural stagnation.

Much of our popular culture is now imbued with an air of self-reflexive, nostalgic yearning. There is constant recycling of tried and trusted form and substance, so that only in the realms of high or elite art is innovation possible, and then at the whims and favours of wealthy patrons or the dispensers of what remains of state subsidy. This is why British popular culture today largely consists of repeats, remakes and re-mixes, paradoxically at a time of ever-proliferating modes and techniques of cultural delivery. We have a million new ways of saying the same old thing. The only apparent novelties are the freak-shows of celebrity and reality TV, sad and sordid parades of exhibitionists and attention-seekers, craving fame for its own sake rather than for any discernible talent or achievement. Even these are simply hi-tech versions of much older forms of ritual public humiliation and titillation.

With the decline of shared – or even inter-connecting – ways of life, experiences and values, we are all left to fend for ourselves, in our enclaves of class, ethnic or more loosely defined lifestyle identities. The upper and upper-middle classes do pretty well for themselves, as they always have done, with their extensive networks of social and professional support, at a time when societal forms of mutual support are being consciously dismantled. Golf club membership doubled every five years since the mid-1980s, while all mainstream political parties have shrivelled. Gym membership, presently at 14 per cent of the British population, is fast approaching the 16 per cent who belong to trade unions.[8]

Much of our new 'knowledge economy' of media, fashion and art, the so-called creative industries that make up an increasing proportion of our productive activity, relies heavily on US-style internship systems to perform the necessary but routine gofer roles that hold it all together. The interns are paid next to nothing and have to rely on the continuing support of their parents. These are confident, advantaged and well-placed young people, encouraged and recommended by their families and broader social networks. They will learn the ropes and then, in turn, rise to the top of their chosen fields and dispense the same favours to selected underlings among their own or their friends' offspring. It is effectively a system of bourgeois apprenticeships, at a time when openings for self-advancement for working-class kids – such as traditional craft-based apprenticeships or even decent jobs for school leavers – are fast disappearing.

The prison population – at an all-time high of well over 80,000 – has increased in exact proportion to the decline in secure facilities for the mentally ill. No doubt the old mental asylums needed to be closed, but without serious prison reform and rehabilitation of offenders, we are simply locking up our mad people without any pretence at therapeutic treatment, and then chucking them back out at the end of their sentences. More people leave the prison system with a drug addiction than enter it. There are currently 3000 children in prison at any one time in Britain, an 800 per cent increase since 1993 and the highest proportion in the developed world. Over thirty have killed themselves since 1990.[9]

Britain has the highest rate of premature birth in Europe – primarily, a Leicester University study suggested, because of stress amongst women in the mid-to late stages of pregnancy.[10] Stress in pregnancy has also been identified as a prime cause of learning and behavioural difficulties among children. We also have the highest rate of teenage pregnancy, partly because of poor sex education and sexual health promotion, but also because of low levels of general education and health, diminished expectations and achievements, and a quest for at least a kind of socially recognised identity amongst some young mothers. They frequently report, when interviewed, that having a baby turned out to be much harder than they expected, but that they thought it would give them some sense of purpose in life and 'someone to love'.

Alongside this, many better-off, older women are struggling to conceive, not least because many postpone the decision to have a child while they are working hard to establish their careers. Our general birth rate is in historic decline (although this may have been checked in the last few years) – a profound historical expression of loss of confidence in the future and a sure sign of chronic imbalance between the household sector of the economy, where human beings are born and nurtured, and the business sector, which is only interested in us as earners and spenders.

Levels of personal indebtedness in our credit-fuelled economy are at an historic high, while personal savings are at an historic low, something which has become a major economic and social problem as the credit-crunch bites hard. Most people now understand that good times do not last forever, and it is not surprising that opinion polls are revealing widespread worry and pessimism, reflected in statistics on family and relationship breakdown. Other indices of social breakdown appear in the quality press on a daily basis, and in more hysterical and simplistic terms in the sensationalist press, thus adding further layers of disquiet to our public discourse. Even Conservative leader David Cameron can refer to Britain as a 'broken society' without any fear of rebuttal – though his policies for healing verge on the risible. These trends can only get worse as the financial and economic crisis deepens and unemployment, insecurity and anxiety increase.

THIS IS A POLITICAL CRISIS

If there is a growing, uneasy awareness that Britain today is slipping deeper into social crisis, exacerbated by the economic crisis, there is less understanding of how and why. In the absence of any convincing alternative, people seek explanations in their own immediate surroundings and preconceptions – the alleged decline of good manners and civility, immigration, drugs and drink, hoodies and burkas, some basic flaw in human nature – but they usually identify what are, at most, symptoms.

We would argue that this social crisis has quite specific political causes within what passes for our political culture, now a largely degenerate and discredited arena which has itself become a major political problem. New Labour ministers endlessly recite a mantra of targets achieved, money spent, growth delivered and jobs created. Yet at the same time, these same ministers oversee a continual process of denigration, reorganisation and structural change, which implicitly denies any success in the past and offers only a vague hope of success in the future. No wonder everybody thinks everything is getting worse, even when it isn't. In the absence of much real political or ideological discussion or action about the future of our society, government needs a steady supply of 'problems' to 'solve', just to look as if it's doing something.

To take almost random examples: a new system of school examinations is painstakingly developed and agreed by virtually every responsible agency and person in the field. It is presented to, and then contemptuously rejected by, an education minister a couple of weeks into the job on the fiat of an adviser in Downing Street possessing neither wisdom nor authority, but with the ear of his master. Then, another new minister restores the rejected proposals, but removes most of their original purpose. Adding to the chaos, a system of testing imposed against the advice of most educational professionals is handed over to a private company which proves incapable of even marking the tests, whilst the minister suggests that the tests may be abandoned.

An energy policy is adopted which essentially lets the market have free rein. Then, within a couple of years a new policy is devised to allow the nuclear industry a bite of the cherry the markets will not give it. It is then discovered that a nuclear-industry consultancy was employed to carry out the policy consultation process. A new green turn to limit carbon emissions is announced without any reference to previous policies, which have in general served to increase just these emissions. The new limits are then wiped out at a stroke by projected aviation growth, which is just accepted as inevitable.

A large chunk of NHS services concerned with bulk purchase is handed over to an American company already under investigation in its home country for massive fraud totalling billions of dollars. We lurch from regional to local health authorities and back again, and express surprise at the resulting financial and administrative chaos in the NHS. An entire department of state is condemned by its minister as 'not fit for purpose' and threatened with being broken up, even as it attempts to carry through the conflicting and chaotic policy initiatives of its previous ministers. In a culminating farce, no fewer than thirteen government ministers support local campaigns against hospital closures that are a direct, planned consequence of government policy on NHS reorganisation: an extraordinary new twist on 'the politics of protest'.

In the midst of this confusion, ministers are appointed with new names such as 'Minister for the Third Sector' or for 'Communities', 'Social Inclusion', 'Innovation' or 'Business

Enterprise', as if new forms of government can be devised first by giving them names and then discovering their purpose. For much of its more than ten-year history, there has been no readily discernible principle or coherent strategy in New Labour government, other than a relentless determination to introduce markets or market principles into ever more areas of social life, whatever the cost. The result has been a string of unrelated and often contradictory initiatives. Increasingly, much of what government does from day to day is not even policy but a series of wheezes, soon forgotten after they have, it is hoped, achieved their purpose of an unchallenged TV sound-bite and favourable newspaper headline.

And why should we be surprised? New Labour has had remarkably little real, lasting impact on the country it purports to govern. Its period in office has been preoccupied with appearance, surface and spin. It has proved wholly conjunctural, to use Antonio Gramsci's useful distinction, rather than epochal. The only major exceptions are the wars in Iraq and Afghanistan, which have proved all too epochal for Blair, Brown and the rest of us. Otherwise, underlying the frenetic activity and spin, the continuing hegemony of Thatcherism (which was and remains a truly epochal force) has been explicitly accepted by New Labour, and given a further insidious and deepening twist, consolidating and extending the neoliberal agenda. This is what, beneath the spinning and the wheeze-ing, New Labour has really been up to. It is only when confronted with a real and immediate threat – like the collapse of the financial system – that minds are concentrated and the government comes up with an emergency short-term partial solution (to a crisis that Brown's own policies as Chancellor, of deregulation and labour market flexibility, helped to create).

THE NEW LABOUR STORY

The dominant common sense of our times runs like this. In 1979, a Britain gripped by economic and social crisis accepted the leadership of a strong right-wing ideologue, Margaret Thatcher. She pushed through a set of necessary, if unpalatable, remedies in the face of aggressive opposition from a die-hard left unable to recognise the necessity of change. In the 1980s the British economy was transformed, but society was deeply divided. The early 1990s was a period of drift, in which an alternative but ineffectual right-wing leadership under John Major failed to heal the country's social divisions. Then on that golden dawn in 1997 a new centre-left government, having repudiated the failed socialism of the 1970s, took over with policies that would both consolidate the economic changes of the preceding years and create a more inclusive and cohesive society.

This story has sustained the New Labour government for over ten years. It has become the unquestioned – indeed *unquestionable* – hegemonic principle of our times, the backdrop to the tide of daily news and comment. But it ignores two fundamental problems. First, the British economy today is more exposed to destabilising external forces than at any other point in its recent history, and than any other major economy. The decline of manufacturing has been accepted as necessary whilst financial services have been praised as a mark of international excellence. This was accepted without question as an irresistible consequence of market forces, even though no other country allowed its financial sector quite such licence. Indeed, ironically enough, a CBI leader recently pointed out approvingly that Britain is uniquely exposed to globalisation and chided the rest of the world, including the US and all other European countries, for clinging onto outdated forms of national protectionism.[11]

Second, however, and more central to our argument here, has been the deliberate extension of market forces into all aspects of social life. This is the main cause of Britain's social malaise. There has been a basic contradiction at the heart of New Labour policy. Under the rigid control of Blair and Brown, variations of the market principle have been driven into all areas of British life, creating the very social tensions other policies purport to remedy. The result, far from 'government that works', is government that is almost totally dysfunctional. This is what explains the policy-itis, spin and wheezes – increasingly desperate attempts to square this circle.

As effective government fails, its obverse – a knee-jerk authoritarianism – becomes more obvious, a further extension of Thatcherism. From the very beginning Thatcher specifically targeted any centre of power outside central government, whether voluntary, such as trade unions, or elected, such as local councils. She routed the miners, using orchestrated police violence in a manner that was unprecedented in post-war Britain, casting a long shadow over large parts of the country and its population. She overcame resistance from elected councils by a combination of centralised administrative and financial diktat. This meant, in the case of the Greater London Council (GLC) and Inner London Education Authority (ILEA), simply abolishing them. Elsewhere local democracy was fatally undermined by capping the budgets of local councils and dismissing resisters, including New Labour luminaries David Blunkett and Margaret Hodge, as the 'loony left'.

Local councils became little more than branch offices of central government and, in whatever political function they retained, pointless talking-shops. In inner-city Britain, Thatcher resisted outright civil uprising by physical force and racist policing. In all these cases her government introduced, none too subtly, the idea of the 'enemy within', the forces which oppose all things proper and British and are traitorous to the British way of life. In the end, Thatcher was brought down by the inner-party machinations of Conservative MPs worried about retaining their seats in the face of widespread opposition to the poll tax, but her ideological legacy lives on.

Labour manifestos from 1983 onwards all included some form of resistance to this imposition of central authoritarian control. Even in 1997, Scottish and Welsh devolution, an elected London assembly, and a vague resolve to reverse some anti-union legislation remained. New Labour was unable to dodge these commitments entirely, despite the evident distaste for them felt by both Blair and Brown. However, the results of devolved elections provided nasty surprises, and in response New Labour developed the same attitude as Thatcher had had towards any concentration of power outside Downing Street. This time, though, it lacked any clear, easy targets or institutional scapegoats, given the wasteland created in civil society and the public sector over the previous two decades.

Rhetorically at least, New Labour chose to pursue the same internal enemies – the unions, public sector workers, the poor, though these had been left much chastened and weakened by Thatcherism, and to court the same allies in big business. The refusal to contemplate any significant change in the legal framework of employment relations was one feature of this. But its main objective has always been to limit and where possible diminish the power of agencies outside central government. Blair famously claimed that the entrenched power of professionals in the public services had stymied his plans to modernise them, leaving him with 'scars on his back'. Successive education ministers, from Blunkett to Balls, have made it clear that they regard teachers as the problem, and some grotesque form of market forces (targets, league-tables, parental choice, academies and so on) as the solution.

Financial control over local authorities and other semi-autonomous spending agents has been extended beyond the capping introduced by Thatcher. Brown brought in much more complex and detailed measures, including ring-fencing and the panoply of 'service-level agreements'; most notoriously, he introduced various forms of private financing in order to keep public debt-obligations off the public sector borrowing statistics. There is little evidence that Private Finance Initiatives (PFIs) yield any public benefit in return for massive long-term commitments of public funding, whilst obvious defects in their terms are simply ignored. It cost £455 million in external fees to set up the PFI contracts for London Underground, when a virtually cost-free financing alternative was on the table. The problem was that it would have augmented the authority of a power-centre outside central government. The private-sector alternative then collapsed and, lo, it was discovered that it was the public purse that bore the ultimate risk after all, and a further £2 billion then floated out of the Treasury. There is much talk in New Labour circles of 'the new localism' and of 'empowering communities'. But without any practical steps to release central financial control, this is just another example of the government saying one thing and doing quite another.

Accompanying this centralism has been continuation of another of the key impulses of Thatcherism, the identification of the 'other', the 'enemy within', alleged to threaten some British way of life. This now includes the key Thatcherite ideological folk-devil of the scrounger, the hard core of benefit claimants who, according to the then minister responsible, John Hutton, 'can work but won't work'. The gradual assumption of a *Daily Mail* agenda, obsessed with the threat of aliens of all kinds, has also shifted the focus, moving from asylum seekers to illegal immigrants and, most recently, to all immigrants. Thus John Reid sought to blame them for defects in local education and health service provision, without the slightest supporting evidence.

Some types and levels of immigration can place a real strain on parts of our social fabric. New immigrants inevitably gravitate towards neighbourhoods and areas where poor people are already clustered and compete with them for low-wage and semi- or un-skilled work. This is the experiential basis for xenophobic and racist prejudice and violence, and for the revived political fortunes of groups like the BNP. Political renewal and measures to combat inequality and social fragmentation would remove this experiential basis for racism, but in the meantime real inter-ethnic tensions have to be carefully acknowledged and resolved. To acknowledge this, however, is not to excuse Labour politicians who pander to such grievances. Brown's slogan, 'British jobs for British workers', marked a new low, stolen not from the Conservatives, but from the BNP.

A similar racism has underpinned the demonisation of Muslims, so that even a Deputy Commissioner of the Metropolitan Police felt it necessary to protest, while civil liberties are whittled away to the point where the judges seem to be our best bulwark against arbitrary detention. Another insidious 'other', created by a combination of a malign press and a government clinging to any explanation for social problems other than its own actions, is the hooded youth. The nation's adolescents, barely out of childhood, are now supposed – despite an eight-fold rise in their numbers in jail, and constant proclamations of their improved efforts and achievements at school – to be at the root of the generalised fear and uncertainty that mar the lives of many individuals and communities. The old-fashioned clip round the ear has been replaced by the ASBO, which the warped logic of our fractious and fractured society then converts into a badge of honour among many of its recipients.

War, terror, economic and social threat and environmental doom have become the commonplace of news headlines. We are encouraged to believe that we have very little protection against looming Armageddon. For the last twenty-nine years, the social infrastructure of solidarity and support in Britain has been systematically stripped away and undermined. Trade unions, social housing, welfare systems – all have been reduced to shadows of what they were even thirty years ago. Education and health have been turned into competitive pseudo-markets in which, to quote Sennett on health, 'the reformers are impatient with the messy realities of being ill; they instead treat the sick like entrepreneurs'.[12]

Sennett's comment is specifically aimed at American health policy, though, like so much about the US, it is now readily applicable to British experience. Indeed, this approach was eventually explicitly adopted by New Labour, with the Department of Health advocating a move towards 'patients as entrepreneurs'.[13] However, Sennett also has a more general comment about the New Labour project, which he suggests has produced anxiety that could be described as 'ontological insecurity', a term he derives from Margaret Mahler:[14] 'This is not a piece of jargon; she [Mahler] aims to describe the fear of what will happen even if no disaster looms. Anxiety of this sort is also called "free-floating" to indicate that someone keeps worrying even when he or she has nothing to fear in a specific situation'. Feelbad Britain is beset with such free-floating anxiety, now complemented by the real fears and anxieties arising from the current financial and economic crisis.

ONTOLOGICAL INSECURITY

It is reasonable to suppose that ontological insecurity, fear without any real cause, is compounded when real disasters loom. The furore about climate change provides a good example. For over ten years, the government has treated environmental issues as peripheral. Policies such as green taxes have been studiously ignored or, as in the case of fuel taxes, actually reversed. The result is that when the scale of the disaster of climate change becomes obvious in the weather we all live with, as well as in increasingly conclusive scientific research, there are neither policies nor mechanisms available even to begin to cope with it. Alarming rhetoric abounds, Prime Minister Brown advocates a speedy agreement on what is to succeed the Kyoto agreement, but the government remains trapped by its own ideological bias and political habits.

The social crisis of Britain is real and close to hand. It has been carefully documented in terms of mental disorder and anxiety. But if it is treated in terms of individual psychology, it can easily be dismissed as pathological. The responsibility can then be laid at the door of inadequate or disordered individuals, who are blamed for letting themselves – or in a subsidiary moral panic, their children – become fat, ill, incapacitated, old, sad and lonely, or simply defective. The remedies proposed usually involve similarly individualised therapies, which people have to seek out, purchase and administer for themselves, because they are not readily available on the NHS. This is the response of those, like Professor Layard, who can see a problem but cannot provide societal solutions.[15]

Our epidemic of unhappiness sustains a burgeoning, multi-million pound industry of self-help books and courses, complementary medicines and therapies, and anti-depressant or mood-altering drugs. The popular psychologist Oliver James has coined the term 'affluenza' to identify precisely the kind of consumer-driven malaise we are talking about. He attributes this 'virus' directly to unrestrained capitalism, and offers the sensible – albeit individualised – solution of simply buying, using and owning less. James considers affluenza to be 'a contagious disease of the middle-classes', which may be partially true, but it is also true that the capacity and confidence to implement the major 'life-changes' he prescribes are certainly middle-class attributes.[16] Yet the masses also experience malaise, possibly to an even greater extent, but their therapies are largely confined to prime-time TV. A huge proportion of this has been given up to makeovers aimed at de-cluttering our houses or revamping our selves, or to experts sorting out dysfunctional families and providing other forms of so-called life-coaching, with a current emphasis on 'fatties' losing weight.

We have no problem with any of this if it does actually make people feel better. We all have to live in this world and our own small parts of it as we find them. Likewise, we accept the use of the word 'happiness' to describe both a state of mind and a general social condition, and we have no difficulty with taking the pursuit of happiness to be a proper goal of public policy. We do, however, have serious reservations about recent research on happiness. Efforts to track changes in personal happiness over time, to compare patterns of happiness across countries and to gain a better understanding of what makes people happy can undoubtedly improve public policy. But unless researchers recognise the pervasive influence of neoliberal capitalism on the way we live and relate to each other, their work will fall short of its full potential.

More fundamental opportunities for reducing human misery and increasing human happiness by reorganising society will be missed.

Nor will it do to concentrate on happiness as a transient subjective feeling and on the factors that determine it. The proper timeframe for the study of human happiness is a whole human life. This shifts the focus away from owning, earning and spending – the central preoccupations of consumer capitalism – towards the questions that concerned moral philosophers in the ancient world and which still exercise many today: How should we live our lives? What is ultimately worth doing? What kind of care do children need to grow into useful, independent, well-adjusted adults? How can I ensure that I will die with no unnecessary regrets? How do we acquire the skills and wisdom to live well? Traces of these age-old questions can still be discerned in Layard's 'new science', and even in New Labour's welfare-to-work programmes, but they are crushed or distorted by the crass materialism of the global marketplace.

Layard writes: 'A society cannot flourish without some sense of shared purpose. The current pursuit of self-realisation will not work. If your sole duty is to achieve the best for yourself, life becomes just too stressful, too lonely – you are set up to fail'.[17] It is impossible to disagree. But when he goes on to say that: 'The secret is compassion towards oneself and others and the principle of the Greatest Happiness is essentially the expression of that idea', he comes very close to the banality of a self-help manual offering life-long contentment in seven easy steps, or the shallow guff of New Age religion. It is not as simple as this. In order to understand the roots of the crisis we must first look at the way in which our society has developed, how it is ordered and, then, how it can be changed.

To sum up: contemporary Britain is a deeply troubled place. It may not seem that way from the metropolitan perspectives of New Labour's luminaries, advocates and dwindling band of supporters. A striking feature of our social crisis is the detachment of our political/media class from the lives and realities of the mass of British people. Ordinary people find little echo of their daily experiences, problems and passions in the official accounts, unless it is filtered through the weird distorting prisms of reality TV, tabloid press and celebrity magazines. This in itself is a dangerous failure in our systems of political representation, and leads people to seek fulfilment and expression on the darker margins of our culture.

It is revealing that the policy which appeared to have finally broken the myth of the caring and healing New Labour project was so very simple – the removal of the 10p tax band to pay for an overall reduction in the main tax band. The gross inequity of this was immediately obvious, yet its implications appear to have escaped the Labour leadership. When Brown asserted that no-one would suffer as a result of the change he was, probably, not lying; he simply had not thought about it. Yet even after a series of electoral setbacks, relieved only by the Glenrothes seat held against the SNP challenge in November 2008, he and his acolytes seemed unable to get the basic message: that the increasing inequity of British society is felt as a deep social wound.

This breakdown in popular political representation is accompanied by a kind of historical amnesia, a great forgetting, which distorts and downgrades or even dismisses altogether the lessons of our past.[18] This is not accidental. New Labour has imposed a kind of foundation myth on the rest of us, with various 'Year Zeros' to choose from: the 'suicide note' manifesto of 1983; Kinnock's defeat of the hard left in 1985; the 'successful defeat' of the 1987 election, then the 'surprise defeat' of the 1992 election; the Blair/Brown ascendancy of 1994; the landslide victory in the 1997 election. With passing time, it becomes ever harder to present New Labour as 'new' (now its major marketing problem). But wherever you start from, we are expected to believe that New Labour sprang phoenix-like from the ashes of Old Labour and the wastelands of Thatcherism, without historical antecedents or causes of its own.

This is simply not true, but it serves the purpose of absolving New Labour from responsibility for what it has actually done or failed to do. If you deny your past and dwell in a perpetual present, you cannot be held accountable for either. Devise a new policy; announce a new initiative; appoint a new minister (or leader); reshuffle the cabinet; re-launch the new leader – and watch the great British public stifle a yawn. Even before a spate of spectacular council and by-election defeats confirmed the Conservatives in a commanding lead in the opinion polls and suggested that voters might have already made up their minds about the next election, there were plenty of signs that the old tricks were not working any more.

What comes next and what is to be done? We shall return later to these questions. First, however, having described the symptoms of Britain's social malaise, we need to find a diagnosis.

THE ROOTS OF CRISIS

In search of further explanation, we need to turn briefly to some theoretical considerations. In the nineteenth century, the major achievement of Karl Marx was a perceptive analysis of a social system in which the increasing scale of commodity production led towards an increasing concentration of property ownership. This was a highly dynamic but also destructive process, which led to recurrent economic and social crises. Marx also showed how capitalist production turns social relations into commodities and human beings into things. Classical Marxism emphasised economic crises and mass unemployment, but Marx himself also noted the resistance that capitalist development provoked and the consequent emergence of countervailing forces, like the factory inspectorate and the trade union movement, which sought to protect living standards and create a more civilised social order. These insights were generalised in the 1940s by Karl Polanyi, who argued that the development of capitalism, which he called 'the self-regulating market', was so destructive of human society that it created a recurrent societal crisis and called forth a historical counter-movement. For this reason, Polanyi described the attempt to create a fully self-adjusting market, today's neoliberalism, as 'market utopianism', in the sense of being impossible to achieve.[19]

More recently, James O'Connor has emphasised the dynamic of capitalist accumulation as the cause of ecological crisis, which in turn has given rise to the green movement and the environmentalism of the poor.[20] These different forms of crisis – economic, societal, ecological – interact in different ways to shape the underlying contradictions manifested at each stage in the development of capitalism. Michael Burawoy has outlined three principles of a contemporary *sociological* Marxism, drawing heavily on Polanyi and Gramsci, which goes beyond classical Marxism, and revises its basic tenets:

'Capitalism creates the conditions for its own demise through deepening crises and the creation of an industrial reserve army' becomes 'capitalism generates a society which contains and absorbs its tendency to self-destruct';

'Capitalism creates class consciousness and class organisation, as antagonisms intensify' becomes 'struggle within capitalism takes place on the terrain of hegemony';

'Capitalism creates the material conditions for a new socialist/communist order' becomes 'the struggle for socialism is a political project for the subordination of the economy to a self-regulating society'. [21]

In this formulation, capitalism generates a society that acts as a kind of social shock absorber, tempering its inherently destructive effects. Struggle takes place over the ways in which this defensive reaction occurs, on the terrain of hegemony or political leadership. The struggle for socialism is a longer-term political project for the subordination of the economy to a self-regulating society, rather than merely the defensive, temporary amelioration of its destructive dynamic. It is about extending the basic principle of democracy, the involvement of everyone in making decisions, to every area of our lives, rather than the destructive competitiveness of the market. This brings us to the central importance of Antonio Gramsci, the great Italian Marxist, for understanding today's gathering economic, societal and ecological crisis.

Gramsci distinguished three forms of social consciousness – corporate, class and hegemonic – concerned respectively with narrow sectional interests, economic class interests and with the presentation of a particular class interest as the interest of society as a whole. For him, politics takes the form of a struggle for 'hegemony', in which different classes seek to present their interest as the interest of all and thereby establish their claim to leadership over a whole society. This struggle predominantly takes the form of what Gramsci called a 'war of position', a kind of political and ideological trench warfare characteristic of advanced capitalist economies with developed civil societies and a relatively consensual democratic state. It is fought on a wide front, taking in ideological, cultural, moral, legal, and political, as well as economic, conflict. Alliances are built with the object of constructing a 'historic bloc' of social forces gathered around the dominant class and held together by that class's hegemonic ideology which then becomes the 'common sense' of the age, constantly and creatively adapting to changing circumstances. Breaking the hold of this dominant ideology then requires the deliberate construction of what can be called an 'anti-common sense', a new vision of what society could be.

In order to create and sustain a historic bloc, the dominant class has to make a 'historic compromise', in the form of concessions to the subordinate social forces, giving them a material interest in its maintenance. Elites among subordinate or 'subaltern' groups are recruited into the ruling group's historic bloc, in what Gramsci called a process of 'transformism'. They in turn facilitate the maintenance of hegemony, not least by reinvigorating the dominant culture with their own fresh energies, insights and supporters. Meanwhile, the lower orders are maintained in their position of subalternity, a kind of grudging, grumbling acquiescence in the prevailing common sense. They might complain about the conduct of the '*signori*', whom we might call the 'toffs' or the 'establishment', but in most times and circumstances they have neither the capacity nor the confidence to mount a serious challenge to the ruling order.

To be historically specific, the British Labour Party has provided numerous examples of subalternity and transformism (Gramsci himself cited Ramsay MacDonald as one of the most obvious), and has thereby contributed to the deep and lasting hegemony of capitalism in this country. By and large, Britain's economy and society have remained remarkably stable and cohesive for long periods of our history, through repeated re-negotiation of our own particular historic compromise to reflect the prevailing relations of class forces. It is when this process ceases to be possible that an organic crisis sets in. What Gramsci called a 'war of movement', of manoeuvre and sudden thrust, then takes place until a new historic bloc is created, society is re-stabilised, and social relations revert to a more settled war of position. Gramsci was among the first Marxists to understand that this historical process of crisis and resolution is not necessarily progressive.

As early as 1919, in the pages of *Ordine Nuovo*, he adopted the slogan for which he is perhaps best known: 'Pessimism of the intellect, optimism of the will'. What this slogan represents was central to his thinking, because of his insight into the complexity of civil society, its inextricable meshing with the state, and the depth and solidity with which the leading class's hegemony is entrenched within society. Whilst he might hope that a new, revolutionary hegemony would be developed from below, he recognised that by far the most likely outcome of any organic crisis was a 'passive revolution': change imposed from above by elements within the ruling bloc. This would have the effect of containing the new social forces and pressures that had built up, adapting the social order to accommodate some of their lesser demands and personnel, dismissing others, and punishing or disciplining the recalcitrants. In time, this would create a new and stable historic bloc. In Gramsci's own time and society, the outcome of Italy's organic crisis and passive revolution was fascism, which led to his own imprisonment and premature death.

Such historic moments in capitalist societies can appear tumultuous, with everything up for grabs, and we remain almost morbidly fascinated with them. The only thing that is not negotiable, in this creative/destructive process of organic crisis and passive revolution, is the continued domination of capital and the continuous reproduction of the underlying social relations of capitalism. Yet even as these social relations are reproduced, any capitalist society exhibits deep contradictions. Capitalism, at bottom, is irredeemably undemocratic. The market is not a democratic agent in any respect. Yet, in most capitalist states, democratic rights of various kinds have been conceded as the price paid by capital in times of social crisis for the restoration of order and stability when its subordinate opponents have been relatively strong and well organised. Capitalism is hostile towards any kind of social organisation which might restrain commodity formation and accumulation, yet labour and various other forms of association have over the years won particular legal rights which seek to do precisely that.

Early Marxists saw the state as a mechanism whose essential function under capitalism was to defend national capital against international competition and to repress internal dissent. Yet with the development of democracy, the state has become a much more ambiguous agency, dispensing both benefit and repression in forms that vary widely between countries. In this respect, capitalism has had to make democratic concessions that constrain market forces, thereby limiting their effectiveness. Otherwise, the system would collapse under the weight of social dissent. Simultaneously, such concessions, once granted, are always under threat, either from direct political intervention by reactionaries or from spontaneous market forces. The history of post-war Britain provides a clear example of this process.

1945-79: FROM POST-WAR SETTLEMENT TO ORGANIC CRISIS

In Britain, as elsewhere in Europe, the post-Second World War settlement involved a three-way deal between capital, labour and the state, at least in the economic and industrial spheres. It also had major implications for our society and culture. This deal or 'social contract' was more implicit and informal in Britain than in most other European countries, precisely because Britain won the war and enjoyed institutional continuity. It rested on three pillars: the maintenance of full employment by means of Keynesian counter-cyclical demand management; a mixed economy with a major role for public ownership, planning and regulation; and, most significantly, the welfare state which provided a wide range of tax-financed social services and cash benefits, the former available mostly free of charge, the latter subject to various qualifying and means-tested conditions. The ongoing management of the national economy became the joint responsibility of government and the corporate organisations of employers and workers, though this tripartite arrangement was largely informal and operated behind closed doors.

This post-war historic compromise was unavoidable, following the near-collapse of capitalism as an economic system in the pre-war period and the victory against fascism in which the decisive factor – lest we forget – had been the armies of the Soviet Union, then widely seen as a new, socialist state. The conduct of this total war had required levels of popular involvement, democratic consent, state intervention and a command economy that could not just be brushed aside. The social-democratic consensus produced a period of twenty five years or so that remains, in many respects, a capitalist golden age, when economic growth was unprecedentedly high, inflation and unemployment low, and social dissent minimal. It seemed as if the business cycle of boom and bust had been tamed. Elsewhere in Western Europe, some form of this settlement still holds, though by now much battered. In Britain, it broke down decisively and catastrophically in the early 1970s, leading to an organic crisis and a growing sense of national disaster as the decade wore on.[22]

British capitalism was on the ropes. From 1973 onwards, price inflation accelerated sharply, peaking in 1975 at an annual rate of 26 per cent. Thanks to the system of index-linking introduced by the Heath government in 1973, many workers' wages were rising on a monthly basis. Profits were in free fall whilst large sections of society were in a kind of general mutiny. The most prominent part of this was trade union activity, emanating not so much from national head offices as from local rank-and-file activism. But there was also a widespread sense of social disaffection, a decade-long 'winter of discontent', ranging from women dissatisfied with their status in society, through black power activists and small groups of violent anarchists, to groups with aims as specific and traditional as Irish nationalists.

By the end of the 1970s, as two of us wrote at the time, the situation in Britain could best be summarised as follows:

> British society has been gripped in a state of socio-political dead-lock. Neither the dominant social groups and their political leadership, nor the subordinate groups and theirs, have proved able to develop, to win broadly based support for, implement and, if necessary, impose a decisive solution to the country's problems. Each side has possessed the defensive capability to block and frustrate the other's designs. But neither has shown the directive, constructive capacity to alter the social and political balances in its favour and set the economy on a new course.[23]

The fundamental crisis of Britain in this decade was a breakdown in the post-war consensus that some form of tripartite collaboration could sustain a rate of economic growth sufficient to satisfy the divergent aspirations of government, capital and labour. The breakdown of consensus made itself felt in a series of inflationary crises, which from the late 1960s onwards brought the British economy to its knees.[24]

In a sense, the struggle between the left and the right in 1970s

Britain was fundamentally unequal, as it almost always is. The left needed to make a complex and difficult adjustment if it was to bid for national leadership. Up to then, it had pursued a political strategy of 'militant labourism', as one historian has recently put it. Trade unions would demand higher wages from their members' employers, whilst simultaneously pressing government for more social regulation and welfare spending. The hope was that this contradictory and unrealisable strategy would force a final and successful showdown with the entire capitalist system.[25] The strategy failed totally and ignominiously. The 1970s was the decade in which the left lost its historical role as the moral standard-bearer of freedom and progress, and, instead, espoused a form of left-wing conservatism now so sharply derided as 'Old Labour', a narrow, sectional, and increasingly outdated subaltern class interest. Control over the political agenda passed to the new radical right. *Unless we grasp this, we cannot begin to understand our present predicament, let alone build a progressive democratic counterweight to the dominant neoliberal ideology.*

Yet there exists widespread historical amnesia about the political economy of the second half of the last century, in particular the way in which the right achieved a new hegemony around neoliberal economic ideology. For them, there was no fundamental problem over the cause of the crisis in the 1970s. The increasingly mutinous working class, no longer corralled by the niceties of the official trade union movement, and in growing if undefined alliance with other disaffected social groups, provided a convenient explanation. Nor was the immediate remedy a problem: a crackdown on class militancy and unions, together with associated disaffected groups, had been touted for some years within the Conservative Party. The issue for the Tories was how to give such an approach sufficient legitimacy to ensure success over at least two elections. This was the heart of the matter. The whole of the 1970s can be seen as a complex legitimacy crisis, with neither the leading nor the subordinate class being able to win out. The right needed to find a legitimate authority on which it could base its decisive assault. It found this in the 'market', as formulated in the work of resurgent neoliberal political philosophers and economists such as Friedrich von Hayek and Milton Friedman.

Friedrich von Hayek was an Austrian political economist whose most famous work, *The Road to Serfdom*, published in

1944, rejected any form of socialism root-and-branch. However, it was a later book, *The Constitution of Liberty*, which Margaret Thatcher is famously reported to have produced from her handbag and brandished when asked in what she believed. Hayek's pitch was freedom of the individual. He believed that true freedom only existed in conditions when the individual alone faced and participated in the market. The sole legitimate role for the state was to protect private property. Hayek believed, for example, that private business could take over from government the job of issuing currency. Just why he never suggested that state-organised security should be supplanted by private armies and police forces is not clear. He would, no doubt, have been much cheered by recent developments of this type in Iraq and a number of gated communities in the US. Hayek was also opposed to any form of collectivism, even of a voluntary kind, and particularly trade unions, which caused 'stickiness' in money wages and generally impeded market adjustment. He blamed the global inter-war depression on precisely this role of British trade unions.

The classical liberal concept of negative freedom, being left alone to find one's own way, and the related commitment to a minimal state, were one strand of the right's ideological story. Another, of quite separate provenance, was the monetarist economics of Milton Friedman. Friedman started his professional life working for Roosevelt's New Deal and thereafter acquired a reputation of sorts in mainstream economic theory. But his fervent belief that 'business knows best' was non-economic, even anti-economic, and unashamedly ideological. In almost any situation, Friedman believed, the most important thing government could do was to get out of the way. Instead of trying to fine-tune the economy, he proposed that government should set a fixed rate for the growth of the money supply in line with the long-term rate of growth of GDP – around 2.5 per cent per annum in the UK – and then instruct the central bank to maintain that rate year in and year out. All other government efforts should be directed towards dismantling any kind of state control over any kind of market on the grounds that business, not government, knows best. The re-naming of the old Department of Trade and Industry as the Department for Business, Enterprise and Regulatory Reform reflects the obsessive way in which the Labour government has taken Friedman's mantra on board.

To these two strands, one further ingredient was added: the idea that the market is 'efficient'. Economists continue to debate exactly what this claim means and in what conditions it might hold good. In any case, scholarly disputation is beside the point. Abstract propositions such as this form part of what J.K. Galbraith called 'the conventional wisdom'.[26] They resemble ritual incantations in religious worship, providing policy- and opinion-makers with intellectual balm and psychological reassurance. And for more than two and a half decades since the watershed of the 1970s, the notion that free markets are inherently efficient bewitched the political class.

These three basic ideas – markets make us free, business knows best, and markets are efficient – derive from quite distinct intellectual positions, which are sometimes contradictory. But then, we are not discussing consistent economic theory here but ideological formations, condensed into what Polanyi would have characterised as 'market utopianism'. The Conservative government elected in 1979 was willing and, more to the point, able to adopt and deploy the whole package amid the political wreckage of Britain's social-democratic consensus. Hayek's faith in individual freedom justified the attack on the trade unions, which he largely blamed for the alleged ills of all European states. Friedman's belief that business knows best allowed the industrial destruction of the 1980s to be conducted in the name of rational restructuring. And the alleged efficiency of the market justified any form of privatisation of public utilities and state enterprises, as well as initial steps towards privatising both the health service and state education.

Although most closely associated with the Thatcher era, neoliberalism and its three basic ideas had long been germinating among right-wing think tanks. Prominent amongst them was the Institute of Economic Affairs, which, under the influence of Hayek, developed a radical right-wing alternative to the social democratic welfare state. As real incomes rose and memories of inter-war deprivation and instability faded, the right's new ideology caught the popular mood. In particular, it resonated with people's rising impatience with state paternalism, their aspirations to own goods and property and run their own lives, and their desire for more responsive public services. However, the right sought to articulate these popular frustrations and aspirations in terms of neoliberal individualism, rather than in any kind of popular democracy. And it now had a clear field of operations. Both corporate capitalism and militant labourism had effectively collapsed in the organic crisis of the 1970s. The radical neoliberal conservatism of Thatcher stepped into the vacuum. It won out, though initially only just, assisted by splits within the Labour Party and the contingencies of the Falklands war.

1979 was the moment when the breakdown in the post-war social democratic consensus finally entered the nation's common sense. Not fully – no Conservative government ever commanded majority popular support – but there existed a sullen acceptance among the majority that 'we can't go on like this'. The left had failed to provide the radical alternative needed to revive and carry forward a stalled collectivist project, and had little more to offer than militant workerism. The Wilson and Callaghan governments had conducted a prolonged holding operation in a desperate attempt at crisis management, but had gradually been worn down by mounting popular discontent and Labour's own loss of purpose. The new Conservative government, particularly when purged of its faint-hearts, offered a twin-track approach: moral regeneration of a nation in crisis and reform of an economic system stifled by a supposedly socialist or statist straitjacket.

THATCHERISM

Capitalism offers for most people a life of recurrent unease and tension. This is precisely its dynamic, celebrated by its apologists as the creative force of market competition. Constructive resistance to this tension generally takes two forms: the creation of voluntary organisations of mutual support and, often arising from these, the mobilisation of democratic power to pressurise the state into providing some form of defence against market forces. Collective self-help is now sadly much reduced relative to state protection, but it is worth taking the time to appreciate the role of such institutions as the once-important friendly societies, and just why they were so named. Limited financial support in hard times, health care, education, compensation claims for industrial injury: all these were provided by mutual support agencies. One can also include the mutual building societies set up to help house purchase for regular savers. This was the basis of much early socialist politics. It extended into every aspect of its proponents' and beneficiaries' lives and – via pre-figurative struggle to build a new society amid the ravages of the old one – into the hoped-for future.

At a moment when Conservative ideologues are attempting to claim the virtues of 'fraternity' as their own policy, it should be remembered that one of the few places where 'brothers and sisters' is the common mode of communal address is trade union conferences.[27] In time, the state took over many of these mutual support functions, commonly through local councils rather than central government. Except in the workplace, voluntary mutual support tended to diminish. But what was left was the concept of a network one could trust, which would guarantee healthcare, education, welfare benefits and housing on a lifetime basis. Furthermore – and this is important – it was both created and controlled in some degree by a democratic process. Much of this popular trust and sense of democratic ownership persists, especially around 'our' NHS, and explains the outbursts of wary protectiveness whenever changes – however intrinsically sensible they might be – are proposed. State collectivism has deep roots in Britain, even if only on a sentimental and last-resort basis.

The Thatcher regime had at its heart the dismantling of this system and its replacement by its alleged alternative: looking after oneself, saving for the future, encouraging individual enterprise, charity begins at home, all the nostrums of the Rotary Club and Alderman Thatcher. There were numerous strands to this programme, but one was central: allowing unemployment to rise unchecked to whatever level was required to rein in inflation and curb the power of the trade unions. The mass redundancies of the early 1980s, primarily amongst working-class men in manufacturing and allied sectors, did more than anything else to disrupt and fracture our society. Even now the shock-waves continue to make themselves felt in family and community breakdown, ill health and premature death, persistent inter-generational poverty, and above all a pervasive sense that a whole generation, gender and social group were at a stroke declared useless. As someone once colourfully put it, 'the salt of the earth' was all of a sudden 'the scum of the earth'.

The second feature of Thatcherism was an assault on local authorities, aimed at curtailing their ability to provide practical social assistance, which had formed a large part of their activities. The best known example was the enforced sale of council housing at below market prices and the refusal to allow the proceeds of this to finance further social housing. This particular policy can be seen to parallel the other public sector privatisations of the time and, like them, it had several motives. One was to provide a temporary boost to public finances. In the case of local authorities, the proceeds of council house sales were firmly ring-fenced but still appeared on their balance sheets. Another aim was to enable a section of the population to acquire assets at below their full price: in the case of council housing, at a deliberate discount; in the case of state enterprises and utilities, by setting a flotation share-price at a level which would guarantee immediate windfall profits. A third objective was to promote an ideology of self-interest. The fact that the personal gains of a section of the population were acquired at the expense of those unable or unwilling to participate in the bonanza was obscured by huge expenditure on advertising campaigns and a chorus of excited support enlisted in the mass media.

The underlying process, the sale of state assets at knockdown prices followed by concentration of ownership, as the 'little people' cashed in their handouts, was little different to the blatant rip-off in post-communist Russia ten years later, followed by the rise of the oligarchs. But in Britain, at least, it was accompanied by assiduous promulgation of the myth that these public sector agencies had been wasteful and inefficient, a drag on society. In fact, as any glance at national income accounts showed, most public industry made a substantial profit remitted to the Treasury, whilst most council housing showed a balance of income and expenditure.

Of course there were genuine problems with the public sector. Some parts were over-centralised whilst others were under-resourced and poorly maintained. Public servants were often arrogant and paternalistic, and usually more inclined to block than facilitate change. There were deep currents of hypocrisy and, occasionally, corruption. Far too often, one size was indeed deemed sufficient to fit all. Thatcherism, like all successful hegemonic projects, tapped into genuine popular grievances and frustrations. Again, council housing and 'the right to buy' provide an instructive example. The ambition to own one's house is not ignoble, but there were plenty of ways in which this could have been accommodated within the rented council sector. Some of these are now popping up within private housing developments where, to obtain planning consents in some of the hottest property zones, so-called 'key workers' are being offered part-rent, part-buy deals to allow them to live in places otherwise inaccessible on their incomes. The current crash in the housing market has exposed the lack of precisely any such intermediate mechanisms for housing. But sorting out the problems of a council-house sector that had expanded rapidly and needed radical overhaul was not part of the Thatcherite agenda. Nor was any serious evaluation of the role of public industry.

Finally, careful but systematic inroads were made into the twin bastions of the public sector, education and health. Public support for these was far too entrenched for any frontal assault. Instead, the Conservative government embarked on a confidence-sapping war of attrition, encouraging private-sector health and education both directly and by none too subtle hints that their public equivalents were second-rate. Ministers made no secret of their use of private health and education services, and reinforced the message with the appointment of Chris Woodhead as Chief Inspector of Schools, a man – kept in post for some years under New Labour – who departed after years of denigrating state schools and teachers and immediately took up a professorial post at the only fully private university in the country, and became chairman of a company running a string of private schools. Meanwhile, direct private-sector involvement and forms of market competition were introduced into both health and education.

The prevailing response on the left, especially the 'softer', anti-Bennite elements around Neil Kinnock (a key transitional figure in the emergence of New Labour), was to decry the 'dogma' of Thatcherism. In fact, Thatcherism was never mere dogma, a body of fixed and abstract principle, which inevitably loses touch with changing reality. Simple dogmatism is rooted, and eventually stuck, in the past. With its ideological commitment to the market, neoliberalism was always more forward-looking than traditional Conservatism. Thatcherism projected us towards an ideal future quite unlike anything in the past, when hard-won experience had shown that markets never work perfectly and society always requires some level and form of state intervention. This was precisely why Thatcherism was abhorred by more traditional, 'one-nation' or 'wet', Tories, and why those few still left have never wholly accepted the brutal ramifications of unfettered, global neoliberalism.

Thatcherism was (and remains) a kind of market-utopianism, easily discerned among contemporary right-wing commentators, especially those uneasy with David Cameron's blatant attempt to reposition the Tories in the centre ground of British politics. Thus David Green of the Thatcherite think tank Civitas could write, on the last day of 2006 and without any supporting evidence or examples, that: 'The political process ... can't manage schools and hospitals. A market system can. It invites innovation and creativity among diverse suppliers who compete to find better ways of meeting human needs and thereby provoke a chain reaction of mutual learning from the successes and failures of others'. This is highly seductive nonsense, with no historical or theoretical basis other than the popular loss of faith in politics and politicians, but, as Green astutely notes, it seduced 'most thoughtful people, including some in the Labour Party'.[28]

Such is the power of neoliberal ideology. It hardly seemed to matter if it had no basis in historical reality: indeed, faced with the tawdry realities of the modern world, it serves a transcendental, almost religious function. Neoliberalism has always been a curiously abstract, vague and ultimately utopian creed. As so often, they spell it out more clearly in the USA, unhindered by our British niceties. Ronald Reagan famously lauded 'the magic of the marketplace'; his critics called it 'voodoo economics'. Reagan set in chain a process of deregulation, privatisation and profiteering that led directly to the false accounting and outright fraud of Enron, arguably the most spectacular single confidence trick ever perpetrated within capitalism.[29] Back in the 1980s, this was all (literally) still in the future. Market utopianism swept all before it. It took the 2008 global crisis of financial markets to show just how illusory are its promises, with the largest act of state economic intervention ever undertaken, nationally and internationally, necessary in order to bail out the banks and stave off financial collapse.

But amid the collapse of the various political projects of the left, which had themselves always contained utopian elements, neoliberalism after the 1970s offered an exhausted society a glimpse of a better or at least different future. The result was a decisive ideological victory for Thatcherism, though, in electoral terms, it was won quite narrowly. It required the defection of the Social Democratic Party from Labour in 1981 to lift persistently minority popular votes for the Conservatives into clear parliamentary majorities. In 1983, the Labour Party fought a general election on a manifesto much derided since as 'the longest suicide note in history'. It was in fact a detailed plan of conservative, quasi-nostalgic social-democracy: a substantial increase in public expenditure to lift the economy out of recession, progressive policies on education, health, social services, women's rights, and the arts, cancelling the Trident programme and removing American bases from Britain.[30] There was almost no nationalisation and no unilateral nuclear disarmament, though there was a commitment to phased withdrawal from the European Community. The programme was actually less radical than the manifestos that had won Labour two electoral victories only nine years before. But with a narrow military victory in the Falklands and a split left-centre vote, the Conservatives won 42 per cent of the popular vote and a Commons majority of 144.

Beyond electoral politics, the Thatcher government routinely demonised various particularly vulnerable sections of society, a practice previously eschewed by respectable, moderate one-nation Tories. The targeting of 'enemies within', assiduously carried on by New Labour, would prove a crucial stepping-stone towards the current crisis of social relations in Britain. Young people, students, single parents, ethnic and sexual minorities, so-called scroungers of any kind, were all singled out quite systematically. Thus began the process of social fracture of a previously relatively cohesive nation. It is important not to romanticise the past of our British nation. It has always been highly stratified on class lines, and undercurrents of prejudice and intolerance run deep through our culture, occasionally erupting into sectarian or ethnic violence. They are all still there, alive and occasionally kicking, alongside counter-balancing traditions of respect and diversity, best summed up in the phrase 'live and let live'. Perhaps this nastier side was easier to accept as a shared moralism, embodied in the tribal, judgmental collectivism of the 'respectable' working class. It generated a social discipline alongside the broader systems of mutual support, and made daily life broadly bearable for those within its firm, if sometimes stifling and occasionally punitive, embrace.

However, the respectable working class was Thatcherism's biggest and most significant victim. It was shattered into fragments, some edging upwards into the lower middle class and some free-falling into lumpen, underclass drudgery. What we see now is that old, national-popular moralism freed from its natural constituency and coupled with the individualised, aspirational, materialistic appetites of Thatcherism's new petty bourgeoisie, and unrestrained by any collectivist values. Detached from its traditional social class moorings, good old-fashioned British 'decency' makes for a much more toxic brew, which the *Sun* and the *Mail* articulate daily.

THE NEW LABOUR TURN

In 1997, the Blair government was elected on the basis of a new start for a country worn down by years of outright Thatcherism. There is little need to rehearse the euphoria of that moment, except to emphasise the extent to which it was based upon popular expectation rather than any concrete shift in policy. One important, though largely overlooked, aspect was that it was not based upon any popular enthusiasm for Labour. John Major achieved a higher popular vote for the Conservatives in 1992 than Blair and Brown did for Labour in 1997. The Labour vote simply held up better, reflecting general weariness with the Conservative administration.

New Labour's 1997 manifesto promised a new path beyond the old left and new right, a transcendence of previous division.[31] 'In each area of policy a new and distinctive approach has been mapped out, one that differs from the old left and the Conservative right. This is why new Labour is new.' Thus in education, 'we reject both the idea of a return to the 11-plus and the monolithic comprehensive schools that take no account of children's differing abilities'. In the health service, 'we will safeguard the basic principles of the NHS, which we founded, but will not return to the top-down management of the 1970s'. In economic management: 'The old left would have sought state control of industry. The Conservative right is content to leave all to the market. We reject both approaches. Government and industry must work together to achieve key objectives aimed at enhancing the dynamism of the market, not undermining it'. On crime: 'we believe in personal responsibility and in punishing crime, but also tackling its underlying causes'. And so on through all the various areas of policy and the comforting balm of the Third Way, which would 'put behind us the bitter political struggles of left and right that have torn our country apart for too many decades'. These struggles were presented as 'conflicts [which] have no relevance whatsoever to the modern world'. It is a sign of New Labour's loss of confidence that Brown as prime minister was still warning, in words that could have come from the mouth of any old right-wing Labour fixer, against left-wing drift. In 1997, we were supposed to be beyond all that.

Additionally – and as it would transpire the trademark feature of first Blair's, then Brown's, government's style – there were the eye-catching wheezes: the partnership with Premier League football clubs to attack underachievement in urban areas; the Internet National Grid for Learning; the University for Industry. This was a set of carefully selected new ideas with the common feature of bringing together the public and the private into a synthesis that would, painlessly and without cost, heal the wounds of the past. That is, if they were ever to happen.

It would be too easy simply to dismiss the New Labour 'project' as vacuous. Its attraction lay in the fact that it correctly identified many problems of British society, assiduously tested their resonance in focus groups, and then laid out a set of targets to resolve or, at least, alleviate them. It suggested that government could be reduced to appropriate management, freed from ideological preconceptions. 'New Labour is a party of ideas and ideals but not of outdated ideology. What counts is what works. The objectives are radical. The means will be modern.' In fact, there was little that was new in this approach. It had many similarities with that of the Wilson government in 1964, which itself drew on the old Fabian predilections for 'scientific' social democracy and technocratic 'expert-ism'. These had long been a strong current within Labourism, something for its intellectuals to busy themselves with while the movement's hard core of ex-councillors and trade union officials got on with the mucky business of running the party and, in its brief periods in office, the country.

Blair and Brown were essentially re-using Harold Wilson's rhetoric of a dynamic modernism, but in a crucially different context. Wilson came to power at a time when the post-war settlement had delivered the most successful epoch of capitalist growth in Britain, before or since, but was beginning to show the first signs of internal fracture. New Labour came to power, some thirty years later, at a time when resurgent neoliberal capitalism had re-stabilised the economy, but at the cost of massive social damage. The career politicians of New Labour were prepared to embrace the new order as the price for electoral success. 'I want to renew faith in politics by being honest about the last 18 years. Some things the Conservatives got right. We will not change them. It is where they got things wrong that we will make change. We have no intention or desire to replace one set of dogmas by another' was Blair's personal affirmation.[32] Gordon Brown's invitation for Thatcher to visit 10 Downing Street was his way of re-affirming this pledge.

Unfortunately, the market utopianism of Thatcherism was a seamless garment. It contained internal inconsistencies, and the compromises necessary to retain popular support. But it repre-sented an ideology a good deal more complete and worked through than anything devised by Old Labour in its death-throes or by Kinnock's soft-left, which emphasised what Labour would not do, but offered little positive strategy of its own. Blair and Brown seemed to believe that they could cherry-pick bits of the Thatcherite legacy and ditch the rest, but they seriously underes-timated its vigour and its reach, and massively overestimated their own.

It remains for future political historians to decide whether Blair and Brown appreciated that they were adopting Thatcher's full outfit rather than naively stumbling around in her wardrobe trying on the hats. It is possible that Brown was more aware than Blair, which rather belies his supposedly greater attachment to Labourist values. Brown's enthusiasm for the economic aspects of neoliberalism was apparent from the start, as was his attachment to the moral values of Hayek. Ceding control of interest rates to the Bank of England was an early indication, a classic Friedmanite gesture of relaxing government interference, and a convenient technical cloak for dispensing with a key piece of democratic control. This decision, much praised at the time, now looks distinctly dodgy. The Bank of England's Monetary Policy Committee misread the growing indications of a developing recession and, mesmerised by the illusory danger of inflation, resisted pressure for interest rate cuts for far too long, only then to announce a panic stricken 1½ per cent cut, unprecedented in modern times.

New Labour's embrace of neoliberalism was stealthy but consistent and became, in effect, total. It was a tortuous, complex process, not without internal opposition within the Labour Party, but its outcome is clear and rather simple. Before Thatcher, Britain was a relatively democratic capitalist society in which people had a number of roles: as employees, employers and consumers; as voters, taxpayers and users of public services; as members of households, families and friendship circles; and as members of voluntary associations of different shapes, sizes and purposes. The various components of the welfare state – whether education, health, social services, housing or social security – all served to provide a nexus of social solidarity which transcended the atomised limits of individual self-help. Additionally, the public sector provided growing numbers of people with employment which, whilst in some ways very similar to the private sector, always had an aspect of public service. These were state functions achieved by various forms of democratic collective political activity and formed the basis of the post-war settlement in most western European countries. It wasn't particularly democratic in its day-to-day operations, or even especially popular, and it certainly wasn't socialist; but it felt like a kind of progress.

This old regime is often presented as though it was a privately negotiated agreement between defined agents: trade unions, employers' organisations, political parties, and so on. Indeed, one of the faults of the post-war social-democratic settlement (especially in Britain) was that it was mostly conducted behind closed doors, famously over 'beer and sandwiches at Number 10'. This was the downside of corporatism or tripartism, but for all its lack of democracy, its necessary precondition was some level of popular and democratic involvement by all citizens in the operations of society. Everybody, especially after the nationwide efforts and sufferings of the first truly total war in the country's history, had a new, shared stake in the state and its future.

Conversely, the assault of the neoliberal politics of Thatcherism thirty years later, although ostensibly an attack on specific institutions such as trade unions or local authorities, was in fact intended to undermine this system of social citizenship. At the heart of

Thatcherism was Hayek's contention that individuals are only truly free when entirely dependent upon their own resources, and that any social provision of services or benefits is just a step along the road to totalitarian dictatorship. This was what Thatcher really meant when she famously declared 'there is no such thing as society', a declaration of ideological belief and political intent, rather than a description of the world as it is.

This view was sufficiently deranged and brutally anti-social – not to mention 'un-British' – to require considerable camouflage, initially by raising such a cloud of social and economic mayhem that it was difficult to grasp what was really going on. The problem with these diversionary tactics was that specific and open attacks induced direct and frequently violent confrontations, which at times in the 1980s reached outright civil disorder. Subsequently, into the 1990s and beyond, a more sophisticated justification was required, a re-branding which would hide neoliberalism's most vicious aspects and provide at least a veneer of social unity. It is this, a classic piece of Gramscian transformism within a larger historical project, which has been the historic mission of New Labour and its small elite core.

To appreciate just how this works, one can start with a statement of the role of government, as set out over Blair's signature in the last stages of his reign, in the capability reviews of four government departments.[33] After the usual vainglorious affirmation that 'the Government has delivered unprecedented and sustained increases in funding for key public services' which have 'brought about major improvements in our public services', Blair asserted that:

[H]aving achieved this, the public's focus is already moving on. Globalisation is profoundly changing the nature of our society. It forces businesses and people to step up a gear simply to keep abreast with the pace of change: commercial transactions are completed without delay; communications happen instantly; goods can be moved rapidly across huge distances. Government is not immune to these changes. For it to continue to maintain its legitimacy, it needs to change its outlook radically. The techno-logical innovations driving global change have not just opened up new opportunities for delivering services, but increased people's expectations of what they want from those who serve them. To meet these challenges the State must provide the same level of customer service as the public have [sic] come to expect in every other aspect of their lives. To achieve this, the role of the State is not to control but to enable – where the State provides strategic direction not micro-management – and this requires a transformation of how we deliver our services.

This attempt to explain and justify the New Labour state is revealing. First, there is the ritual affirmation that it has already done wonderful, indeed unprecedented, things. However, global market forces are inexorably working to alter the foundations of social life for the better, not just because service delivery improves, but because individual expectations of service delivery rise. The state, necessarily lagging behind in satisfying heightened customer expectations, must seek to meet the performance standards set by global business. To this end, it must constantly transform itself. That then becomes the central task for the New Labour government, having withdrawn from any serious attempt to reshape or even protect the society around it. Hence the dizzying resolve to keep its own departments, committees and 'units' under constant review and reform.

Now, even if we accept this retreat of government into itself, it is easy enough to point out the internal logical and factual problems in its programme of 'constant self-improvement'. Why, for example, having achieved such huge improvements in public services, are sudden transformation and permanent revolution required all over again? And just what are the expectations of public service delivery which are now so much higher than they were ten or twenty years ago? Nor is it clear just how 'strategic direction' as against 'micro-management' improves customer service. We might also wonder just how the tender attentions of the security services can be seen as 'customer service' delivery, outside the world of Terry Gilliam's film *Brazil*.

However, pointing out the logical flaws in this line of argument fails to get to the heart of its message. The world, it claims, is in the grip of inexorable market forces. These are ultimately irresistible but also beneficial provided one moves with them. This is held to be self-evidently true for businesses, individuals and also the state, which in this discourse is simply a kind of laggard business. There is no collectivity possible within this perspective, no kind of social response to external change, which takes us back to our earlier CBI leader, Mr Sunderland, and his rather curious statement that Britain alone has embraced globalisation: global capitalism in one country perhaps.[34] But the most revealing sentiment of Blair's capability review lies in its grammatical solecism: even 'the public' is plural. Society has disintegrated to the point where each individual consumer is his or her own public.[35] Truly, as Margaret Thatcher (echoing Hayek) affirmed, there is no such thing as society, just individuals and the markets wherein they buy commodities and sell themselves.

Blair's rant is capable of further interpretations, most obviously as a circular, self-justifying, but also self-defeating apologia for the actual weakness of the British state and the ineffectuality of its government. For much of the post-war period the state has ultimately failed in the developmental or directive tasks it has set itself. This was, of course, another facet of Thatcherism: that free individuals neither could nor should put any abiding faith in a failing state except, paradoxically, when the state was doing Thatcher's bidding by suppressing resistance, waging war or selling off bits of itself.

Politicians' exasperation with the state they were nominally in charge of, coupled with deep and recurrent spending cuts, amounted to a peculiar, almost masochistic, round of admonition and punishment of public services and the slow destruction of any public-service ethos. Inevitably, fewer capable people wanted to work in public service, so competence and morale fell into a downward spiral. This resulted in further deterioration in the quality of services, which justified a further round of denigration, constraint and cutbacks and ultimately, wherever possible, privatisation. Again, New Labour gleefully sustained this central Thatcherite refrain, even while apparently boosting public spending. In fact, much of New Labour's extra spending of the last five years has simply disappeared in dodgy PFI deals, changes in accounting procedures, or in heavy pay increases for certain favoured public-sector workers.

The shift in leadership from Blair to Brown, once hoped for by some on the left as a moment which would release Brown's hidden virtues, has proved to be no more than a continuation of the same policy. Until the financial meltdown in the autumn of 2008, deference to City financial interests increased even in the face of mounting evidence that these interests had been guilty of staggering incompetence and, at the very least, corporate malfeasance, whilst always relying on the state to bail out their greed. Rather than take failing banks into public ownership, Brown and Darling sought private sector solutions until it became clear there were no takers. Even then, the equity stakes in the banks taken by the government were seen a temporary and carried no control, so that in the absence of formal powers the government had to rely on the force of public opinion and moral suasion to persuade the banks to pass Bank of England interest rate cuts on to borrowers, and to curb the payment of bonuses out of public money to failed market operators.

NEW LABOUR: CONSUMER THATCHERISM

What symbolised New Labour's determination to drive market principles into the heart of the welfare state was its insistence that public services rename their clients 'customers', a development which reaches full, self-evident absurdity in areas like social services that offer very little real choice to their 'service-users'. Arguably, they cannot and should not: how can you treat as customers a seriously dysfunctional family, a dementing elder or a sectioned schizophrenic? But the point was to impose a *faux*-market ethos on the public services which successive governments had cut back and run down. This enabled New Labour to allot the British citizenry the economic and social role that fitted most snugly with the new needs of capitalism, and to elevate this above all else: that of the individual as consumer.

This shift towards re-branding the individual as a consumer/customer was, initially, a smart one for the Blair/Brown project. It gave a friendly face to what had, at that point in the mid-1990s, come to seem an inhuman and blatantly profiteering process of allowing market forces free rein. Consumers have rights, customers have choices, and New Labour seemed to be standing up for them in the marketplace. Blair, Brown et al were the champions of the 'consumer interest'. This piece of image-making was a crucial device in consigning Old Labour – the champion of the 'producer interest', canonised in Clause 4 – to the historical dustbin.

Under the Conservatives, the individual had had precious little role except as the hapless, subdued recipient of greater 'efficiency'. Manufacturing industry had collapsed because it was more efficient to operate overseas: by the 1990s, 'Made in Britain' was a rarely seen label, let alone a guarantee of quality. Schools had been given greater control over their entry criteria, and market forces had been allowed to penetrate the health sector, but most people saw little appreciable improvement in achievement or treatment. Discounted council house sales had sparked an initial flurry of proprietorial pride and then an upward house-price spiral, which crashed in the late-1980s and left many locked into a negative-equity trap or with their homes repossessed. Full-blooded Thatcherism had become increasingly unpopular in its social consequences.

But far from seeking to overturn the new common sense of Thatcherism, New Labour chose to pursue a particular strand within it. While Thatcherism had destroyed the old consensual historic bloc and created the basis for a new neoliberal era, it had also unleashed forces of social disorder which, at times, threatened to undermine the state. It had not yet wholly enlisted a new and stable social coalition in Britain for global neoliberal principles and policies. This was to become the historic mission of New Labour. Economically, New Labour pursued a relentless neoliberal free market strategy, seeking to create and consolidate a corporate business-friendly domestic and global environment. It set about extending the 'business state' into every aspect of our lives. However, it is in relation to the welfare state that the distinctive character of New Labour's neoliberalism is most apparent. This is where it has been able to bring elements of its own tradition to the mix, albeit in an inversion of the traditional social democratic nostrum about re-shaping the market to fit the people. Instead, as Roy Hattersley and others have pointed out, New Labour has set about re-shaping the people to fit the market.

After an initial period in which it accepted the public expenditure plans of the Conservatives – and incidentally frittered away much of the goodwill that swept it to power – New Labour significantly increased public expenditure, but on strict conditions. It sought to impose these conditions through an unremitting centralisation of power, the proliferation of unaccountable charitable or not-for-profit agencies, and the further sidelining of local government. And always, they transmitted the message, loud and clear, that the public services and the people who deliver and receive them are not good enough for the shiny new world of market competition.

The organising principle of New Labour's so-called modernising reforms has been the replacement of the ethos of public service by market principles and 'value for money'. Patients, students, passengers, clients and citizens have been redefined as consumers and customers. Wherever possible, public servants have been replaced by business people, by managers of marketised state and non-state agencies, and by 'social entrepreneurs'.[36] A late portent of this process was the proposal by hired management-consultants, ever sensitive to their clients' aspirations, that head-teachers should be drawn from the business community. Even the funding of Blair and Brown's own political party has switched from collective and to some degree accountable agencies – primarily the trade unions and Labour's own membership – to compliant, venal elements amongst the new business-elite (with embarrassing consequences). In such a context it is entirely natural that a General Secretary of the Labour Party appointed in 2008 after the forced resignation of the previous incumbent should be a hedge-fund manager rather than a trade unionist. It is also quite natural that this appointee should then run for cover when the true scale of Labour indebtedness was revealed to him.

The rationalising spin for all this has been ending the power of bureaucracy and vested professional interests, transferring power from producers to consumers, 'personalising' services, and giving people control over their lives by providing choice. This ideological thrust was initiated by Thatcherism, but was generalised and universalised by New Labour, and given a material basis by the increased public expenditure. Freedom from the paternalistic state, empowerment, assuming personal responsibility for one's own life through the exercise of market or quasi-market choice: this has been the gloss under which the role of the state has been transformed. It has been changed from collective provision and solidarity on behalf of society as a whole, of people as citizens, into 'helping people to help themselves' in the marketplace, as individual consumers.

Policies to encourage or coerce those not working back into the labour force initially resulted in some reduction in poverty, especially child poverty, though this then showed signs of stalling.

However, even this initial success was accompanied by an increase in inequality as corporate directors and managers also helped themselves, irrespective of corporate success or failure, to massive bonuses, capital gains and golden handshakes. The process of elite self-enrichment reached obscene extremes in the City of London, but it happened less spectacularly right across the economy, with hugely enlarged pay differentials even in education and the health service. Those who can, really have helped themselves. What remains of citizen-based solidarity principles is confined to the provision of a safety net for those who cannot, for whatever reason, be brought to fend for themselves.

New Labour's attempted recasting of the welfare state's central metaphor of the safety net as a trampoline was a characteristic piece of clever wordplay. But it cannot disguise the fact that those who fall into it, or supposedly bounce back up, are already deeply disadvantaged by the cumulative historical effects of the capitalist economy. Thus, New Labour consciously created a two-tier system, in which those who can, look after themselves, and those who cannot or will not, receive charity provided by a reluctant and disapproving state. When anybody can be bothered to ask recipients of New Labour welfare, in Sure Start, Welfare to Work or the various supposedly New Deals, what it actually feels like on the receiving end, the demeaning multiple stigmas of inadequacy and dependence quickly emerge.

The consumerist edifice constructed by Blair and Brown is illusory, particularly with regard to choice. The so-called consumers of public services were not looking for some balance between quality and quantity, the kind of choice that weighs twenty frocks from Primark against one from Harvey Nichols. What they want is a single, indivisible thing: a timely and competently performed heart operation or an adequate pension or a decent education for their children. They are not generally interested in the technical detail of where or how it is delivered, or in accountancy-style calculations of its strengths and weaknesses. The illusory exercise of choice is reduced in this situation to some form of quality differentiation between different institutions. This requires setting up external, quantifiable and, ultimately, artificial, criteria that get nowhere near the real human experience of living, learning, being treated and recuperating inside these institutions. Instead we are supposed to measure our 'customer-satisfaction' by the proportion of A-C GCSE passes, percentage of post-operative deaths for heart bypasses, or whatever takes the fancy of the consultants hired to set up measures of quality and accompanying league tables. Then, given that each unit 'succeeds' according to its place in this 'quality' hierarchy, it in turn sets about choosing its customers according to those who contribute most to 'success'. 'Quality' begins to select itself.

This is another factor that differentiates public services from the high street: the 'quality' of the product depends on the 'quality' of the customers themselves. Take education, for example. Given that by far the best indicator of success in any public examination is the income of the family from which the student comes, all schools try to maximise the proportion of children they take from high-income backgrounds. This is not cheating but a rational and predictable response to market forces, and explains why middle-class flight is the ultimate nightmare of any half-competent head-teacher. The best schools or universities or hospitals or general practices become not those best at teaching or curing, but those best at choosing their 'customers'. The highest GCSE grades, the lowest rates of heart disease, the most marked improvements in exercise and diet are delivered by the highest income parents, the least socially deprived families, the more physically fit and mentally healthy, and so on.

The only barrier to such 'cream-skimming' is the level of professional scruple and social responsibility among the staff of the various institutions plunged into this pseudo-market. But the New Labour state has devised and deployed a new and largely unproved science of performance-management, some of it drawn from the private sector and some of it simply made up, to deal with such resistance among public sector employees. They are subjected to twin pressures to conform: first, hugely increased rewards to those who actively champion the new way of working and meet their performance targets; and second, the constant denigration of public-sector workers who stand in the way of 'progress and modernisation', whether from genuine principle or cussed, sectional or tribal defensiveness.

The social consequences of converting public services into quasi-commodities are subtler than the brutal class conflict prompted by Thatcher.[37] Experience both in Britain and in other countries during the 1980s demonstrated that direct application of neoliberal policies can lead to levels of civil disorder which come dangerously close to social breakdown, if not outright civil war. New Labour's carefully orchestrated introduction of 'consumer Thatcherism' largely avoided this, but led directly to social problems more insidious, and just as dangerous, as the confrontations of the Thatcher era. The New Labour project to reduce all citizens to consumers by systematically introducing market forces into all corners of social life has engendered an especially malign form of Sennett's ontological insecurity.

One form this has taken is a kind of consumer panic: each person is lost in a crowd of frantic searchers after the best bargain, the lowest price, the latest fashion. And just like the January sales, the best bargains have always just gone, you can never reach the right counter in time, the crowds are always too thick in one place, too thin in another. And when you get the thing home, you realise you've already got one just like it anyway. We have already made much use of psychological pathologies to illustrate our analysis of feelbad Britain. At this point, it seems apt to mention one with all too obvious physical manifestations, to illustrate the effects of rampant consumerism. The spectacular increase in clinical and morbid obesity during the New Labour years makes a vivid metaphor for the prevailing mood: as constant consumers, with ever-expanding appetites and waistlines, we can never be finally satisfied. No matter how much we take in, we soon want more, not least because those around us, our consumer-competitors, seem to be doing so much better and feeling so much happier than we are.

At one level, New Labour gradually became aware of Britain's social crisis. Government policies became full of references to empowering communities, to the third sector of voluntary organisations, to developing mutual respect and understanding. The trouble is that all this rhetoric floats like froth on the ocean of market ideology, devoid of institutional anchorage. Just where the ocean currents are carrying us is unclear, not least because the social and economic instability created by consumerism has become intimately mingled with various external threats, real or exaggerated.

The dangers of climate change are a real and imminent threat and the government has recently been converted, in words, to the need to act to forestall it. However, despite the fact that this is a crisis demanding a social and political response on a global scale, the most audible government reaction lays almost total emphasis on the tweaking of market mechanisms and on individual green-consumerism. What needs to be stressed is that the government's feeble response to global warming stems not from inadequate short-term policy-making, but from the market-driven changes that have reshaped our society, with New Labour's knowing encouragement and acquiescence.

The exaggerated threat is that from international terrorism and the associated assault upon the social status of Muslims and all of our civil liberties. It is universally accepted, if not always acknowledged, that the main source of such threat as exists derives from British foreign policy in the Middle East. Our participation in the invasion and occupation of Iraq and the ensuing civil war put us all at serious risk from terrorist attack. And the fact that the Blair government chose to ignore the biggest demonstration in British history in 2003 did immense damage to British democracy, as well as to the credibility and standing of the government itself. Yet all that ministers can offer by way of explanation is facile comparisons with the threat from Nazi Germany and the perils of 'appeasement'. Tough talk and posturing seem for a while to play well in the opinion polls, but do precisely nothing to bring about sustainable peace and security.

The vicious circle of state repression and terrorist outrage we are embarked upon is wearyingly familiar from the thirty years of the 'troubles' in Northern Ireland. The New Labour government is rightly proud of having brought an end to that, but now seems willing to turn Britain into the most intensively 'surveillanced' society in the world. It is unclear just why this deliberate policy of increased scrutiny and suspicion is being followed, but the fear it engenders is being used to justify a massive erosion of civil liberties extending far beyond anything necessary to counter possible terrorism. The combination of a socially divided, dissatisfied and fearful country with a central government prepared to use unprecedented authoritarian control to suppress real or imagined dissent provides, at the very least, a cloudy prognostication.

THE FINANCIAL AND ECONOMIC CRISIS

Until the surge in food and fuel prices and the credit crunch turned the boom into bust (despite claims by Brown when chancellor that he had abolished boom and bust), New Labour boasted endlessly about the sustained growth recorded by the British economy during its period of office. Yet, as is now evident to everybody, the period of unbroken growth relied on a booming retail sector based on rising personal debt and an inflated housing market. In both cases, continued buoyancy depended on a consumer-confidence trick. Put simply, the economy kept going because most of us kept shopping and moving house, in many cases way beyond our means.

In a bizarre double twist, we were made to feel that our social and political obligation to the new globalised economy was to borrow, shop and consume. Saving, thrift and restraint became irresponsible, deeply unfashionable and by implication unpatriotic. But most of us knew at some level that we could not go on like this. That was the real political challenge of the dawning green common sense: consumerism is unsustainable. Moreover, even if it posed no threat to the environment, sooner or later boom is inevitably followed by bust, and those economies that boost consumption beyond realistic limits are the ones liable to suffer the deepest and longest recessions.

Year after year, the UK's burgeoning personal debt levels and balance-of-payments deficits were brushed aside, with blithe disregard for the future. Indeed, paradoxically, unregulated capitalism and unbridled consumerism harm not just the environment and society, but also capitalist business itself. Yet history moves in mysterious ways. Despite having presided over a decade of deregulation, and evangelised for the virtues of a flexible, business-friendly financial and economic system, giving market buccaneers carte blanche to enrich themselves, Gordon Brown suddenly emerged in the autumn of 2008 as the saviour of the international financial system by taking an equity stake in failing banks rather than buying their toxic debt, as had been initially proposed by then US Treasury Secretary Paulson. He then adopted a rather manic version of Keynesian reflation, attempting to stimulate consumer demand by a temporary cut in VAT and accelerating various infrastructure projects.

At the same time, faced with a rapidly deepening global recession and rising unemployment, governments around the world began to draw up reflationary packages to stimulate economic activity by lowering interest rates, cutting taxes and increasing public spending, with growing acceptance of the need to re-regulate the national economy and to reform the international monetary system. In the 1940s Polanyi not only characterised the attempt to create a self-regulating capitalist economy as 'utopian'; he also identified a counter-movement in the form of resistance to the destructive effects of free-market capitalism, and the creation of a legal and regulatory framework to save capitalism from itself. However, such interference with the logic of capitalist production for profit eventually causes the system to seize up, which is what happened in the 1970s after the post-war era of welfare state Keynesianism. The result was the neoliberal epoch of privatisation and deregulation.

This raises the question of whether the present neoliberal era is now coming to an end. Are we at the beginning of a second Polanyian counter-movement which, given the extent to which globalisation of the world's financial and economic systems has occurred, will this time need to involve global rather than national regulation? Can we expect a twenty-first century version of Roosevelt's New Deal, perhaps this time in the form of a Green New Deal? It seems likely that the capitalist world as a whole has entered an organic crisis which will involve a prolonged period of experimentation, innovation, trial and error, until a new historic settlement is arrived at as the basis for a new period of relative stability. But we must remember Gramsci's adage – 'pessimism of the intellect, optimism of the will' – with the most likely outcome being a passive revolution which may not be at all progressive.

Of course, the actual outcome will depend on struggle and the balance of forces, within each country and globally. It took ten years after the 1929 Wall Street crash for an effective new deal to be created and implemented, and even then it was only the advent of the Second World War that finally brought about full employment and created the conditions for the post-war settlement that ushered in the major advance of the social democratic Keynesian welfare state. It is against this historical experience that our analysis of the social crisis – caused by the neoliberal erosion of trust and mutuality; by the redefinition of people as workers, customers and consumers, rather than as citizens; and by the replacement of a solidaristic society by frightened, anxious, atomised individuals – becomes so important. The forces for progress were in many ways much stronger in the 1930s than they are today, although the election of Barack Obama as President of the United States offers some hope for the possibility of change. If the turbulent times ahead are to be shaped in a democratic and progressive direction, we need to recognise how we have arrived at the present situation, to be realistic about the social forces on which such a movement depends, to think clearly about the obstacles that will have to be overcome, and find ways to build a new sensibility of mutuality and common purpose.

So, while analysis is essential, in itself it is not enough. The question, as always, is: What is to be done? For most of the past hundred years in Britain, all serious answers to this question have taken the Labour Party as a central point of reference, variously calling for a change of leadership, direction or party organisation. In the next section, we argue that the emergence and now bankruptcy of New Labour renders the old map of politics obsolete and that the democratic left needs to rethink its entire project. When Tory leader Cameron can position himself to the left of Brown on a range of social policy issues, we have to acknowledge that we are indeed in a strange place.

WHAT ON EARTH IS TO BE DONE?

As we have described, after three decades in the political wilderness after 1945, the free market right began in the 1970s to overturn the post-war settlement. A full thirty years on, the remnants of the British left are an endangered political species. Beyond a few small groups and fringe publications, it is hard even to see any consciously, recognisably left-wing political force in Britain. Since 1989/91, the end of the Cold War, and the final collapse of what passed for communism in the east, all conceptions of socialism – whether as a form of society wholly beyond capitalism or as a transforming presence within it – have been largely written off as the late, unlamented pipe dreams of the twentieth century. A mood of deep disillusion with ambitious plans for social improvement has set in. As the logic of the market swamps the logic of citizenship – to the point where even the principle of progressive taxation is called into question – it has become fashionable to argue that politics has now moved beyond established notions of left and right, or any kind of transforming purpose, to become merely a process of administering given realities. There are challenges to the state from a new generation of activists. But, in the main, they do not see socialism any more than other kinds of organised politics as relevant to their causes. If anything, they are informed by a new kind of anarchism; the flag they march under is green and black not red.

Until the 1970s, it all seemed so simple. The left-right axis coincided with the radical-conservative axis: the left was radical, the right conservative. The emergence of a new political phenomenon, the radical right, tore the ideological map apart. The single line of British politics became a four-cornered cross. From Peterloo to the General Strike, the right's reflex response to social unrest was to demand firm action to suppress it and restore the old order. In Thatcherism, this atavistic, repressive impulse clearly existed, but it was coupled with a radical programme for unleashing market forces. The old Tory aversion to big ideas, bold initiatives and wholesale regime change was simply cast aside.

Conversely, having no hegemonic project of their own, the left and the labour movement were forced onto the defensive, vainly seeking to resist or retard reforms that had once been unthinkable and were still unpalatable, but were widely if reluctantly accepted as inevitable. And just as Mrs Thatcher and the new radical right, in presiding over the first wave of the neoliberal revolution, killed off one-nation Conservatism, so Tony Blair and New Labour, in completing Mrs Thatcher's unfinished business, has killed off British Labourism, our own peculiar national variety of left-conservatism.

With the demise of the two class-based traditions that had dominated British politics for sixty years after the First World War, Britain has acquired, for the first time since the industrial revolution, a thoroughly bourgeois pattern of politics. The mainstream parties, jostling to win votes in the crowded centre ground, respond to the financial and economic crisis by vying to offer minor variations on the best way to resume job-centred consumerism and boundless economic growth. They may acknowledge that our lives are insecure, our society atomised and our planet at risk, but they seem to think that these problems can be tackled without restraining the growth machine itself. Their ideal, we might say, is an inclusive, cohesive, sustainable yet endlessly expansive capitalist cornucopia.

This *is* a pipe dream. There is no need to rehearse, accept or dispute the whole of Layard's argument. It is enough to point out that Gross Domestic Product (GDP), the dominant measure of a society's success, can no longer be taken as a reliable proxy for human happiness and arguably never should have been. The idea that capitalism is still a broadly benign, if manifestly disruptive, engine of progress is further undermined when one considers the most recent phase of capitalist development. The spread of market forces, relationships and commercial norms to social activities in which their role was previously circumscribed – from child rearing and education to postal services and pensions – weakens social cohesion. It further undermines the sense of belonging to a wider community, essential if the culture and practice of democracy are to flourish. The rampant commercialisation of what were previously protected, private spaces cheapens and brutalises what should be sources of intimacy, pleasure, joy and consolation. If everything is for sale, nothing is sacred. And now in a bitter irony, homes are repossessed, jobs lost and savings and pensions are threatened, while all the time the environmental damage caused by unlimited growth is so serious as to endanger the future of life on Earth. In short, capitalism has outlived its useful social purpose and the democratic left should say so.

This is not an outrageous conclusion. In the 1980s, it might have seemed so, when consumer capitalism still held some genuine allure, especially to those who had grown up amid post-war austerity and the paternalistic state. It clearly offered a quality of service and quantity of product never had before, at little obvious extra cost, and seemed like some sort of compensation for the social and industrial devastation wrought by high-period Thatcherism. For all those whose livelihoods were lost and whose lives were blighted, there were others who saw real improvements in their personal and family fortunes. But we have now come to the end of that line. The allure has faded and been shown to be an illusion. From almost any perspective, capitalism is now doing far more harm than good.

PROJECTS AND POLICIES

What might a sustainable post-capitalist world look like? Is it attainable? How long would it take to construct? And how can it be brought closer? How can the majority of people, with daily lives to lead, jobs to do, families and households to maintain, and the usual bundle of personal hopes and worries and preoccupations that we all carry around, embark upon such a huge, historic undertaking? What use can be made of existing democratic arrangements and political structures? What new arrangements and structures are needed?

These are big questions and it would be presumptuous to suggest that the answers we offer below are anything more than rough sketches and examples. We do, however, maintain that these are the right big questions to be asking. Max Weber once said that there are only two questions in politics: What should we do? And what shall we do? What we are saying is that, while there are undoubtedly tensions between 'should' and 'shall', between morality and practice, between visions and realities, they all need to be considered together if we are to begin making a political difference.

Every political tradition invokes certain distinctive values that convey some image of the good society, however sketchy, and provide adherents with a sense of direction amidst the flux of events. Old Tories, for example, argue that social hierarchy is both inevitable and desirable because human beings are naturally unequal: some people just are more able, intelligent, wise or forceful than others. Liberals and socialists both reject this view, but disagree about what equality entails. The liberal ideal is a society in which all members have equal moral standing – 'each counts for one and none for more than one' – and everyone is assured the same basic liberties and opportunities. Socialists argue that this is not enough. There are wide, persistent and historically determined inequalities in the distribution of resources and power: notably by class, gender and race. Such systemic inequalities are both unjust and divisive, making it impossible to build a self-governing democracy in which people's shared identity as citizens tempers the individual or sectional interests that divide them.

The democratic left seeks to combine the characteristic socialist belief in social equality and human solidarity with the civic republican ideals of positive freedom and democratic self-government and the green commitment to sustainable development and post-materialism. Do these values cohere? Could a society embodying them exist? Or is it a chimera? Two issues need to be distinguished here. One is whether a society with the requisite features would be able to cope with the perennial problems facing all human societies – such as how to handle conflicting claims on available resources – and thus maintain itself as a going concern. The other, more obviously political, issue is whether such a society can be brought into being, starting from where we are now and taking into account probable barriers and sources of resistance.

There is one important reason why this process is not just a political dream but a practical necessity. Climate change is already upon us and will come to dominate our lives in a very few decades. Either we alter the way we live by progressive change based on social recognition of the problem or our lives will be wrenched into new and almost certainly dire paths by the compelling force of nature. The need to pursue an 'ethical' or 'green' lifestyle is already becoming a common ambition. The difficulty is that at the moment, there is little on offer to achieve such aims save versions of green consumerism.

There is, however, a difference between visualising possible worlds and pursuing political projects. In politics, we have to reckon with constraints and pressures that can – indeed *must* – be set aside when articulating visions: institutional inertia, cultural habits, structural bias and political resistance, including the complex games that ensue when political agents try to anticipate the moves and counter-moves of their opponents. Thus, while values and visions are the stars we steer by, we still have to navigate in real time and space.

By way of illustration, we might cite a model developed by one of us of a post-capitalist economy, in which the co-ordinating principle is neither market forces nor central planning but a system of democratic decision-making called 'negotiated co-ordination'.[38] The model combines social ownership of the means of production with stakeholder democracy. Current production decisions would still be reconciled beyond the workplace by means of market exchange, but bigger, strategic issues affecting the pattern of economic and social development, such as major investment projects and the adoption of new technologies, would be decided beforehand through co-ordinated processes of collective deliberation, problem-solving and negotiation in which all stakeholders are involved. Market exchange exists in the model but market forces do not. This model certainly describes a possible world, but it is far removed from the world we are in, and could not come into being without a long process of institutional and cultural change.

To take just one aspect: before people can govern themselves, they must acquire the requisite outlook, attitudes and experience. At present, democracy is more or less limited to voluntary organisations and periodic parliamentary and council elections to decide which party or coalition should form an administration. Private business firms are accountable only to their owners, not to any other groups of stakeholders. Public bodies are accountable only to central government. As a result, very few people gain experience of running things, whether in politics or the business world. But if people are not involved in making the policies and decisions that govern their lives, they are unlikely to feel any responsibility for them. In fact, they're liable to behave irresponsibly, putting their personal or sectional interests – especially as jobholders, wage-earners and consumers – above those of their fellow citizens and society as a whole. The case for enabling and persuading more people to play a bigger part in running a wider range of social organisations is not just that it makes for better government, but that it makes people better citizens.

It is clear that New Labour is dimly aware of the social problems that arise when those agencies which used to provide scope for democratic involvement have their hearts ripped out. The mantras of 'community empowerment' or 'local involvement' are repeated endlessly. But the neoliberal Hayekian project, to which Gordon Brown et al subscribe, has no room for collective social agencies. Indeed, it is specifically and totally opposed to them. One fundamental reason for the incoherence of the Labour government under Brown is precisely that it seeks to remodel society according to principles which are, even now, impossible to spell out in public discourse.

In the socialist tradition, it is customary but misleading to describe the period during which a new society is emerging as 'transitional'. History has no terminus or timetables and all historical journeys involve a leap into the unknown: we are perpetually poised between an irrevocable past and an uncertain future and no outcome is ever final. So we must accept that social transformation of the kind and scale we are after is unlikely to be achieved straightforwardly, or within our own lifetimes. On the other hand, it will not do to say, with Keynes: 'In the long run we are all dead'. If transforming society is to be more than an aspiration, then our short-term actions and choices must be framed accordingly. In tackling the urgent problems of the present, we must acknowledge that we are also creating the future.

It helps to keep this point in mind if we distinguish between policies and projects. Policies are not just practical responses to perceived social problems: they are also political acts that impinge on the prevailing balance of forces. Hence, correctly judged, they are instruments for changing the political landscape, building new institutions and securing vantage points for further advance. But timing is crucial. Policies need to be tailored to specific situations and adapted, dropped or picked up again as the situation changes, normally within an electoral timeframe. A project, by contrast, is a long-term undertaking informed by deep and lasting values. It should make sense of the past, identify the main problems facing society in the present and propose a strategy for tackling them in the future, including general principles and guidelines for producing policies (a policy paradigm).

To be effective, any political formation needs both these things – flexible policies and a firm project – but the latter is vital for two reasons. It provides a sense of direction and purpose, essential for maintaining morale in the face of unavoidable compromises and setbacks; and it provides a framework for building a new, hegemonic, historic bloc. Furthermore, it makes sense not to be too prescriptive on policy, because the new allies you wish to recruit to your bloc/project will have views and needs of their own that you will need to accommodate.

From this standpoint, Thatcherism and New Labour make interesting contrasts. Thatcherism was above all a project, to transform the terrain upon which its politics were to be conducted and its specific policies advanced. It did not need to be rational, thought-through or even wholly conscious, because it worked at the level of ideology, the deep and complex ways in which people make collective sense of their daily, individual, lives. Besides, Thatcherism was never a wholly transformative project – a large part of it was about restoring aspects of the past, even if only at the level of popular mentality. As Stuart Hall put it in his definitive 1980s analyses, its attempts at 'modernisation' were simultaneously 'regressive'. It touched the souls of important sections of the British population precisely by voicing their griev-ances at 'the way things are going' and their nostalgic yearning for 'the way things used to be', while at the same time propelling them towards what we have already described as a 'market utopia'.[39]

Nor did Thatcherism need to be democratic, because it was a top-down process of change, determined and implemented by the ruling elite: in Gramscian terms, a classic example of passive revo-lution. It had no need to engage people in continuing discussion or decision-making, or even really change their minds. It merely had to chime in with what they already thought and co-opt them into its market utopian ideology, or bully them into submission. Indeed, its primary beneficiaries, the petty bourgeoisie who form the classic audience for passive revolution, were only too happy to be told what to do by 'her', the conviction-politician, the ultimate strong man.

Thatcherite government policy was also often almost wilfully confused, especially when it touched upon persisting differences within the ruling bloc. But this did not necessarily matter either, so long as policy served the broader project of deepening the hegemony of neoliberal capitalism, sustaining the alliance behind it and further marginalising its opponents. On the policy front, Thatcherism could be surprisingly non-prescriptive and prag-matic, strongly focused on 'what works' in furthering the grand project. Every policy area of the 1980s and 1990s Tory govern-ments contained surprising pockets of progressive practice, even if only because the Tories' basic disdain for the detailed business of government allowed for experimentation in its more marginal niches and some creativity amongst its paid operatives.

New Labour, by contrast, has produced a torrent of 'policy': a lot of it finely wrought and detailed, mulled over by sympathetic think-tanks and committees of the great and the good, refined and sound-bited for media transmission and public consumption. Barely a day has gone by in the last ten years without some new policy initiative, often a repackaging of an old one, but buffed up and refashioned for the morning papers and news broadcasts. Then, within a day or two, we get another 'bold' new departure from some other department or agency. New Labour government is afflicted with policy-itis, an epidemic of proposals and targets and executive summaries. It assumes a kind of political Attention Deficit Disorder on the part of the British public, who are not supposed to notice that it's all been said before and that it doesn't really amount to much anyway – the essential feature of the New Labour decade.

Policy-itis also helps to explain why the New Labour government has steadily lost the support of so much of the anti-Tory coalition that propelled it into office in 1997. Every new 'policy' provides at least something for someone to disagree with and cite as reason for their broader disenchantment, even without reckoning the most common final straw of all, the ultimate policy disaster of Iraq. There is precious little to hold people in the coalition, because New Labour has completely lacked any true overarching sense of a project. This has left it incapable of challenging Thatcherism, of developing a strategy for constructing a new historic bloc and transforming British society in any meaningful sense.

The original New Labour clique of Blair, Brown and Mandelson might have called what they were up to 'the project', but this was always a slightly flippant, self-conscious in-joke. All they were doing was mounting a palace coup within a historically ailing party. New Labour's only discernible historic mission has been to expose our society and economy to the full force of neoliberal capitalism under the rubric of globalisation. In the process they have consolidated the truly historic project of Thatcherism in ways the Tories either could not attempt or would not have dared, by driving consumer capitalism into aspects of our lives previously considered sacrosanct.

Again, it is clear that some grasp of this problem has penetrated the recesses of the metropolitan New Labour think tanks and policy-movers. The call is for a new 'narrative' to underpin the plethora of policy. But, again, there cannot be any new narrative without some renunciation or at least reformation of the old. Most New Labour acolytes seem unaware that they already possess a narrative which is itself the problem. In any significant policy sense, it makes little difference whether current Labour or Conservative rules. The danger is that the British political system has become unstable and could shift into uncharted, probably authoritarian, territory. Within the current neoliberal hegemony, and now its crisis, Britain cries out for a 'strong' leader, a new 'Caesar'.

The left needs to recognise both the urgency and also the complexity of its problem. What we now need on the democratic left is a renewed sense of our project: where we want to go and how we propose to get there. It will be harder for us than it was for either Thatcherism or its New Labour offspring, because we need a project which is both radical and progressive; truly democratic rather than merely electoral; popular rather than populist; and which amounts to more than wheezes, fixes, spin and sound-bites. It will have to offer genuine, not regressive or superficial, modernisation of our country; challenge the existing common sense of the age and not just pander to existing prejudices; catch people's imaginations as well as their eyes; reach their souls and not just their pockets. We need to transform our social relations, not to freeze them. In the following sections, we look at some specific aspects of the overall passage to a new society with, very briefly, examples of the kind of policies required to bring it about. We shall return finally to the issues of agency: what kind of politics and project might take us towards where we need to be, firmly on the road to a sustainable and socially just society.

CONVERGENT GLOBAL DEVELOPMENT

The pattern of economic development that has prevailed for the past two centuries is no longer sustainable. The challenge of our age is to limit and repair the damage caused by unbounded economic growth – to society, nature and humanity. Cleaner forms of energy and increased energy efficiency will buy us more time. The same goes for recycling and other ways of reducing materials used or wastes produced per unit of output. But however much we succeed in greening capitalism, efforts to conserve resources and protect habitats are bound to be an uphill struggle as long as global business keeps on growing and we remain its willing slaves.

Moreover, it is not just the *future growth* of output that we need to worry about, but its *current scale* and the cumulative consequences of our own past profligacy. The effects of global warming, daily more obvious and troubling, accrue from two centuries of unchecked industrialisation – just a foretaste of what is to come if we do not bring it within conscious social control. There is an often-overlooked political dimension to this. The poor invariably bear the brunt of environmental disaster, such as the flooding of low-lying land in Bangladesh, New Orleans or even

East Anglia. We need political action to share both the current effects of global warming and the adjustment costs of dealing with it on a fair and equitable basis.

Nearly everyone now accepts that we have a serious environmental crisis, but there is a general sense of powerlessness about what can be done about it. Many feel that these are global problems beyond personal, national or even human solution. Recycling and ethical consumerism are all well and good, but compared to the effects of China's headlong dash towards industrialisation, they can feel like isolated, conscience-salving, token gestures. Tony Blair alluded to this, but typically used it to justify the reluctance of elected politicians like himself to propose serious action, thereby reinforcing the general sense that nothing worthwhile can be done.

This sense of powerlessness is hardly surprising, given the scale of the challenge and the loss of faith in democratic politics, but there is a real risk of apathy, or worse, of a yet further deepening of the ontological insecurity we spoke of earlier. Green politics needs to focus on the social as well as the environmental, and on ways of involving as well as alarming people, two political techniques that do not always sit comfortably together. It also needs to celebrate rather than oppose the modern and the urban, to engage with the popular mainstream as well as the variously disaffected, and to demonstrate that a sustainable society and life style would offer a better, not worse, quality of life. That's also a pretty tall order, which no established political forces – red, green or otherwise – measure up to.

What on earth is to be done? We might start with some clear and, in principle, feasible demands of our national and international political institutions. One possibility is to build on the emergent response to climate change. Critical thresholds for atmospheric concentrations of greenhouse gases have provided a baseline for constructive international negotiations aimed at reducing overall carbon emissions and sharing the costs of adjustment fairly, with the aim of each country agreeing to a specific quantified target, even though the United States under Bush and some other countries refused to join in.[40]

Given the political will, the same approach could be applied to restraining economic growth, the underlying cause of environmental damage. An international commission could agree on a trajectory for sustainable global GDP, based on the best available scientific knowledge of what was needed to combat global warming and manage other environmental risks. Inter-governmental negotiation would then establish growth paths for each country consistent with this global trajectory according to its current per capita income. The aim would be to equalise living standards across the world at the highest sustainable level by some distant but definite target date. For the sake of argument, suppose that no country is prepared to lower its GDP and that this stance is compatible with environmental constraints.[41] On these assumptions, the sustainable global growth curve would rise towards an upper limit, the agreed growth of per capita income in rich countries would slow down or stop – not just temporarily but for good – while incomes in poor countries would gradually catch up. This is what we mean by convergent global development.

Needless to say, there is little chance of getting national governments to agree a plan for convergent global development and then act upon it unless people in rich countries come to accept the moral and practical imperative for poorer countries to catch up. This is where political action comes in. If, for example, the US or the Anglo-Saxon bloc refused to participate, it would still be worthwhile for the rest of the world to work out national growth paths consistent with convergent global sustainability, but the purpose of the exercise would be to build up political pressure to get these wealthier states to join in. Similarly, if governments in rich countries persistently broke their international undertakings by exceeding agreed growth targets, in the end only peer pressure could bring them into line and that, in turn, would presuppose that most countries endorsed the global plan.[42] Any engagement by Britain in this project on a unilateral basis would, of course, have limited physical impact. However, this is not the point, for it is clear that whilst supranational institutions such as the EU must ultimately adopt a common policy, it is also clear that they will only do so if individual nations within them pursue more than rhetorical policies.

In this sense, supranational institutions lose traction if the nations they purport to serve lose confidence in them: witness the fate of the EU constitutional treaty. All the same, trans-national governance is a necessity, not a luxury, let alone a burden: efforts to restrain economic growth in any one state are unlikely to succeed unless they are embedded in a supportive global regime. And institutions charged with protecting the biosphere and steering global development must be flanked by complementary arrangements to regulate cross-border trade, migration and capital flows. Neither so-called free trade nor go-it-alone protectionism affords a viable basis for building a just and sustainable world order, any more than the old idea of indivisible and inalienable national sovereignty affords a viable basis for safeguarding inter-national peace and security.

It should be emphasised that this is a social and political project, not a market-based one. It focuses on the central issue of how world poverty is to be eliminated within the context of avoiding climate change. In this sense it is similar to, but distinct from, the concept of contraction and convergence (C&C) of carbon emissions, which has emerged as a leading principle for the next round of international negotiations on climate change. The current western interpretation of C&C is that whilst there is a long-term ambition of equalising per capita carbon emissions worldwide, during the transition period poor countries will assist the wealthy to achieve their target levels of emissions, at least nominally, by selling their 'surplus' emission rights. The funda-mental problem with this approach is that whilst providing the poorer countries with some immediate financial compensation for not exercising their full rights to carbon emissions, it also mort-gages their future paths of economic growth by limiting the accumulated carbon emissions required to achieve such growth. Consider, as a simple example, the huge volumes of carbon which have been required to produce the mass of steel and concrete locked into the long-lasting infrastructures of rich countries. How can poor countries similarly develop such infrastructure of energy-rich materials if they are selling part of their annual carbon emission rights?

Such a grand global plan has to be socially and politically based, rather than centred on market-based solutions, which emphasise only individual responsibility and action. We accept that the idea of convergent global development is radical and hugely ambitious. Some might suggest that it is utopian, though compared to the market utopianism that has held sway for the last thirty years it is a model of practical realism and common sense. It is at least based on the best of previous experience, on the available scientific evidence, and on a clear sense of what can be achieved by people working together for the common good. And unlike neoliberalism, it will benefit everyone: globally, nationally and individually.

Of course these global objectives need to be based upon equally far-reaching programmes in Britain. Take one particular example: that of road transport. Any major reduction in carbon emissions requires the gradual adoption of electricity-based vehicles, which will be less powerful than current hydrocarbon-fuelled vehicles. In a small country, the alternative of biofuels is simply not a realistic option of any significance. In fact recent experience suggests that development of crop-based biofuels will actually have malign effects not just on the environment but also socially, as food prices are driven up by agricultural shortages. This is a good example of how market-based 'solutions' to reducing greenhouse gas emissions often bite back in unexpected ways. As a nation, we must become accustomed not just to driving less but also to driving more slowly. To achieve this there must be, alongside massive investment in public transport, a large investment in both the vehicles themselves and associated fuelling facilities. There must also be serious controls on the speeds at which vehicles are allowed to drive and huge investment in sustainable electricity production to match the increased power consumption from such vehicles. Planning and house-building policies must ensure that jobs, essential services and utilities, and leisure facilities, are within short, or preferably walking or cycling, distances.

The extent of the cultural change required for this kind of shift is enormous. They range from shifts in social awareness about powerful cars and fast driving to long-term planning of low-carbon electricity generation and the expansion of rail and bus transport. We need to generate the same sort of moral public opposition to unnecessary car journeys and speeding as applies to smoking. There will be resolute resistance to such changes, both explicitly from the motorist 'Jeremy Clarkson' lobby and, implicitly, from private sector interests in the car, electricity and transport lobbies. The changes will require a combination of strong government intervention and equally strong social support of the required changes in life-style. We will all need to slow down, right across our lives, but as the 'Slow Food' movement has shown, there are real benefits and pleasures to be had from a more relaxed and sensuous approach to life.

In this fashion, policies for a low-carbon sustainable future become part of a global project both to resist climate change and to raise living standards in the poorer parts of the world. Utopian? Well, it is worth noting that these twin projects engage active and widespread political enthusiasm in a way that the tired politics and politicians of New Labour can only envy and are only too anxious to be associated with. Blair at Gleneagles and Brown in his new-found enthusiasm for the poor of Africa could see a genuine political cause even if their attachment to it is both shallow and transitory.

CITIZEN'S INCOME

How can the competitive rivalry and compulsive expansion that drive the capitalist mode of production be tamed? How can people living in affluent societies move beyond their addiction to getting and spending and aim at a better quality of life? Can they be convinced that once material sufficiency is assured, lasting happiness comes from pursuing non-material goals? And how can the transition from boundless economic growth to balanced social development be achieved within a democratic framework?

The social transformation we are envisaging would be as profound as the industrial revolution that launched the modern era, yet, potentially, as popular as the practice of birth control that spread across Europe between about 1870 and 1930 and improved family life immeasurably, especially for women and children. The international setting in which it might unfold was considered above. The domestic problems that have to be resolved *en route* to a slow-growth or steady-state economy can be subsumed under three headings: the work-income nexus, distributional conflict and public finance.

The work-income nexus consists of socially determined rules and unspoken conventions governing what counts as work and how entitlements to income are established. Even in wealthy countries, most people have, at best, only modest financial assets and continue to depend on regular employment throughout their working lives as their main source of income. Moreover, in a capitalist economy, both the overall level and detailed pattern of employment are largely determined by the decisions of profit-seeking firms. How, then, might the work-income nexus be organised in an economy where public policy seeks to curb the restless dynamic of capitalism? For instance, as a society, we have grown accustomed to relying on regular output growth to maintain employment in the face of rising productivity, which would otherwise reduce the demand for labour and lead to a 'shortage' of jobs. How can we unlearn this habit and pay more attention to the alternative way of enjoying the fruits of productivity growth: work less and live more?

Changes in the duration and pattern of working time impinge on the distribution of income, the division of labour and the balance between the business, public, household and voluntary sectors of the economy. They cannot simply be imposed: they would have to be negotiated and agreed by all concerned. But if, as seems plausible, perpetual growth is a way of avoiding or alleviating conflict among competing sectional interest groups, what will happen when this safety valve is closed? Public finance could also present problems. In a growing economy, governments can cut tax rates, whether for ideological reasons or in response to competitive pressures, and still maintain or even increase total tax revenue. But how will they cope in a steady state?

To reduce the risk that restrained growth will provoke social strife and fiscal crisis, political exhortation and agitation would never be enough. The work-income nexus needs to be radically reorganised. A key step would be to replace the existing social security system by a Citizen's Income (CI): a recurrent, tax-financed money transfer payable on a lifelong basis to every individual member of the community, each in his or her own right, with no means test and no work test. Thus defined, CI could be paid on any feasible scale, from a purely token amount up to the highest level that can be permanently sustained. Clearly, however, the official poverty standard, inscribed in current social security schedules, marks a critical threshold. Only if CI were paid on at least this scale would it be possible to phase out all or most social security benefits without plunging anyone into poverty.

More generally, to make a real difference to people's work-life options, the scale of payment, graduated according to age and disability, would have to enable people to meet their basic needs, defined according to prevailing social norms, without having to participate in the labour market. CI, paid on this scale, is generally known as Basic Income. Would it be viable? How would people use the enhanced freedom it brings? And would they be willing to pay the requisite tax costs? The short answer is: no one knows. It depends on the answers to four questions: Is the idea ethically defensible? Is it socially acceptable? Is it economically sustainable? And is it capable of mobilising enough political support to put it into effect? Though logically distinct, in practice these questions are interdependent.

Suppose, for example, most people – or at any rate, most jobholders – are addicted to getting and spending in the sense that such a lifestyle seems the only one which brings them necessary social esteem and personal satisfaction, the condition characterised by Oliver James as affluenza. Then even if the ethical case for Basic Income is impeccable, any attempt to introduce it would have adverse consequences for business firms and the labour market. Since these would probably be anticipated in advance, it is most unlikely that any political party advocating BI would be elected to government in the first place. In these circumstances, economic progressives must play a long game, pursuing initiatives designed to change the prevailing culture and modify existing institutions in ways that anticipate the more distant future. This very much follows Gramsci's concept of prefigurative struggle, inserting elements of socialism into the cracks in capitalism. In this case, it would almost certainly mean settling for piecemeal reforms of the tax and social security system that fall short of the ultimate goal, but bring it closer to the horizon of political possibility.

The consolidation of Child Benefit, Education Maintenance Allowance and the Basic State Retirement Pension into Junior and Senior Citizen's Incomes, respectively, would be one example of such a reform. Another would be the replacement of university tuition fees and student loans by a system of finance combining funding from general taxation, as at present, with an earmarked graduate tax. This would be levied as an additional charge on the taxable incomes of all working age graduates, including those who had gained their degrees in the past as well as future cohorts. Persuading graduates to support such a scheme is a challenge of the same general kind as persuading well-heeled citizens to support CI. Say the aim is to raise enough revenue to cover tuition costs and provide undergraduate students with modest maintenance grants. Then most graduates would end up with marginally lower disposable incomes over the course of their working lives. On the other hand, students and many parents would be financially better off, market forces would be expelled from higher education and inter-generational solidarity would be strengthened. Moreover, once bedded in, the scheme could be extended to all forms of post-school education, including the payments currently made to encourage students to attend sixth-form. Thereafter, it could be converted into a Young Citizen's Income, establishing a bridge-head from which to engage with the problem of extending entitlement to the rest of the working age population.

But in fact we really have little idea whether James' affluenza virus is pandemic, epidemic or just a minority illness, nor whether there are vaccines or treatments. This is why the distinction between project and policy is so important. The pace at which society will move towards a different order is hard to know in advance and policies have to be proposed which are politically acceptable here and now. At the same time, accelerated change can occur at moments that are impossible to predict, but for which we need to be prepared.

CI will become feasible to the extent that *homo economicus*, that benighted denizen of the neoliberal universe, gives way to *civis socius* (and *socia*), the social citizen for whom, in Ruskin's phrase, 'there is no wealth but life'. And reconstituting social citizenship calls for a suitably democratic system of finance and management. From this point of view, the best arrangement would be one in which CI is financed exclusively by an earmarked personal income tax, with public services financed by revenue from other taxes – VAT, excise duties, corporation tax etc. An integrated tax-transfer system would be simple to administer, easy to understand, socially inclusive and fiscally disciplined. It would also open up the prospect of democratising the annual public budget and changing the terms of public debate: both about questions of distribution – who does what, who gets what, who decides what; and about questions of value – what things are worth having, being and doing.

With CI and income tax locked together in a self-contained system, proposals to raise or lower transfer scales and tax rates are bound to take account of the probable repercussions for the economy as a whole. Most people nowadays equate the 'economy' with the activities of business firms and public agencies – or even just the former alone. Likewise, when they think of 'work', they automatically form an image of paid employment. In what we might call a 'Citizen's Income Democracy', unpaid work in the household and voluntary sectors of the economy would finally enter the framework of social accounting. And this in turn would facilitate efforts to establish a multilateral system of policy negotiation covering all aspects of social reproduction, involving all relevant stakeholders and providing a regular procedure for steering the economy, managing conflict and building a post-materialist civilisation.

SOCIAL OWNERSHIP

Historically, the question of ownership became the defining feature of twentieth century socialism to the point where it pretty much excluded all other aspects. Moreover, ownership under socialism came increasingly to mean state ownership, literally nationalisation. The problems with this definition of socialism became apparent in the 1970s, as nationalisation in Britain became a byword for last-ditch and usually doomed efforts to revive failing capitalist enterprises alongside unaccountable bureaucracy in established state industries. The neoliberal response to this was privatisation and deregulation, to which the increasingly beleaguered labour movement had no answer other than to defend the ailing status quo.

As part of the democratic left project, ownership has to be placed firmly back at the centre of political action, not as a series of state acquisitions, but as a strategy for extending popular democratic control over productive assets and for protecting society and the environment against the harmful consequences of private control over key sections of the economy. Nationalisation was a major step forward in its day, imposing checks on the socially destructive effects of unregulated capitalism after the bitter experiences of the 1920s and 1930s, but it was not social ownership. State-owned enterprises were not subject to democratic control by their workers, customers and the communities in which they operated. Nor, of course, did they exhibit the ruthless dynamism of exclusively profit-motivated private business. Thus they tended to combine the worst of both public and private worlds. As their shortcomings became increasingly apparent, change was inevitable.

In the 1980s, privatisation of state and municipal assets was promoted as the key to greater economic efficiency. It also brought substantial windfall profits at huge discounts for those lucky enough to have the capital to participate. The collapse of state communism after 1989 seemed to be the final nail in the coffin of nationalisation and, by extension, of socialism itself. The largely symbolic campaign to repeal Clause 4 of the Labour Party constitution summed up this shift. However, the economic benefits of 1980s privatisation are highly debatable. In the electricity sector, for example, cost savings estimated at about 6 per cent were effectively given away in profits and have to be set against the destruction of the coal industry and the very rapid depletion of British gas reserves. Recent huge price rises by the privatised energy companies have resulted in outrage but, in the end, the lack of any clear levers of control and a reluctance to engage with business have meant that the government has done almost nothing. New Labour's acceptance of the ideology of Thatcherism has meant that far from carefully analysing the pros and cons of privatisation, the government has plunged further and further into it. It has barely bothered to justify such measures, whether in terms of economic benefit or even short-term electoral bribes. It has been able to do this without more than defensive, sectional opposition because, in effect, the issue of social ownership has been removed from the political agenda.

The unhappy saga of Northern Rock is illustrative. Once it was a small, provincial mutual society which provided a useful service to its members. They saved on a regular basis and once they had acquired a sufficient base, the society offered a long-term mortgage at interest rates a little above that paid to savers. Such institutions proliferated throughout Britain well into the twentieth century. Of course, it can be argued that the building societies were conservative and often discriminatory. They lent to 'respectable' couples, either married or soon-to-be, and were notably sniffy about any deviation from this social norm. They were also, often, agents for the better-off, at best serving the skilled working class. But they did a useful job in a limited way. In the mania for privatisation, the de-mutualisation of building societies was accepted as just another obvious practice. Windfall cheques dropped through the letterboxes of many surprised savers, and the newly formed 'banks' were either swallowed up by larger fish or turned into expansionary predators capable of resisting absorption and preserving high-paid executive posts. Expansion required borrowing short on international markets to lend long on domestic mortgages, a practice lauded at the time by City analysts in comparison with the old fuddy-duddy style. Then came the crash with the results we all know.

The most striking aspect of the Northern Rock collapse was New Labour's total bafflement at what had happened. Their tutors from Goldman Sachs had never mentioned this. The obvious solution, clear to the social democrats among the Liberal Democrats, was to nationalise the hulk, safeguard depositors and wind the sorry mess down. Yet unable to place this in their political mindset, Brown and Darling hesitated month after month, searching for a suitable private-sector solution, unable to see that when Richard Branson is one's only salvation it is time to look for the exit. Social ownership in any form simply failed to register until a mutilated form of it was effectively forced on them, and then only as a short-term crisis measure. And the emergency measures by the government in autumn 2008 to take an equity stake in three out of the five main British retail banks to stave off the collapse of the financial system were seen as temporary, with social control nowhere on the agenda.

Yet the issue of social ownership urgently needs reviving. At one extreme, the necessary massive reductions in carbon emissions to mitigate climate change cannot be achieved without direct and stringent state intervention in a number of industrial sectors. This is most obvious in the electricity generation sector, but is also likely to be required in transport. The current ludicrous situation of the rail network, effectively bankrupt and state-owned but pretending to be private, can only be resolved by a modern, more democratic and socially-aware form of re-nationalisation. The original privatisation and break-up of British Rail was, even by the standards of Tory privatisation, seriously botched. Just about everybody, outside the current government and the Tory ministers who oversaw it, agrees on this.

Even so, state ownership of enterprises which play a key role in the economy, the original reason for nationalisation, can only be a minor part of the overall project to transform ownership relations in this country. One of the many tragedies of twentieth-century socialism was that an originally very wide-ranging set of ideas and

indeed practical policies was compressed into a single big idea;
nationalisation of the 'commanding heights of the economy', as
expressed in Clause 4 of the Labour Party constitution. There
were obvious and, at the time, apparently convincing reasons for
this. The persistent under-investment in industries such as coal-
mining and steel and in the rail network meant that the state was
virtually forced to take them over in the post-war period, having
already nursed them throughout most of the preceding two
decades. The new network industries of electricity, gas, water and
telecommunications would have been stillborn without direct
state control, though the centralising tendencies of the British
state killed off most local municipal involvement, still common
throughout Europe. Alongside this, the apparent successes of the
Soviet Union in industrialisation convinced much of the left,
social democratic as well as communist, of the inherent benefits of
centralised economic planning.

Nationalised industries pulled Britain through the post-war
period and were an important part of the social democratic settlement, but they crowded out other, decentralised, conceptions of
social ownership that had been part of the development of
socialism in Britain. A key example is the co-operative movement,
which had its origins in the provision of decent food to the
working class. Now generally seen as a minor group of old-fashioned supermarkets, the Co-ops attempted to develop a complete
food chain, from agriculture through food processing and into
their shops and customers' homes. The aim was to provide good-
quality food at affordable prices, with ethical standards of
production and delivery and all profits returned to regular shoppers in the form of dividends. Today this seems a very modern
idea. Similarly, the idea of partnership groups, in which employees
own the organisation for which they work, was once a key
element of British socialist thought. Though now represented on
any scale only by John Lewis, it suddenly seems to embody much
of the rhetoric of workforce empowerment espoused in recent
years by fashionable 'business gurus'.

Another casualty of post-war nationalisation was the tradition
of municipal socialism in which local councils, directly and immediately accountable to their electors, owned and operated a range
of local facilities, from housing through energy and transport
supply to support for local small business. The early 1980s saw

belated attempts to revive a popular municipal socialism in such places as London and South Yorkshire. They were quickly suppressed by the Thatcher government, which clearly understood their popular appeal. Local autonomy was also viewed with great suspicion by the leadership of the Labour Party, which was no more prepared than the Tories to tolerate rival poles of authority. Whilst the well-publicised actions of Liverpool's Militant council were used to justify this position, what is less publicised is that the general leftward shift in Labour councils at that time was a revolt against complacent and often corrupt right-wing local Labour leaderships. Since 1997, the Labour government has, if anything, intensified control over local authorities by imposing even tighter financial and legal restrictions. The refusal of Gordon Brown to allow municipal financing of London's underground or any other city transport system is notable only in the catastrophic financial consequences of the collapse of Metronet, the principal contractor for the renovation of the underground.

Nationalisation also diluted the various powers of inspection, regulation and consultation won by organised workforces from their employers. There is a long history of such control, going back, for example, to coal-miners employing their own check-weighmen at pitheads. But the practice effectively died out with the belief that the managers of nationalised industries would act in the best interests not only of the country at large, but also of their workforce. And in the private sector, strong unions preferred to conduct collective bargaining outside any joint worker-management industrial democracy structures. Again, there was a brief flowering of interest in workers' control in the 1970s, but this did not survive the long, hard winter of Thatcherism and by the time of the New Labour spring the idea that 'business knows best' was entrenched.

There are many strands to the project of enlarged social ownership. They all need to be carefully thought through and given an appropriate democratic basis. However, in many areas of life the preconditions already exist. A small example of what can be done is shown by the enthusiastic popular response to the land reforms introduced by the Scottish Executive during the Lib-Lab coalition's term of office. Now that local communities have the right of first refusal and can apply for public loans to buy privately-owned land when it comes up for sale, half the land area in the Western Isles is under some form of state or communal ownership. The next step is to establish community land rights in urban areas, building on efforts of local volunteers to reclaim the streets, restore derelict land or conserve green islands.

Similarly, the idea of an ethical food chain based on social ownership is grounded in an already existing movement and could quickly mobilise widespread public support. Workforce partnership schemes or co-operatives are another example of radical but wholly practical initiatives. There are various plans for small-scale social development of urban spaces in, for example, the Permaculture network. The greening of energy supplies to housing and commerce is already on the political agenda, but so far with a dominant emphasis on individual action. Yet this is something which cries out for local municipal involvement, carrying through democratically agreed local plans for carbon emissions in housing and transport. The developing transition towns and rural areas movement might provide a framework for drawing up such plans. Nationalisation may be a largely discredited idea; true social ownership has hardly been tried.

CHILDHOOD UNDER ARREST

How free was your childhood? Chances are, if you are an adult or even a teenager, it was a lot freer than it would be now. We monitor, organise, escort, restrain and fear for our children more intensely than ever before. We keep them under virtual house arrest, only letting them out under our anxious supervision, strapping them firmly in our cars and ferrying them to school, where we hand them over to the charge of another set of anxious adults. In the evenings or at weekends they are only allowed out with us or to attend activities organised by yet more anxious adults, then home again before darkness brings out another, even more fearsome set of threats and spectres. If none of this applies to you and your children, well good for you, but all the evidence is that you are in a shrinking minority. Or, by the standards of our current state of moral panic about children and childhood, you are likely to be judged a seriously neglectful parent.

The only children now allowed any freedom from adult supervision, any real independence, are derided as neglected or even 'feral', the children of the underclass in what we might call (after the TV series) 'Shameless Country'. As they grow up and start to 'hang-out', as adolescents always have, exploring their own and each others' emerging personalities and possibilities, we call them yobs and ask our New Labour-approved neighbourhood wardens and community support officers to come and sort them out, move them on or, preferably, give them a New Labour-devised ASBO. We forget that these are adolescents just as we were, children in adult-sized bodies, practising their new abilities and desires, confronting their own fears and worries and often feeling over-whelmed by them, growth-spurting out of themselves and their clothes, waking up every morning and wondering who they've turned into overnight; and annoying, unsettling and challenging the adults around them – just as we did.

And that is the main point we want to stress: that children today are not so very different from previous generations. They have pretty much the same interests: playing, learning, the natural world when they're little; then as they become teenagers, music, sport, fashion, their own and their peers' budding sexualities, and usually mild forms of personal rebellion that help them establish their own individuality. They have pretty much the same basic needs too: food and shelter and pocket money; someone to rely on, to back them up and help them out when things get tough; available and attentive adults to establish secure boundaries for them to bounce against, but also to encourage them to find their own way and eventually venture out into the world on their own.

What has changed dramatically over the past thirty years is childhood, the conditions under which children live and grow up. Families have become more fragile; road traffic has devoured safe spaces; fast food has transformed eating habits; television and the internet dominate children's leisure time; advertising exploits their sexuality; and schools have been retooled to train and test them. In a world of winners and losers, the fear of failure is pervasive, driving out trust and co-operation. The anxious encounters of daily life no less than the violent fantasies of computer games teach children to trust no one, least of all anyone who offers support or kindness.

At the same time, adults have withdrawn into their own sepa-rate spheres of (over-) work, competitive consumption and private leisure. Parents are expected to give more and more 'quality time' to their children, to worry about them, to help them 'consume' education and to compete against others within this education; to warn them about all the dangers which face them 'out there'; and more generally, to turn them into model owners, earners and consumers. Parents are constantly warned about failing in this task.[43] The message is clear: shape up or face further impoverishment and family breakdown, without the slightest recognition that families may be going 'off the rails' because they live in a deformed and damaged society.

What is new and disturbing about our present age, the age of the child as consumer, is that it blurs the difference between children and adults. Whatever its cultural setting, childhood is a period of latency, when children have not yet developed the capabilities required to make wise, informed and responsible choices, and need the freedom to play, explore and learn in conditions that are welcoming, safe and supportive. If we fail to provide an appropriate combination of license and protection, we risk turning our precocious kids into infantilised adults.

It will take at least a generation to achieve a more balanced and less confused preparation for adult life, but as tokens of a project that stretches across the whole of childhood experience, we offer three modest proposals.

Playing out: In the 1950s and 1960s, children of all ages were routinely sent to 'play out' for much of their free time. There were undoubtedly dangers and temptations in the streets and fields, but they learned to look after themselves and out for each other. Why can they not do that today? Moral panic about 'stranger danger' can be allayed by public education. Apart from that, the only serious new risk is traffic. But it is not difficult to calm traffic down or eliminate it altogether from residential areas. This is actually one of the few important new functions local authorities have taken on in recent years, and on occasions performed rather well. There are also some very good examples in other European countries, where – without being too starry-eyed about it – they still seem to like their children. No expensive new facilities are required either. If anything, children and young people prefer to create and occupy their own niches within general public spaces, as skateboarding demonstrates. In the process they learn valuable lessons in co-operation, consideration for others and creative improvisation.

Common sense on sex-abuse: The unleashing of capitalism from the mid-1970s onwards gave free rein to the commercialisation of sexuality. Yet our sexual attitudes and practices remain mired in deeper psychic complexes and much older, generally repressive traditions. This conflict between trade and taboo helps to explain why we constantly fret about our children's 'loss of innocence'. Then there are the social consequences of Thatcherism. The factory closures and redundancies of the early 1980s brought men into direct contact with their families and communities in a way that absentee fathers had not previously experienced. Sent ignominiously home, these men harboured deep inhibitions and prejudices about children, caring and women, and their families had little idea what to do with them. This was an unaccustomed and uneasy intimacy.

Most sexual abuse occurs within families, as a consequence of generally inappropriate relationships, the freedom and power accorded to exploitative and inadequate adults, and the relative weakness and vulnerability of children growing up in these situations. Families are not always safe places for children. There are specific interventions that can be made to tackle these problems and genuinely protect abused or at-risk children, primarily by enabling their families to function properly and learn how to look after each other appropriately. That's what children want: to be loved by the people they love. But in the prevailing atmosphere of hysteria whipped up by a malevolent press, with department store Father Christmases forbidden to sit children on their laps, nobody is especially interested in practical solutions. Far too often, abused children are themselves punished by being placed in the functional, sometimes abusive care of pressured local authorities. Real paedophiles are driven underground or on to the internet, and the freedom of all children is even further curtailed by our over-anxious 'child protection'. However, this is a very complex issue. Overworked social workers inevitably sometimes make mistakes, intervening when they should not, or not intervening when they should. The present trend towards actually listening to what children say needs to be encouraged.

We also need to integrate men into children's lives, as a caring, benign and necessary presence. Decently paid paternity as well as maternity leave should be extended; the right to flexible and well-paid part-time work should be guaranteed. There is no reason why fathers cannot be as involved in caring for their children as mothers, and indeed, the time fathers spend with their children has increased dramatically, though it still falls well short of that spent by mothers. Given the historical taboos against it, fathers need help and support in relating to their children, enjoying and loving them in their own distinctive ways. Positive discrimination should be practised in the recruitment and training of child carers and early years' teachers, at least until 50 per cent are men.

Above all, we need major socio-economic, cultural and attitudinal changes, to enable, accept and welcome the presence of men in their children's lives. This was after all one of the central demands of the women's liberation movement in the 1970s. And there remains a common and justified sense of grievance about men 'not pulling their weight at home', which generally means housework. We have already referred to the need for changes in the work-income nexus and the work-life balance, which would facilitate more involvement by men in children's lives – as fathers, grandfathers, carers and teachers, or just friendly neighbours – and would make our whole society a happier, pleasanter and more child-friendly place.

Testing times: Under New Labour, schooling has turned into testing, as if you could fatten the pig by repeatedly weighing it. In England, children are subjected to a battery of tests in virtually every year of school from the age of three upwards. But as is now recognised almost everywhere except the so-called Department for Children, Families and Skills, there is no evidence that this has improved the quality of education. On the contrary, 'teaching to the test' narrows the curriculum and stunts children's faculties, putting them off learning and turning them into cynics. Testing is, however, a useful ideological tool: it sends out a signal that teachers cannot be trusted to do their jobs and need to be audited by techniques imported from the business world; and it provides raw data with which to construct league tables of school performance as the basis for 'parental choice', a futile exercise given that the results obtained by schools depend primarily on the social composition of their intake.

We should scrap all external tests, apart from those taken when students leave school. To measure students' progress and identify further learning needs, we should rely on teachers' judgements of their pupils' achievements and aptitudes, and on the evidence of the work the pupils themselves produce. We should give children the time and space to explore their interests and abilities, basing decisions about next steps and subject choices on internal exam results and portfolios of work taken through a whole school career. In short, we need to start trusting our teachers and nurturing our children.

THE PARTY QUESTION

There is more to politics than parties, but parties give politics its edge. Straddling the boundary between state and civil society, political parties perform certain core functions for which there are no real substitutes. They frame political choices and structure political competition; they aggregate interests and views, making elections more coherent and meaningful than they would otherwise be; they recruit and train political organisers and leaders; they produce disciplined parliamentary groupings without which it would be difficult to enact legislation or hold the government to account; and by doing all these things, they help to legitimise representative democracy.

Political parties also perform certain other social functions not unique to them. They seek to inform, educate and persuade the public; they provide a focus for social identity and allegiance; they offer channels for lay people to participate in public life; they forge links between otherwise disparate issues and forces, creating coalitions of mood and opinion; and in the past – though this is scarcely true today – parties rooted in the working class gave a voice to social groups who would otherwise have been excluded from national politics.

In all these respects, we are less well served by our parties now than during the golden age of post-war capitalism. As parties have become more professional, their popular base has shrunk, while their links with the media and with professional political managers have grown. This would matter less than it does if the media showed some sense of social responsibility, but their infantile preoccupation with personality, sound-bites, splits, scares and sleaze trivialises and degrades the political process. Trivialisation is not just confined to the gutter tabloids either, but has also begun to infect all the broadsheet and broadcast media. And in an age of professional polling and electronic campaigning, party members are no longer essential for fighting elections.

The ending of the twentieth century's 'wars of religion' has also taken its toll, with waning party tribalism reflected in falling party membership, declining electoral turnout and an increasingly volatile pattern of voting. At the same time, thanks to the concentration of power in the hands of the leadership, political parties today offer scant opportunities for unpaid volunteers to express their aspirations and make a mark on the world. And since New Labour no longer seeks to contain capitalism and master the market, but instead projects itself as the natural party of business, the party's traditional supporters – the organised working class and the liberal intelligentsia – have been rendered politically homeless. In the last century, the fact that both of the major parties were essentially coalitions meant that political debate and choice within them kept the two-party structure from becoming overweening. This was particularly true of the Labour Party with its competing and combative socialist and reformist wings. But with the effective elimination of this internal competition, in the name of 'electability', Britain's first-past-the-post electoral system serves to stifle political creativity.

The decay of parties as *social* institutions impairs the performance of their core *electoral* functions. Falling electoral turnout and the alienation of the poor are producing a skewed pattern of political participation. As the political battleground contracts, the techniques that parties use to poll or target voters and to communicate grow ever more sophisticated, while their messages and images grow ever more simplistic and manipulative, with generally baleful consequences. Critics of first-past-the-post elections have long argued that they exaggerate the winning margin, handicap minor parties and force millions of citizens to choose between voting for no-hope candidates, voting tactically, or not voting at all. Now a fresh charge can be added to the indictment: that the system encourages tactical electioneering in which parties effectively ignore most of the electorate and target swing voters in key marginals. This allows them to assign their dwindling band of foot soldiers to the ground-war in marginal seats, while the professionals fight the air-war in the media; but it corrupts the democratic process. Some Trotskyist critics of the former Soviet Union used to describe it as a 'degenerate workers' state'. We might characterise contemporary Britain as a 'degenerate bourgeois democracy'.

The health of our political system is just one side of the party question; the other is the future of the democratic left. How can what is currently little more than a loose-knit, generally disgruntled body of opinion become a force to be reckoned with? To put the issue starkly, there are three possible answers: transforming the Labour Party, assembling a rainbow alliance around Labour, and founding a completely new party.

For the Labour Party to become the party of the democratic left, it would have to repudiate neoliberalism once and for all, while resisting the temptation to revert to labourism. This would require an openness to ideological debate which has hardly been prominent during its hundred-plus years of existence. It would have to re-launch itself under a new name, something more than the marketing term 'new' tacked onto the old one. It would have to reform its internal structure, reinvent its political culture and gear itself up for the politics of the long haul, reaching out to social movements which share its direction of travel, while respecting their differences, and above all reconnecting with ordinary people and everyday life. It would also have to embrace the cause of electoral reform and announce its willingness, in principle, to form coalitions with other parties prepared to agree on certain priorities for government.

None of these things seems remotely likely. They run wholly counter to the party's history. Labour would have to become something utterly different from what it has become: a vehicle for carrying a small number of career politicians into parliament with the institutional support of special interests – originally trade unions, now increasingly business. To some degree this has always been its function. It was, after all, founded precisely to protect the special interests of the unions, and only acquired the full trappings of a political party after 1918. But for some sixty years after that it provided the central focus for left-wing politics in Britain, especially for the various socialist organisations inside and outside the Labour Party, which formed the core of the left. However, the collapse of the post-war consensus exposed the bankruptcy of the workerist strategy that had sustained nearly all sections of the socialist left. In the desperate political struggles of the 1980s, one of the least edifying spectacles was that of the Labour centre and left turning upon itself in a suicidal feeding frenzy. It was this that gave the Blair/Brown/Mandelson axis a free hand to reconstruct the party as a 'modern' – that is, essentially authoritarian – political machine, finally destroying the party's social roots in the process. By the mid-1990s, the party was an empty shell, easily taken over by New Labour.

As a political organisation the Labour Party is moribund, but it still has a huge electoral presence, largely obstructive to serious, progressive political change in Britain. Its membership organisations at local and national levels are aimless and demoralised, increasingly inhabited by people who have nothing much else to do but grumble amongst themselves for most of the year, then spring to life with the approach of local or national elections. The party leadership relies overwhelmingly on the media and professional campaigning to communicate with the public.

In the absence of any effective challenge from the left – now a marginal, if still noisy force – the party is not going to abandon the positions that New Labour has staked out: a fundamentally neoliberal economic policy, domestically and internationally; a neo-imperialist foreign policy; and an illiberal, xenophobic and populist stance on 'homeland security', law and order, social cohesion, immigration and multiculturalism. Disputes within the party are now reduced to leadership power struggles devoid of any real policy content. So powerful is the control exerted by the central leadership over the party's activity and so demoralised are its remaining members that it is quite impossible to mount any kind of political challenge to the ruling order from the inside.

Some would argue that Labour has never been a truly progressive political force, but there have been moments when the party has adopted genuinely progressive perspectives and, more to the point, acted upon them. Labour governments in the 1920s, the 1940s above all, and even the 1960s and 1970s, made worthwhile and lasting improvements to British society, even if they all ended in disillusionment and recrimination. The important historical point is that these were periods of generally progressive change across our whole society and culture – unlike today – which Labour governments were forced to reflect in their political and administrative practice. They were simply responding to the popular hopes and fears expressed by the various social movements and coalitions – the rainbow-alliances – of their day.

The idea of a rainbow-alliance appeals now to the very many people who despise party conceit and yearn for electoral reform in the hope that it will normalise alliance politics and coalition government and create a more grown-up political culture. But professional politics is a rough old trade, and coalitions that are little more than marriages of convenience based on parliamentary arithmetic have a habit of falling apart amidst mutual recrimination. Within our debased political culture, cross-party alliances tend to bring together opportunists and technocrats whose only real common ground is distaste for democratic politics and the size of their own egos. The various Lib-Lab pacts of the last thirty years, which is what alliance politics has usually amounted to at Westminster, have been neither fruitful nor lasting. The last serious attempt to break the Westminster mould, the 1980s Social Democratic Party, is an even more dispiriting precedent.

However, there are signs that in Scotland, Wales and Northern Ireland various forms of coalition politics are emerging. The Lib-Lab coalitions which initially governed Scotland after devolution achieved some limited, but worthwhile results: notably, in resisting university top-up fees, introducing free social care for the elderly, combating religious sectarianism and enacting a modest measure of land reform. Similarly, the minority SNP government which took office in May 2007 with the qualified support of the Scottish Greens, has played down its long-term goal of independence and concentrated on demonstrating its competence to govern, adroitly outmanoeuvring or negotiating with the opposition parties in order to stay in power. Its social democratic social policy and pro-business economic stance is not, in truth, all that different from Labour's, but it enjoys high popularity ratings, thanks in no small part to the sheer ineptitude of the Scottish Labour Party, which has failed to come to terms with defeat, and whose successive leaders have paid the price for deferring to London. The SNP also deserves credit for opening up debate about enhanced devolution and fiscal autonomy, though its vaunted 'national conversation' about constitutional arrangements has yet to bridge the divide between parliamentary politics and civil society, and remains disconnected from the parallel initiative launched by the pro-Union parties in the form of the Calman Commission.

Enduring and, more to the point, successful coalitions must either be bound together by some overriding external imperative – fighting for national survival, say, or recovering from national catastrophe – or be strongly committed to a common political project. A national emergency may of course trigger the formation of a hegemonic bloc: it is naturally difficult to keep inter-party hostilities at bay unless the problems facing government and society are of a high order of importance. Either way, the whole point of the democratic left is to unite diverse social forces and political groupings around a radical programme aimed at creating a happier, fairer, greener, more cohesive and more democratic society. We have no interest in some quick electoral fix or stitch-up between career politicians.

If any kind of rainbow-alliance is to take shape and succeed in British politics, it will need a genuinely new set of political perspectives and practices, including forms of organisation and action usually considered the preserve of political parties. Besides agreeing on general aims and specific objectives, it will require effective co-ordination to link its separate components. If a political party of the democratic left existed, this is the role it would play. However, for the foreseeable future, it is difficult to see how such a party could hope to succeed, even if it could be launched. What is really needed is some form of coalition of all the various components of the left outside the Parliamentary Labour Party with the aim of devising a new democratic strategy to oppose the current market-based 'common-sense'.

The elements of such a coalition clearly exist, both among smaller parties such as the Green Party and part of Respect and within some of the remnants of the old socialist left; but also, and more importantly, they can be seen among the various activist groups which in the past ten years have provided the main practical opposition to neoliberal policies. These are centred on the environmental and anti-war movements, but also include other groups seeking to resist the march of the market and the erosion of social citizenship. There are also signs that some trade unions would support such a coalition.

A coalition of the left could not expect to make much headway at Westminster until some form of proportional representation is achieved. However, local elections offer more fertile ground, as the modest success of the Green Party has shown. There is also scope for progressive alliances and policies in Scotland and Wales, which would help the cause of political realignment in England, whatever happens to the Union. More generally, the work required to unite the fragments of the left would help to create the social and cultural preconditions for the eventual formation of a new party, in much the same way as happened in Western Europe in the late nineteenth and early twentieth centuries when various different kinds of organisation coalesced to form socialist parties.

The nearest British equivalent to what we are proposing is the Green Party. It has taken over thirty years of incredibly dedicated activism to get to its current electoral strength, with councillors in a number of cities, MSPs in Scotland, MEPs in Europe, and some realistic chance of electing an MP or two at future general elections. However, the Green Party battled its way into national politics at a time when Britain still had a centralised, two-party state and when electoral reform was widely regarded, even on the left, as an issue for policy wonks, an optional constitutional extra at best. Now Britain's political system is unstable: the Union itself is in flux, voting behaviour is volatile and people are disillusioned with both politicians and politics. In this situation, campaigning for a fairer electoral system could emerge as a centrepiece of a new popular and radical strategy.

Any kind of significant political realignment requires several factors to come together, and depends, therefore, on contingencies. Opportunities missed may not recur. If in 2005 several Labour MPs had had the courage of George Galloway and stood in their constituencies as independent Labour on anti-war platforms, it is possible that most would have won. This could have led on to the formation of a much wider and more resilient grouping than the ill-fated Respect. This is pure speculation, but it is probable that any future realignment will also require public figures from various walks of life to take decisive and courageous steps that could lead to public oblivion.

We are left, then, with a project in search of a party. But the fact that the party question cannot, for the moment, be resolved does not mean that it should not be continually posed. Many thousands of intelligent, constructive, socially aware and well-informed people in Britain have no ready-made political home. If it is to avoid extinction, the democratic left sooner or later will have to form a new organisation for these people to join and support. Under the existing electoral system, the scope for doing this is limited. But it is not non-existent, and even where there is no point in contesting parliamentary elections, we can still engage in preparatory talks about our broad, strategic purposes, and encourage the ideological and cultural shifts we need to create a democratic majority for radical progressive change in Britain. If this chapter succeeds in promoting this process, it will have served its purpose.

POLITICAL GENERATIONS

We are fully aware of at least one possible response to this chapter: that we are just the wreckage of a previous epoch, unable or unwilling to come to terms with the demands of a new global age. This may or may not be true: readers must judge for themselves. We all of us carry the burdens of our past, which shape the stance we take towards the present and the future. But those who refuse to learn from the mistakes of the past are doomed to repeat them. Amnesia is a disabling condition. To be cut off from your own past is to lack a future. If you don't know who you are and where you've come from, you are stuck in a perpetual present, incapable of forming long-term commitments, making forward plans or pursuing life-projects of any sort.

There is also a personal issue here, which touches all those of us who have taken part in the momentous political struggles of the past three or four decades. It is our responsibility to that new generation growing up in the world we have, in part, created. This is not a particularly new concern. Inter-generational dialogue and misunderstanding, co-operation and conflict have always been features of political life. The generation gap was a major theme of the culture wars of the 1960s. At the beginning of that tumultuous decade, Edward Thompson confronted an earlier generation who had fought a long and honourable battle against fascism but had, after the war, lapsed into what he called 'quietism'. Trapped between Soviet communism, revealed as the very opposite of the progressive socialism they had once admired, and a resurgent and aggressive American militarism, they had opted for a quiet life based on personal virtue. Thompson also saw a new generation refusing to acquiesce in this retreat into quietism and rebelling against the world they had been given. In 1960 he wrote an essay about their 'rebellious humanism':

> And so this rebellious humanism stems outward from the offence which power gives to the personal – the offence of power against

people with different pigment in their skins, the offence of power against people of different social class, the offence of the bomb against human personality itself. The anti-political find themselves once again in the arena of political choice. Because 'love' must be thrust into the context of power, the moralist finds that he must become a revolutionary.

It is not a junction that can ever be whole. It is more like a constant quarrel between morality and circumstance, which is perpetually resumed. But it is a fruitful quarrel which must not cease, or – between the pull of 'integrity' and the pull of 'necessity' – the drift of circumstances will have its way. And it is a quarrel which must engage the conscious mind and the whole will. From the intellectual today a particular dedication is required. It is in his capacity for utopian vision that men's will to change may be contained. If men are paralysed by the horror of their recent history, then it will do no good either to nourish horror or to turn aside and pretend that no horror is there ...

Can the new human nature which has formed beneath the orthodox snows express itself in positive rebellion? Can a new generation, East and West, break simultaneously with the pessimism of the old world and the authoritarianism of the new, and knit together human consciousness into a single socialist humanism? [44]

In our times, our new millennium, there is also a new generation that looks at the world afresh. It sees, environmentally, a world grievously wounded, perhaps dying; socially and economically, a world in which the rich grow ever richer and more confident in their overweening power, whilst the poor live and die wretchedly. And culturally, forms and images are uprooted from their social contexts and beamed across the world, endlessly replayed and recycled, till they lose all resonance, significance and meaning. They see this world and don't much care for it. Some of them have already fought their own battles against what Thompson called 'the offence of power' in Seattle and Genoa. Their protests are often incoherent, usually betrayed, and invariably condescended to by politicians who are happy to take up famine in Africa or the threat of climate change for a day or two. Sometimes their ideals are manipulated by the unscrupulous and the malign.

They deserve better. The future is theirs, but they also need a history to make sense of an otherwise bewildering present. We hope this book, and the democratic left we aspire to form on the back of it, will reach at least some of them and sow seeds of understanding.

Like E.P. Thompson before us, we have tried to name 'The Beast' of our times, neoliberal capitalism, and acknowledge it for what it is: at best a deluded form of market utopianism, at worst a voracious and malicious deformation of the human spirit, which promises endless riches and delivers worthless dust. We are not disciples of the One True Path. There is no one path to the good life, no single set of rules to be imposed, no single goodness. That is one of the mistakes which the left made in the past. But by explaining how we got here, and offering some signs and warnings, we hope to help this next generation find their own way to a better world.

Perhaps we can take Thompson's words as our own:

'Terrible is the temptation of Goodness' wrote Brecht. We have learnt what Wordsworth learnt before us: the good life is 'no mechanic structure built by rule.' Socialism, even at the point of revolutionary transition – perhaps at this point most of all – must grow from existing strengths. No one – neither Marxist vanguard nor enlightened administrator nor bullying humanitarian – can impose a socialised humanity from above. A socialist state can do little more than provide 'circumstances' which encourage societal and discourage acquisitive man; which help people build their own egalitarian community, in their own way, because the temptation of Goodness becomes too great to resist. Socialism can bring water to the valley; but, as Brecht went on, it must give 'the valley to the waterers, that it bring forth fruit.' What else is there to do?

This is a revised version of the essay of the same title available on www.hegemonics.co.uk.

REFERENCES

1. Jonathan Rutherford and Hetan Shah (eds), *The Good Society*, Compass/Lawrence and Wishart, London 2006.
2. R. Layard, *Happiness*, Penguin Books, London 2005.

3. http://cep.lse.ac.uk/textonly/research/mentalhealth/DEPRESSION_
   REPORT_LAYARD.pdf.
4. Jenni Russell, *Guardian*, 19 September 2006.
5. Unicef, *Child Poverty in Perspective: An Overview of Child Well
   Being in Rich Countries*, Unicef, New York 2007.
6. W. Hutton, *The State We're In*, Vantage, London 1995.
7. R. Wilkinson, *Unhealthy Societies*, Routledge, London 1995.
8. *Guardian*, 15 December 2006. It long ago outstripped regular religious observance (a mere 7 per cent).
9. BBC *Newsnight*, 4 December 2006.
10. *Observer*, 7 January 2007.
11. J. Sunderland, quoted in *The Times*, 27 November 2006.
12. R. Sennett, *The Culture of New Capitalism*, Yale University Press,
    Yale 2006, p169.
13. H. Clayton, *Guardian*, 17 January 2007.
14. Sennett, op cit, p175.
15. Layard's work and that of others in the field is analysed in more
    detail in M. Prior, *Happiness*, on www.hegemonics.co.uk.
16. O. James, *Affluenza*, Vermilion, London 2007.
17. Layard, op cit, p234.
18. We are grateful to the American sociologist Fred Block for the term
    'the great forgetting', which he coined in 1999 to describe the way
    in which the progressive impulses of recent American history had
    been written out of the official story during the 1980s and 1990s.
    Like so much else that starts in America, we observe the same kind
    of re-writing or rather obliteration of history happening here now:
    Fred Block, *The Great Forgetting: Neoliberal Globalisation and
    the Unmaking of the Postwar Order*, Center for Research on Social
    Organisation, Ann Arbor 1999.
19. K. Polanyi, *The Great Transformation*, Beacon, Boston 1944.
20. J. O'Connor, 'The Second Contradiction of Capitalism', repro-
    duced in Ted Benton (ed.), *The Greening of Marxism*, Guildford
    Press, New York 1996.
21. M. Burawoy, 'For a Sociological Marxism: The Complementary
    Convergence of Antonio Gramsci and Karl Polanyi', *Politics and
    Society*, 31:2, June 2003.
22. Space does not allow any full analysis of this period. For an
    extended discussion of the transition from the post war consensus
    to New Labour Thatcherism, see P. Devine, 'The 1970s and After:
    The Crisis of Social Democracy', *Soundings*, Spring 2006.

23. M. Prior and D. Purdy, *Out of the Ghetto*, Spokesman, Nottingham 1979, and on www.hegemonics.co.uk.

24. See P. Devine, 'Inflation and Marxist Theory', *Marxism Today*, 1974, and on www.hegemonics.co.uk

25. G. Andrews, *Endgames and New Times*, Lawrence and Wishart, London 2004.

26. J.K. Galbraith, *The Affluent Society*, Penguin, Harmondsworth 1958.

27. See, for example, D. Kruger, *Prospect*, September 2006.

28. D. Green, *Sunday Telegraph*, 31 December 2006.

29. Perhaps the best representation of this is the film *Enron: The Smartest Guys in the Room*, directed by A. Gibney, 2005.

30. www.labour-party.org.uk/manifestos/1983/1983-labour-manifesto.shtml.

31. www.labour-party.org.uk/manifestos/1997/1997-labour-manifesto.shtml.

32. www.bbc.co.uk/election97/background/parties/manlab/labmanintro.html.

33. The full text of this is at www.civilservice.gov.uk/reform/capability_reviews/index.asp.

34. Sunderland, op cit.

35. Linguistic habits and social practices feed each other. In a minor, but telling enactment of New Labour's rhetoric, the Office of National Statistics now publishes an on-line facility that enables each individual to calculate his or her own personal rate of inflation.

36. For an extended discussion of the transition, see Devine, op cit, 2006.

37. Quasi-commodities, not real commodities, as long as services continue to be financed by taxation and are provided free of charge at the point of use. In practice, various hybrid arrangements are emerging. Take, for example, the education of undergraduate university students domiciled in England. This is now financed partly from general taxation and partly from 'variable, top-up' tuition fees. The fees must be paid up-front, but students may borrow the requisite funds at a zero real interest rate, repaying the debt incurred in instalments after they have graduated and are earning more than £15,000 per annum.

38. P. Devine, *Democracy and Economic Planning: The Political Economy of a Self-governing Society*, Polity Press, Cambridge 1988.

39. S. Hall, *The Hard Road To Renewal: Thatcherism and the Crisis of the Left*, Verso, London 1988 and on hegemonics.co.uk.

40. At Bali the USA agreed only to participate in discussions about possible *future* targets.

41. If it were not, the richest countries would face the prospect of a long-term decline in per capita income. Falling incomes, as measured by GDP per head, would presumably be even harder to accommodate than zero growth, but this does not alter the nature of the problem to be solved. Of course, the problem would be easier to deal with to the extent that an increasing emphasis on quality rather than quantity resulted, as we would expect it to, in people experiencing a better quality of life. See, e.g., Kate Soper on 'alternative hedonism', www.sussex.ac.uk/Units/CCE/conferences0607/beyondconsumerism_katesoper.

42. The opposite case, where a poor country persistently fell below its convergent growth path, calls for a different approach.

43. E.g.: 'We are going to have to say to some families before they get into serious law-breaking "you are off the rails, we are not going to carry on supporting you through the benefit system unless you are in a proper structured environment with rules by which you must abide, and if you don't, your liberty is going to be increasingly constrained." That is a very heavy thing to say, but that is what is needed.' T. Blair, 'Evidence to Commons Select Committee Chairmen', *Guardian*, 7 February 2007.

44. E.P. Thompson, 'Outside the Whale' in *The Poverty of Theory*, Merlin Press, London 1978.

2. Re-conceptualising
the economy

David Purdy

What exactly is the economy? Economics offers little enlight-enment. The world's best-selling textbook informs students that: 'Economics is the study of how societies use scarce resources to produce valuable commodities and distribute them among different people'.[1] This definition is admirably succinct, but deeply misleading, for modern economists study only those societies whose dominant institutions are private property, free contract, competitive markets and commercial money, and in which the lure of gain or fear of loss are the prime motives of human action. The suggestion that the principles of economics, as understood today, apply to all human societies, past and present, depends on the ambiguity of the word 'commodities', which sometimes refers to useful things in general and sometimes to articles of trade in particular.

Karl Polanyi distinguishes between what he calls the substantive or material conception of the economy as an instituted process of social interaction for satisfying human wants, and the supply-demand-price mechanism. The former is part of the human condition, the latter a comparatively modern institution.

> To narrow the sphere of the genus economic specifically to market phenomena is to eliminate the greatest part of man's history from the scene. On the other hand, to stretch the concept of the market until it embraces all economic phenomena is artificially to invest all things economic with the peculiar characteristics that accompany the phenomena of the market. Inevitably, clarity of thought is impaired.[2]

The significance of this point extends beyond the study of pre-industrial, non-market societies, for even in mature capitalist societies, markets are embedded in forms of social life that are not themselves governed by market 'laws'.

In what follows, I argue that economy, polity and culture form an integrated complex and need to be considered together if they are to be properly understood. In section 1, I propose a broad definition of social production encompassing unpaid work and non-marketed products. In section 2, I discuss classifications of economic activity and outline a four-sector model based on the distinctive features of business firms, government and public agencies, private households and voluntary associations. Current social accounting systems ignore the role of the household and voluntary sectors in reproducing human beings and 'social capital', respectively; take commodity production as the exemplar for all economic activity; treat the biosphere as an inert, exploitable resource rather than as an organic eco-system; and presume that the growth of GDP is always a good thing. In section 3, I argue that the fantasy of boundless growth in a self-regulating market economy has given rise to serious social dysfunctions and environmental stresses, and outline an alternative regime centred on a democratically managed Basic Income system and geared towards a more balanced pattern of development.

THE CONCEPT OF ECONOMIC ACTIVITY

On the broadest view, people engage in production whenever and wherever they devote time, energy and skills to making objects or serving purposes that are of value to someone – if only themselves – regardless of how their work is controlled, whether they work for pay, what form their product takes and whether it is produced for the market. The trickiest word in this sentence is value. There is no space to discuss it fully here. Suffice it to say that value in exchange – what someone is prepared to pay for something – is not the only criterion for deciding what things are worth producing, acquiring or keeping. Some of the things that most of us desire – and arguably all of us need – are not to be had on any market. Examples are emotional goods such as self-esteem, love and friendship; social goods such as trust, solidarity and civility; and environmental goods such as biodiversity, natural beauty and clean air. Conversely, some of the things that money can buy, such as sex, drugs and guns can seriously damage your health, though this does not stop people buying them, if only as fashion accessories, status symbols or anxiety suppressants.

What about activities that benefit only those who perform them? By definition, their products are not exchanged. Does production without exchange qualify for inclusion in the economy? It seems perverse to exclude the feats of self-provisioning performed by the shipwrecked Robinson Crusoe before he meets Man Friday. After all, the word 'economy' originally meant household management. In the case of multi-person households, Gardiner distinguishes four kinds of activity: 'domestic labour' carried out by and for the members of the household, which could be delegated to a third party or could be purchased if a market for the relevant services existed; 'basic functions' that people normally perform for themselves, such as washing and eating; 'leisure pursuits', which by their nature cannot be delegated to someone else, such as watching TV or reading for pleasure; and time spent 'resting and sleeping', over which people have some discretion, but only within certain limits.[3] Domestic labour is certainly part of the economy; where to place other cases is unclear.

However we define economic activity, the important point is that our lives are variously intertwined with those of others, for we belong not only to organic communities such as households, neighbourhoods and workplaces, but also to imagined communities such as online networks, historic nations and the human race. It is, therefore, practically impossible to distinguish between self-regarding and other-regarding actions. Sooner or later, everything we do – or fail to do – has consequences of some kind – direct or indirect, beneficial or harmful – for our families and friends, neighbours and colleagues, associates and fellow-citizens or fellow-humans, alive or yet to be born. Thus, if I cultivate my own garden, I may give pleasure to others, intentionally or not, just as I may annoy them if I leave it untended, though in neither case is there any question of charging for services rendered or costs inflicted. Similarly, if I become addicted to alcohol, tobacco or gambling, it will not be just me who pays the price.

It follows that there is no sharp dividing line between those activities that benefit others and those we perform only for ourselves. All societies practise some kind of division of labour whereby certain groups specialise in particular kinds of work: men in hunting, women in gathering, for example. This suggests a distinction between those activities that form part of the prevailing social division of labour and those that do not. In any given case, however, it may be hard to tell. Consider the maintenance of personal health, hygiene and appearance. Most of us want to be fit, clean and well turned out, irrespective of whether this pleases or profits others, and in so far as we perform the necessary tasks for ourselves, it could be argued that the work falls outside the social division of labour. But suppose my employer requires or expects me to spend longer washing and ironing my clothes, grooming myself and generally preparing for work than I would if I could please myself. Then some of my 'own time' is really just unpaid overtime. And for whose sake does an expectant mother attend clinics and maternity classes, perform physical exercises, regulate her diet and otherwise prepare for childbirth?

But if the boundary of social production is fuzzy, at least the definition proposed above does not restrict work to paid employment or confine the measurement of the social product to goods and services which command a market price or to which some more or less spurious monetary value can be imputed. It thus avoids the common mistake of conflating the 'economy' with the 'market' and the related mistake of equating value with price.

CLASSIFYING ECONOMIC ACTIVITIES

Economists sometimes pretend that the social product consists of a single, homogeneous, yet malleable good, which can either be consumed today or invested so as to augment production and consumption in the future. This fiction avoids having to deal with relative prices and, in the absence of any differences between products, is usually combined with the assumption that the economy is closed and has no trade or other relations with the rest of the world. A further simplification is to ignore differences between members of the population. This amounts to assuming a society of equals in which average income, output per head and capital per head are meaningful magnitudes and there are no systematic inequalities of income, work and power rooted in enduring social divisions such as class, gender and race. Naturally, at this level of abstraction, no attention is paid to political institutions or cultural norms.

Evidently, a 'one-sector' model ignores all those aspects of the world that can only be understood by distinguishing different kinds of economic activity. But it is not, for that reason, useless. Indeed, it can yield surprising insights: notably, into the problems of development planning in poor countries or into the relationship between growth and stability in mature capitalist economies. However, one-sector models do not get you far and, for most purposes, we need to distinguish two sectors or more. There is, for example, the traditional trinity of 'agriculture', 'industry' and 'services'. Alternatively, we might distinguish between 'public' and 'private' activity or between the 'formal' and 'informal' economies. There is no single, correct model: everything depends on the purpose at hand. But if we are interested in the relationship between capitalism and the wider social framework or, more generally, in the interplay between economic development, cultural change, social institutions and public policy, then two sectors are too few: we need a broader canvas and some additional categories. At a minimum, I suggest, we need four sectors. What we call them is a matter of choice. I propose to call them the business, public, household and voluntary sectors. Their distinguishing features are summarised in Table 1 below.

In the business sector, competing, privately owned and profit-seeking firms employ paid workers to produce commodities for sale on the market. The public sector comprises the state, defined in terms of basic government functions, together with various tax-financed agencies, controlled or commissioned by the state. These are normally, though not necessarily, non-profit-seeking, but either way employ paid workers to produce non-marketed goods and services that are made available to the public (largely) free of charge. In the household sector, individuals perform unpaid provisioning and caring work both on their own account and for the benefit of others with whom they cohabit. The voluntary sector contains a wide variety of charities, membership organisations, civic associations and informal networks which employ paid staff or use unpaid volunteers to express shared values, promote shared interests and cater to social needs that are either not met at all, or not met so well, by commercial, public or domestic producers. The final column of Table 1 indicates the sources of each sector's income. Except for the voluntary sector, which is too diverse to permit any useful generalisation, the principal source is underlined.

TABLE 1: A FOUR-SECTOR MODEL OF ECONOMIC ACTIVITY

Sector	Objectives	Workers	Product	Income
Business	Commercial	Paid	Marketed commodities	<u>Sales</u> Asset income Public subsidies
Public	Political	Paid	Public goods and services	<u>Taxes and charges</u> Asset income
Household	Personal	Unpaid	Social persons	<u>Earnings</u> Asset income Social transfers
Voluntary	Associational	Paid and unpaid	Communal goods and services	Donations Subscriptions Asset income Sponsorship Grants

These profiles represent ideal-types. Actual economies are liable to deviate from the pure forms. In the household sector, for example, we find au pairs, sole traders and family firms. Similarly, just as the public sector used to contain state-owned, commodity-producing monopolies, so nowadays some private, profit-making firms are paid by the state to deliver free or subsidised public services. If such 'anomalies' become sufficiently common, categories must be revised. In that sense, all classifications are provisional. Their purpose is not to provide a 'comprehensive' map of the world – what could that possibly mean? – but to highlight those features of the world that are pertinent for the job in hand: in this case, understanding how different kinds of production involving different social relations and logics of action fit together.

Note also that the table relates only to current activity. Since economy and society have a continuous existence in time – because they are constantly being reproduced by human activity

– the current period belongs to a sequence of similar periods extending backwards into the past and forwards into the future. This may seem an obvious point, but it is worth stressing because it is crucial for understanding the behaviour of business firms and the process of capital accumulation. Unlike agents in the other three sectors, capitalist enterprises are engaged in a Hobbesian war to the death. Each firm is a threat to all the others. Those in the same line of business offer the keenest competition, but all are rivals to some degree, for all offer alternative outlets for capital funds and all are perpetually jostling for a share of the total purchasing power that they throw on the market together. Thus, on pain of extinction by bankruptcy or takeover, every firm must strive not just to make profits on its current operations at roughly the going rate, but also to safeguard its future position. In lawless states, competition may be conducted by predatory methods, including gang warfare. Normally, however, the best way for firms to outdo or match each other is to invest in additional capacity, improved techniques or new products.

The accumulative logic of capitalism tends to damage those non-capitalist forms of production on which both business itself and society as a whole depend. For just as firms produce commodities which are purchased and used in the other three sectors, so the activities of these sectors in turn contribute to business success and social well-being. The state, for example, is responsible for defence and foreign policy; presides over the legal, policing and penal systems; regulates banking and finance; provides or supervises the provision of essential services such as transport, communications, energy supply, education, health care and social security; seeks to maintain macroeconomic stability; and normally makes some attempt to manage social conflict and legitimise the social order. What households, for their part, produce is people – both from generation to generation and from day to day – not, of course, as mere biological organisms or bearers of labour power, but as fully fledged social persons who are more or less well equipped to participate in social life and whose own lives, from cradle to grave, are bound up with those of their families, friends and fellows. And the voluntary sector plays a vital – if as yet imperfectly understood – role in building and maintaining communal assets such as mutual trust, civic vitality, public order and social cohesion – often somewhat confusingly described nowadays as 'social capital'.

Thus, even if we are concerned with riches or possessions rather than with wealth more broadly understood as that which sustains and enhances human life, and even if we ignore those aspects of production and consumption that make life worse – 'illth' as Ruskin called them – any suggestion that business alone creates wealth is specious and self-serving.[4] Yet Ruskin's plea for a political economy that studies the material, moral and spiritual well-being of individuals and communities continues to be ignored by economists.

In textbook accounts of the circular flow of income and spending, the prime movers are business and government. Households feature as owners, earners and spenders, but not as productive agents in their own right. Their role in the production of people is ignored. Thus, in measuring GDP, no attempt is made to impute a value to the unpaid provisioning and caring work performed within the household sector. In part, this is because of the conceptual and practical difficulties involved. How, for example, should we value the time that people – mostly women – spend on household work: by reference to what it would cost to pay someone else to do it or by reference to what those concerned could earn if they spent less time on housework and more in the labour market? Moreover, while some aspects of domestic labour can be replaced by market substitutes without anyone losing out, unpaid caring work is more problematic, for the relationship between carers and their charges is normally an intrinsic part of the care provided. And what are the consequences of marketisation for the rest of society? Does it matter, for example, if income-rich, time-poor parents limit hands-on involvement with their children to 'quality time', relying on paid carers or Playstations to keep them occupied at other times?

Conventional national income accounting avoids these conundrums by definitional fiat, placing the business and public sectors on one side of the 'production boundary' and the household and voluntary sectors on the other. Thus, GDP consists of the unduplicated value of the goods and service that cross the boundary – i.e. pass from the 'productive sector' to 'final demand', where they are not used again in the production of other goods. Final demand is taken to comprise capital formation (capital goods plus changes in stocks), private consumption, public consumption and exports minus imports. These concepts reflect the understanding of the macro-economy that came to prevail in the 1930s and 1940s, when (a sanitised version of) Keynesian theory won the support of most British and American economists, and they have since been routinely used to measure economic welfare, to make comparisons over time or across countries, to diagnose the macroeconomic situation and to assist in macroeconomic management. But the concepts are not sacrosanct, least of all in circumstances where, as argued in chapter one of this book, they tell us ever less about human well-being.

We need a new system of social accounting based on the concept of social reproduction. The commodities purchased from firms by the public, household and voluntary sectors are not passively consumed, but actively used to produce non-commodity outputs: public goods, human beings and communal services. These in turn help to reproduce both the framework of social life and the embodied capabilities that enable people to perform their various social roles: as employees, citizens, volunteers and home-makers. Thus, economic production is a phase of social reproduction: activities reproduce society to the extent that they help to replace (or increase) the human population, to maintain (or expand) productive capacity, to conserve or (reform) social institutions and to transmit (or transform) cultural norms. And since human activity is embedded in the biosphere, social reproduction leaves its 'footprint' on the natural world and is, in turn, affected by 'biofeedback'.

FROM BOUNDLESS GROWTH TO BALANCED DEVELOPMENT

Contemporary capitalism contains two major fault-lines: between the business sector and the rest of the economy; and between human activity as a whole and the biosphere. Competition between rival units of capital gives rise to unlimited accumulation and growth. Since neoliberalism became the ruling paradigm of public policy, this tendency has operated largely unchecked, generating a variety of ever more serious dysfunctions and stresses.[5]

In Britain, paid employment is now characterised by long

hours, flexible contracts, reduced security, intensified work and grossly unequal rewards. There has, it is true, been a partial convergence of gender roles, but progress towards gender equality is glacially slow and the division of paid and, more especially, unpaid work between men and women remains stubbornly unequal. In the household economy, the birth rate has fallen below replacement level, leading to increased reliance on inward migration to relieve labour shortages and restrain money wages. At the same time, parental time budgets and family relationships are strained by the 'work and spend' culture, and childhood itself has been transformed by the relentless commercialisation of everyday life and the attendant social and psychological pressure on children to conform to consumerist norms. The voluntary sector too has succumbed to the invasive spread of commerce. While 'amateur' sport, music and the arts continue to flourish – in part because of the scope they offer for supplementing or replacing earnings from day jobs – religious observance and membership of political parties and trade unions have all declined, active participation has given way to passive subscription and the internal culture and management of voluntary organisations increasingly resemble those of business firms.

In the public sector, traditional tax-financed and centrally planned forms of provision have been replaced by quasi-markets in which services are still largely free of charge at the point of use, but service-providers compete for public contracts and service-users can choose among alternative suppliers. Targets and performance standards continue to be set by central government and, indeed, proliferate, with external audit replacing professional integrity as the preferred means of assuring service quality. Within this centrally imposed framework, public sector executives enjoy greater operational independence than in the past, though they also work longer hours and most of their work consists of making sure that their organisations satisfy external assessors, which may, of course, divert or prevent them from serving the public in ways that are not reflected in the official performance criteria. The objectives of schools, hospitals, universities and other (quasi-) public organisations continue to be politically determined and are, to that extent, qualitatively different from those of business firms. But the widespread adoption of commercial norms and practices blurs the public-business boundary and encourages service-users to think of themselves less as citizens and more as customers or even, in the case of student loans, as walking cost and profit centres.

The environmental damage inflicted by boundless economic growth is so dire as to call into question humanity's long-term prospects of survival, not to mention that of non-human species. Cleaner forms of energy and increased energy efficiency may buy us more time. The same goes for recycling and other ways of reducing materials used or wastes produced per unit of output. But however much we succeed in greening capitalism, efforts to conserve resources and protect habitats are bound to be an uphill struggle as long as global business keeps on growing and we remain its willing slaves – not breadline proletarians, to be sure, but still wage slaves for all that.

Chapter one of this book outlines a regime for managing the transition to a more balanced pattern of development. Here I want to expand on the proposal for reconfiguring the work-income nexus and reconstituting social citizenship by providing every individual citizen with an unconditional Basic Income (BI), financed exclusively from personal income tax (see p80). As pointed out earlier, such a radical reform will not be feasible unless its supporters succeed in changing current attitudes towards what counts as work and convince their fellow citizens that the advantages of BI justify the high level of taxation necessary to sustain it. The effort required to challenge conventional wisdom on these matters and refashion social institutions can be compared to the intellectual and political struggles that ushered in the Keynesian 'revolution' during the 1930s and 1940s: regime change is never easy. But just as active fiscal and monetary policy helped to maintain full employment and the long post-war boom, so an integrated tax-transfer system would bring questions of distribution and the management of the economy into a common frame, pitting the claims of common citizenship against the counter-claims of sectional interest.

A BI system would have to be regularly monitored and managed, in tandem with the annual budgetary cycle. This is because proposals to adjust tax rates and transfer scales are bound to have repercussions for the disposition of people's time and hence for the balance between different sectors of the economy. But whereas neoliberal methods of macroeconomic management are predicated on the primacy of capitalist commodity production and celebrate owning, earning and spending as the highest expressions of human culture, a system that partially decouples income from employment would effectively subsidise work in the household and voluntary sectors of the economy, correcting the current bias towards getting and spending. At the same time, commercial interests would be obliged to justify the expansion of commodity production rather than taking it for granted that what is good for business is good for society. More generally, with the emergence of a less blinkered and more rounded conception of economic activity, submerged questions of distribution and value would come to the fore: who gets what, who does what and who decides what? And what things are worth having, doing and being? The prospects for achieving redistribution without growth depend on convincing people that once material sufficiency is guaranteed, lasting happiness comes from sources such as meaningful relationships, active citizenship and the life of the mind.

Such a regime calls for supportive transnational arrangements, aimed, as we argued earlier, at promoting convergent global development, just as national Keynesian policies were underpinned by inter-governmental agreements on currency exchange rates, international payments and cross-border trade. And just as the problem of reconciling full employment with low inflation and adequate profitability called for some form of tripartite social pact between employers, employees and government to restrain the use of sectional power, so the transition from unfettered growth to a steady-state economy will need to be co-ordinated by a more open and democratic system of social negotiation, covering a broader set of issues and involving a correspondingly wider range of stakeholders. A Basic Income Democracy (BID) would not replace capitalism, but it would put an end to wage slavery, bringing the prospect of a democratic alternative to capitalism on to horizon of political possibility.

REFERENCES

1. P. Samuelson and W. Nordhaus, *Economics*, (14/e), McGraw-Hill, New York 1992, p3.
2. K. Polanyi, *The Livelihood of Man*, Academic Press Inc, New York 1977, p7.

3. J. Gardiner, *Gender, Care and Economics*, Macmillan, Basingstoke 1997.
4. J. Ruskin, *Unto This Last: Four Essays on the First Principles of Political Economy*, Collins, Glasgow 1862.
5. Much of what passes for economic growth neither enlarges personal freedom nor enhances human well-being, but simply extends commodity production to activities from which it was previously absent, from child-rearing and collective self-help to subsistence farming and mutual assurance.

3. Social ownership and democratic planning

Pat Devine

Historically, socialism was seen as an alternative to capitalism, a new way of organising society, not least economic activity, based on a new set of values – a vision of a good society based on freedom, equality and the planned use of society's commonly owned productive resources to meet human needs. The socialist movement was the movement working towards this end, overlapping with the labour movement but not coterminous with it. For the right wing of social democracy, socialism became transformed into a set of values to be achieved through redistribution and equality of opportunity within capitalist society.[1] The rise of neoliberalism and the historic failure of Soviet-style state planning have now resulted in much of the left wing of social democracy joining with the right in embracing private ownership and market forces as the principal means of organising economic activity. Finally, New Labour has extended market principles and values into the heart of the welfare state, deepening the social crisis which has resulted in Feelbad Britain.

The progressive democratic left is understandably not happy with this. In a recent review of three programmatic statements by *Compass*, Michael Kenny addresses the central dilemma anyone thinking beyond capitalism faces: 'if not state planning, nor the market, then what can be the agent and embodiment of progressive economic governance and public management?'[2] This chapter offers a possible answer to Kenny's dilemma in the form of a model of socialism based on the concept of social ownership and a process of participatory planning through negotiated coordination. [3]

Of course, there are people who, while in some sense believing another world is possible, consider attempts to visualise what such a future world might look like as a waste of time, preferring instead to concentrate on understanding the present. However, movements of resistance to the effects of neoliberalism, and attempts to create alternatives, are unlikely to cohere into an effective and enduring challenge to the existing capitalist system unless there develops a broad, widely shared, general sense of what an alternative system might look like. The Soviet model, historically the only systemic attempt so far to build a society derived from the principles of classical Marxist socialism, has failed. The era of the social democratic Keynesian welfare state, the apogee of the Polanyian counter-movement against the ravages of the free market, has also come to an end. Some idea of the architecture of a possible twenty-first century socialism, its principles, institutions and social processes, is urgently needed if the left is to recover its confidence and reclaim its rightful position as the standard bearer of freedom and progress.

A link between present discontents and struggles and a possible future socialism is not hard to find, whether we start from the traditional socialist concern with exploitation and oppression, or the green concern with ecology and the environment. Corporate global business, motivated by the relentless pursuit of profit and shareholder value, tramples on human and non-human nature alike. It destroys jobs, communities and the environment in one place after another as, driven by market forces, it continuously reshapes the world in the face of constantly changing profitability opportunities. People, individually and collectively, are buffeted by forces beyond their control, with little if any say over the direction of development of the society in which they live. Decisions affecting our lives are made in New York, Tokyo, Shanghai, Frankfurt and Paris, as well, of course, as in London. President Sarkozy's attacks on 'free competition' and his argument for some forms of protection are a reflection of the reaction against the destructive effects of global market forces, albeit from a reactionary and Euro-chauvinist standpoint.

THE CONTEXT

My concern is with how economic activity could be organised in a complex modern socialist society, but four preliminary comments are needed. First, such a society must be based on radical participatory political democracy combining direct democracy, through the voluntary associations of civil society, and representative democracy. Politics won't disappear under socialism and political parties will continue to exist in one form or another to provide alternative visions and values for future developments and to determine social priorities, but radical democracy must be rooted in civil society. Second, while the formal economy, with which the model outlined below is concerned, will continue to exist for the foreseeable future, there is likely to be a fundamental change in the 'work-life ratio', with a significant shift to household and local community production and caring. However, this does not mean a subsistence economy, as the two sectors will be mutually dependent.[4]

Third, ecological sustainability and a qualitatively richer life experience each require major changes in social structure and life style in the metropolitan capitalist countries. These cannot be achieved by manipulating the market context that shapes people's individual behaviour, but require instead the active participation of people individually and collectively in debating and creating the society in which they wish to live, through processes of deliberative democracy. Fourth, to participate effectively in deliberative democracy, people need the personal resources that can only be obtained through experience of the different types of socially necessary activity present in society: unskilled and repetitive; skilled; caring and nurturing; creative; and planning and organising. The achievement of this would amount to the abolition of the social, though not the functional, division of labour.[5]

The formal economy is the complex of different enterprises within which production takes place, and the processes through which their different activities are linked, or co-ordinated. This includes changes in the structure of society's productive capacity brought about through investment and disinvestment in response to changing demand and technology. During the so-called 'golden age' of the 1950s and 1960s, many key enterprises were taken into public, in effect state, ownership. Despite their many achievements, a feeling of disenchantment with their hierarchical structure and paternalism began to develop. Faced with these shortcomings, there were two possibilities – to move forward to social ownership, or backward to private ownership. Given the failure of the top-down planning of the Soviet model and the social engineering of social democratic capitalism, there were two further possibilities – democratisation or marketisation. One of the reasons why neoliberalism triumphed – with its programme of privatisation, deregulation, commodification and consumerism – was the failure of the left to develop an alternative perspective of radical democratisation based on social ownership and participatory planning.

SOCIAL OWNERSHIP

Ownership consists of a set of property rights. It is usual to distinguish between different rights in relation to the same property – the right to current use; to the income arising from current use; to transfer ownership; and to destroy the assets involved. These rights may be owned as a whole or each distinct right may be separately owned, and the exercise of each right is usually circumscribed by an external regulatory framework. It is helpful to bear these different rights in mind when thinking about the concept of social ownership.

Social ownership is best defined as ownership by those affected by decisions over the use of the assets involved, in proportion to the extent to which they are affected. It has much in common with the green concept of stakeholding. Following the principle of subsidiarity which underpins, at least in theory, the multi-layered governance structure of the European Community, the social owners will differ according to the degree of generality, the reach, of the decisions to be made. Decisions made at higher levels of generality will involve more assets and affect a wider range of people and interests than those made at lower levels. At each level, the social owners need to negotiate with one another to agree on the use of the assets that will further their collective social interest, as defined by them. This multi-layered process of negotiated coordination is what is meant by participatory planning.

This governance structure can be illustrated in relation to the National Health Service. Each Primary Care and Hospital Trust would consist of representatives of the relevant social owners – those who will be affected by the current use of the Trust's assets and therefore have the right to decide on that use. Some would be elected by local community groups, patient groups, medical and support staff; others would be appointed by related Trusts, relevant Local Authorities, and Area or Regional Health Authorities. Between them they would decide on the use of the resources made available to the Trust through the democratically determined national and regional or area allocation processes.

However, when it comes to decisions over the allocation of resources between Trusts within a region or area, involving the possible redistribution of resources, a wider set of interests will be affected. This new set of social owners would include: community and patient groups; the various Trusts and Local Authorities within the region or area; and representatives of the regional or national government bodies responsible for health policy and monitoring standards. Representatives of these social owners would constitute the Regional or Area Health Authorities, responsible for planning health care provision in their jurisdiction, allocating resources accordingly, and ensuring that nationally agreed universal standards are complied with.

Such a governance structure, combining direct representation of people as members of affected groups and indirect representation of people as citizens, would enable pluralism and universalism to coexist, reaching decisions through a democratic process of negotiated coordination. A comparable structure for education and the public sector more generally can readily be envisaged. Could the same principle be applied to what is currently the private sector? How could negotiated coordination by social owners at different levels be extended to the production of goods and services that are not supplied free at the point of use?

At the enterprise level, social ownership would embrace the workers in the enterprise, the communities in which it is located, the users of its output, other enterprises in the same industry, major suppliers, advocacy groups concerned with equal opportunities and the environment, and so on – all those with a legitimate interest, or stake, in its activities. Socially owned enterprises would normally compete with each other, using their existing capacity, and their performance would be one indication of whether they were producing what users wanted. When it comes to investment or disinvestment, however – to changes in the structure of existing capacity – a different set of social owners is involved.

Investment and disinvestment decisions affect existing enterprises, their workers and the communities in which they are located. In a capitalist (and market socialist) economy this occurs in an unplanned way in response to market forces. The owners of each individual enterprise make their own decisions in pursuit of profit, without regard for the effects on the workers and communities affected. Profitable enterprises expand, less profitable enterprises contract or close, and then, as profitable opportunities and least-cost locations change again, capital once more moves on and the process is endlessly repeated. People's lives are shaped by the imperatives of capital accumulation, over which they have no control, but which to a greater or lesser extent they seek ways of resisting. This is what gives labourism its conservative character and why the socialist movement developed, in order to look beyond capitalism, to another possible world.

In such a world, of course, there would continue to be changes in technology and demand, albeit probably at a slower rate and shaped by society's democratically determined values and priorities. Changes in the structure of society's productive capacity brought about by investment and disinvestment would continue to be needed. In capitalism such investment decisions are made atomistically by each individual enterprise, with coordination only occurring after the event, when it becomes clear whether too much or too little capacity has been created in any line of production. In a socialist economy, by contrast, major interdependent investment decisions would be coordinated in advance of the resources being committed. This would not eliminate all uncertainty, since some aspects of the future are inherently uncertain. But it would eliminate what has been called 'market uncertainty', the uncertainty that arises from not knowing what the aggregate affect of all the atomistically decided interdependent investments of different enterprises will turn out to be.

In the model of participatory socialist planning, the social owners at the level of the industry – the socially owned enterprises outlined above, relevant local communities, trade unions, user and advocacy groups, planning commissions, etc – would negotiate the pattern of investment for the industry as a whole. They would take into account anticipated technological and demand changes, the performance of existing enterprises, and the circumstances of the different local communities potentially affected – the balance between planned new jobs and jobs likely to disappear, housing, transport, congestion, etc. The negotiated coordination body would have available to it not only publicly available information but also the detailed knowledge of their circumstances provided by the representatives of the enterprises and communities involved, allowing an efficient use of local knowledge. The same principles would apply at all the different levels of decision-making, up to the global, as defined on the basis of the principle of subsidiarity.

Discussion of economic systems is often conducted in terms of plan versus market. However, it is important to deconstruct both terms. Economic planning is usually thought of as a top-down process in which the state decides what enterprises are to do and allocates resources to them accordingly. However, there is no reason why economic planning should not be a bottom-up process in which interdependent enterprises negotiate a pattern of major investment which takes into account both their particular circumstances and the more general society-wide circumstances relevant to their activities. When considering the market, it important to distinguish between market exchange and market forces. Market exchange involves the buying and selling of goods and services. The operation of market forces is the process through which resources are reallocated from one use to another by separately taken, atomistic investment decisions, motivated by the pursuit of profit, which Adam Smith called the invisible hand and Marx called the anarchy of production. In the model proposed, market exchange is retained, but market forces are replaced by a political process of participatory planning through deliberative democratic negotiation.[6]

FEASIBLE?

How feasible is this model? A longstanding objection to socialism is summed up in Oscar Wilde's quip that socialism would be impossible since there would be too many meetings; and this might be thought to apply *a fortiori* to the model of negotiated coordination. However, the corporate capitalist world of today is run through meetings, a high proportion of which are concerned with managing alienated 'human resources', sales promotion, commercial secrecy, financial deals, litigation, etc, which would no longer be necessary in a participatory socialist economy. It is also the case that at present the small minority of people who run the economy spend most of their time in meetings. In a participatory society functioning through negotiated coordination, participation in meetings and decision-making would be much more equally shared, contributing both to personal development and a more efficient use of knowledge.

One of the principal arguments used against socialist planning stems from a particular view of the nature of knowledge. Hayek argued that local knowledge of time and place is essential for economic decision-making and that such knowledge cannot be centralised. This argument has been given a new twist by the distinction increasingly drawn between explicit knowledge that can be codified and in principle transmitted, and tacit knowledge that cannot. Tacit knowledge is acquired through experience, resides in the person who has had the experience, and can only be drawn upon by that person in action. It involves knowing *how* to do something, learnt by doing, as distinct from knowing *that* something is the case. Tacit knowledge can also be social, acquired by a group through working together, which is why teams and social or work groups are more than the sum of the individuals comprising them.

It will be immediately evident that tacit knowledge provides a strong argument for generalising participation in economic decision making to all those affected by the production and use of the goods and services involved. Those who produce them are the people who know how to do so most efficiently and those who use them know the extent to which they really meet their needs. The strength of the argument for the capitalist 'market' is that it enables entrepreneurs to draw on their tacit knowledge and back their judgement. However, this interpretation is based on individual tacit knowledge, with those able to draw on their tacit knowledge confined to those with access to capital. Once tacit *social* knowledge is recognised the argument is turned on its head. Private ownership of the means of production gives way to social ownership, so that the tacit knowledge of everyone affected by the activities of the enterprise is drawn on, not just that of the top managers. And atomised individual decision-making gives way to decision-making by those groups in civil society which constitute the social owners. Market exchange remains but at the level of major interdependent investment decisions the operation of market forces gives way to the process of negotiated coordination.

The model also provides a framework within which the increasingly pressing environmental and ecological challenges facing us can be addressed. Market-based 'solutions' within capitalism rely on technology and modifications to individual behaviour to enable the unlimited economic growth required by the dynamic of capitalist accumulation to continue forever. They are a form of greenwash, comforting people with the prospect of business as usual and endless increases in GDP per head, which continues to be promoted as the best single criterion of well being, despite the mounting evidence to the contrary.[7] By contrast, the relatively new discipline of ecological economics advocates a multi-criteria approach based on a deliberative participatory process. The argument is that it is not possible to reduce all relevant considerations to a single, monetary, measure, as mainstream environmental economics seeks to do.[8] What is needed is a deliberative democratic process that takes account of the different issues involved – economic efficiency, bio-diversity, impact on landscape, consequences for people living in vulnerable areas, responsibilities to future generations, etc – and enables the social owners to weigh these different considerations in relation to each other and decide on the best course of action in the light of the available scientific knowledge and their values. As an example, the state of scientific knowledge in relation to key ecosystems is frequently subject to considerable uncertainty, yet decisions in relation to them are urgent. The weight attached to the precautionary principle will have different consequences for different groups of people and decisions will only carry legitimacy and be effective if they are taken by those who will be affected by them.[9]

A further advantage of the model is that it enables the direction of research and development leading to innovation to be shaped in accordance with social needs, rather than by the pursuit of corporate profitability. Innovation is inherently uncertain and this means that a variety of innovations needs to be pursued, as not all projects embarked on will be successful. The crucial issues are the criteria used within research institutes and enterprises to select which proposals for development should be followed up and the criteria involved in selecting across the innovations that emerge. Under capitalism the criterion in both cases is expected prof- itability. In the model of negotiated coordination democratically determined societal priorities would set the framework within which the social owners at each level would evaluate the produc- tive, unproductive or destructive potential of proposed or realised innovations in terms of their own criteria.[10]

The final issue to be discussed in relation to the model is the question of incentives. In the epoch of triumphalist neoliberalism it is now more or less universally accepted that people are innately self-interested and that the belief that they will act altruistically is naively utopian. Instead, we are urged to be realistic and assess insti- tutional arrangements in terms of their incentive-compatibility. However, this lowering of sights should not be accepted by twenty- first century socialists. Whatever the balance between nature and nurture turns out to be, it is obvious that human behaviour is to a very significant extent shaped by the social framework and *Zeitgeist* within which we grow up and live. And even in today's 'me, me' times there are plenty of examples of people acting out of concern for others, not just in their own narrow self-interest. Of course, the fact that people are concerned for others does not mean that they are not concerned with their own interests. Indeed, there is plenty of evidence that our sense of well-being is dependent not only on our own situation but also on the well-being of others.

The model of democratic planning based on social ownership and negotiated coordination is transformatory, in that the deci- sion-making process involves people in each of the affected groups becoming aware of the interests of the other social owners, as well as their own. In the event of a failure to reach a consensus about what is in the best collective interest of all, there would have to be a decision making rule, such as some form of majority voting. But the logic of the deliberative negotiating process is to promote understanding of the overall situation, recognition of the plurality of interests, and realisation that all legitimate interests have to be taken into account. It is in this sense that the process is transformatory. It is not a process of aggregating pre-existing indi- vidual or group preferences, but rather one in which preferences change as the negotiation proceeds. Instead of the outcome being determined by the operation of market forces, an outcome no one willed, or being imposed by the state, it is arrived at by those affected by it. The social interest is constructed by those whose social interest it is.

TRANSITIONAL FORMS

There are many current examples of attempts to create participatory processes involving all with a legitimate interest in the outcome, from participatory budgeting, through community development projects, to proposals to make corporations responsible to a wider range of stakeholders than just their shareholders. There was even initially an apparent recognition of the importance of aspects of civil society by the incoming Brown administration: 'Over the last decade, we have seen changing attitudes and policy on disability, gay rights, debt relief – and, in all cases, the changes were driven by third sector organisations ... The smallest local organisations represent the glue that binds our communities together.'[11] There are also attempts to engage people through citizens' juries, policy forums, and on some issues referendums. However, these developments co-exist with widespread disenchantment with the formal structure and processes of representative Parliamentary democracy. And, with the exception of participatory budgeting, they are not a complementary form of controlling the state but at best substitutes for the shortcomings of representative democracy and at worst empty pretences at consultation and involvement.

One of the clearest lessons of the twentieth century is that twenty-first century socialism must be self-governing, not state-governed or market-forces-governed. Self-government is rooted in the voluntary associations of civil society, alongside the institutions of representative democracy. One institutional form that this might take would be a Chamber of Interests, consisting of representatives of the principal associations in civil society, alongside the House of Commons, representing people as citizens, with comparable structures at local and global levels. But self-government must also mean civil society in control of the economy, and this requires moving from private ownership, and residual state ownership, to social ownership, and from coordination by market forces or a centralised state to negotiated coordination by social owners. Twenty-first century socialism, like any form of socialism, is ultimately about power and power relations, and in the economic sphere about ownership. Power to the people must mean economic as well as political power.

This chapter is a revised version of 'The political economy of twenty-first century socialism', Soundings 37, Winter 2007, pp105-115.

REFERENCES

1. Anthony Crosland, *The Future of Socialism*, Cape, London 1956.
2. Michael Kenny, *Soundings* 35, Spring 2007, p101.
3. For an influential earlier statement of the dilemma, see Alec Nove, *The Economics of Feasible Socialism*, George Allen & Unwin, London 1983, p226.
4. The formal economy referred to here corresponds roughly to the business sector and parts of the public sector distinguished in chapter two. The change in the work-life ratio referred to is roughly equivalent to a move from these two sectors to chapter two's voluntary and household sectors.
5. This is discussed in more detail in Pat Devine, *Democracy and Economic Planning*, Polity Press, Cambridge1988, ch7.
6. For a fuller outline of the model, see: Devine, op cit; Pat Devine and Fikret Adaman, 'Participatory Planning as a Deliberative Democratic Process: A Response to Hodgson's Critique', *Economy and Society*, 30:2, 2001; Pat Devine, 'Participatory Planning Through Negotiated Coordination', *Science & Society*, 66:1, 2002; and Pat Devine and Fikret Adaman, 'The Promise of Participatory Planning: A Rejoinder to Hodgson', *Economy and Society*, 35:1, 2006.
7. See R. Layard, *Happiness*, Penguin, London 2005; A. Offer, *The Challenge of Affluence*, Oxford University Press, Oxford 2006; O. Oliver, *Affluenza*, Vermilion, London 2007.
8. For example, the Stern Report compared the cost of measures to tackle climate change now with the cost in the future of not doing so. Perhaps the major reason for its significant impact was that it cast the problem in economic terms.
9. See B. Ozkaynak, P. Devine and D. Rigby: 'Whither Ecological Economics?', *International Journal of Environment and Pollution*,

18:4, 2002; and 'Operationalising Strong Sustainability: Definitions, Methodologies, Outcomes', *Environmental Values*, 13:3, 2004

10. See F. Adaman and P. Devine, 'A Reconsideration of the Theory of Entrepreneurship: A Participatory Approach', *The Review of Political Economy*, 2002.

11. Ed Miliband, *The Guardian*, 25 July 2007, Society Section, p3.

4. The fulfilments of post-consumerism and the politics of renewal

Kate Soper

Other contributions to this collection, together with the opening chapter, offer extensive commentary on the quality of our current discontents and on the malign forces responsible for them. They also point to the significant economic and political changes that will be needed to alleviate the worst forms of poverty and distress, and to set the country on the path to a more socially just and sustainable order. I do not intend here to add much to this general diagnosis of Britain's ills, nor to consider in any specific way the economic arrangements and transnational forms of cooperation that will be required to remedy them. But in discussion of the sources and agents of any such transformation, I note the stress that has been placed on the cultural shifts – indeed the veritable cultural revolution – that will be the prior condition of the emergence of any sufficiently forceful 'will to change', and thus of any effective political mandate for a new order. And it is this cultural revision of outlook that I want to discuss here: both to take note of some of the signs – admittedly rather few at present – that it may be in the offing, and to contribute something to its further summoning. My remarks are prompted by my own experience of life in contemporary Britain, and have Britain as their main reference. But the cultural shifts I am concerned with are by no means exclusive to this country, and will need, in fact, to come about on a transnational scale and to involve transnational forms of governance (especially in the first instance within the nations of the so-called 'developed' world) as a condition of any remaking of Britain itself. In other words, and in line with the correct stress placed by the authors of chapter one on transnational initiatives as a key lever for national change, the 'cultural revolution' required cannot take place in one country only. Nor will it; for, just as globalisation has contributed to the hegemonic power of the current – 'consumerist' – conception of the 'good life', so it will ensure the contemporaneous diffusion, at least within the more affluent nations, of any countering 'imaginary'.

A REVISION OF THINKING 'IN THE OFFING'?

I have referred to the 'hegemony' of the 'consumerist' way of life, by which I mean the dominance of a mode of consuming definable not only by its rupture with earlier systems of need, but also by its resistance to any non-commodified conceptions of the means of advancing the 'good life' and personal development. It is marked, that is, by all the insignia of the quest for profit: by the mass production and diversification of goods for sale (rather than the promotion of other means of realising well-being); and by the unprecedented investment in branding, packaging, advertising and other inducements to purchase. Its productive mission, one might say, is the multiplication and diversification of 'satisfiers' of already experienced forms of need and, wherever possible, the creation of new 'needs' themselves – provided these are always conceived as satisfiable only through goods or services provided on the market, and are thus means of profiteering. There is no denying that this 'consumerism' is reliant on manipulative methods for much of its appeal. But its success in winning and sustaining that appeal must also be acknowledged. Many love shopping and acquiring new clothes, shoes, sports and leisure gear, household furnishings, cosmetic goods and services, and so forth; and the market for new technology, especially ipods, mobiles, computers, electronic games, and similar items, shows no sign of abating. Much the same is true of the demand for high speed and/or privatised modes of travelling, such as driving and air flight, which are still hugely popular. It is important for the critics of consumer society to recognise this consensus, however much they may deplore it, and to make clear what theoretical line they are taking on the degree of autonomy exercised by consumers and the status of their desires. The left has often in the past been rather evasive about the issue of consumer freedom and accountability. This is because it has been anxious to claim *both* that its critique of the 'falsity' of consumerism (together with its implied knowledge of what people 'really' need) is democratically representative, *and* to explain the mismatch at any point in time between what consumers *actually* demand and what it is claimed they *really* want, by reference to their unfreedom, in other words, their ideological manipulation. But it seems no more convincing to view shopping enthusiasts as merely the unfortunate and unaccountable dupes of the consumer society, than to view them as fully autonomous and self-knowing beneficiaries of it. There is, in short, a tension around the issue of consumer needs and desires that it would be more honest to admit and openly discuss, rather than seek to suppress. We also need to acknowledge fully the complexities and contradictions of a culture in which all of us are thoroughly integrated into the 'Western way of life' and its capitalist provision of our car transport, air flights, fuel, life insurance, pensions, and so forth, even if many of us – for differing reasons and in differing ways – are also alienated, exploited and politically disaffected with this system. We need, therefore, to be cautious about presuming any extensive support for an alternative way of life to that of present consumer culture; and we can be certain that, even if it were to gain wider appeal and hence begin to provide a democratic mandate for change, there will be no quick and easy ways of moving to a post-consumerist way of living.

That said, however, there are also a number of qualifications to be made to this somewhat discouraging picture, and some recent countering trends of which we ought to take account. In the first place, there is a clear distinction to be drawn between forms of consumption that are foisted upon us, whether we would have it or not, in virtue of our collective co-option into the market-driven system of provision, and a simpler – and relatively freer – exercise of consumer choice. There may be little option in some situations but to drive to work (although these situations are probably rather fewer than people like to claim), but the decision to acquire an SUV in which to do it is altogether more voluntary. People will have little say about what happens with the investment of their mortgage payments or pension contributions. But they will have a lot more say in how many home 'makeovers' they go in for, what materials they use, how much they recycle, and so forth. Likewise, in respect of a whole range of goods and services, there is always a space for more or less green or fair trade forms of purchase, and the recent expansion of ethical shopping indicates that there are now increasing numbers who are keen to avail themselves of the opportunity this allows for more socially just and environmentally friendly consumption.

Ethical shopping, it is true, can readily figure as 'greenwash' for producers and retailers, and sometimes functions, as George Monbiot has suggested, as little more than a fashion gimmick.[1] Being associated with dutiful buying rather than self-interest, it does little to invite us to revise conceptions of our own well-being and the role of consumption in securing it, and even ethical shoppers too often remain captive to the 'consumerist' understanding of the 'good life' to the exclusion of other visions of how to live and prosper. But even if it is only a small one, it is a step in the right direction, and should be welcomed as such.

Nor, despite the lure of the shopping malls for so many people today, should we assume that it is only the more extreme No Logo and anti-globalisation campaigners or 'Simple Lifers' who are questioning the wisdom of continuing with the growth economy and its consumerist life-style. It is true that neither in Britain (nor anywhere else) are there many signs of disaffection, but that does not mean that there are none at all, and we can already detect a measure of consumer ambivalence about the 'good life', both in the sense that other conceptions of this are gaining more of a hold among some, and in the sense that there is a pervasive sense of disenchantment with the supposed blessings of consumerism, compromised as these now are by the stress, pollution, traffic congestion, obesity and general ill health that go with them. Today, in short, a good part of the affluent British lifestyle is being brought into question not so much because of its environmental consequences (although these are also deplored), but because of its negative impact on people themselves, and the ways it distrains on both sensual pleasure and more spiritual forms of well being. We can take note in this connection of the many laments for what has gone missing from our lives under the relentless pressure from neoliberal economic policies, and the frequently expressed interests in less tangible goods, such as more free time, less stress, more personal contacts, and a slower pace of life. Whether it be distress about the loss of the forms of convenience and conviviality associated with the local Post Office, or the nostalgia for a nationalised rail service (for a time, as a fellow traveller said to me the other day, 'when we were passengers, not customers'), or the dejection over an educational system so tailored to the needs of industry rather than the intrinsic rewards of learning, or alarm over the commercialisation of children and the evidence of depression among the young – in all such cases, what is voiced is a sense of sadness that none other than monetary values can make any headway in our culture; that little in public life will be guaranteed survival if it cannot make profit.

These voicings of discontent are still fairly low-key, diffuse, and politically unfocused. They are the frustrated murmurings of those who are aware of their impotence to take on the corporate giants, and have little coherent idea of what to put in place of the existing order. But their regrets and disgusts are real enough, and they feed into a now quite widely felt sense of the opportunities we have squandered in recent decades for enjoying more relaxed and less narrowly reductive ways of living. There are a number, too – the 'alternative hedonists' – who are now more explicitly asking why we must always pursue more monetary wealth, and why, when we have done so, it must mainly accrue to the already rich and super-rich, and not be turned into public resources for the benefit of all of us. Why, it is asked, must we further swell the coffers of a handful of magnates and financiers, when we could have otherwise dramatically reduced the time spent working, or provided home insulation for all, or doubled the parks and playgrounds in every town and city, or created a complex of walkways and cycle tracks throughout the land allowing all of us, from the cradle to the grave, to bike or walk in safety – and consider how splendid we could have made these tracks, given the difference between the cost of a metre of the M5 (£35,000) and that of a metre of cycle path (£180).

TOWARDS POST-CONSUMERISM

In the UK per capita emissions of CO_2 are running at 9.6 tonnes a year, whereas a 'sustainable' quota is estimated at 2.45 tonnes.

This means that each of us needs to reduce our emissions by no less than three-quarters, on average. But even if there were no compelling environmental reasons for shifting to a less acquisitive, work-driven and fast-paced way of living, there are many rewards to be had from doing so, and a growing body of evidence to indicate that increases in economic wealth do not, once a certain level has been reached, bring any further enhancement of personal happiness or well-being.[2] Indeed, according to the New Economics Foundation's *Manifesto on Well-Being*, alongside a near doubling of economic output in the last thirty years, there has been a rise in depression and mental illness, and feelings of trust in others have fallen dramatically (whereas some 60 per cent in the 1960s answered affirmatively to the question 'do you think most other people can be trusted', this has now fallen to around 30 per cent).[3] Self-reported stress caused or made worse by work more than doubled in Britain between 1990 and 2001/2, and even in areas where job satisfaction in the past has to some extent compensated for relative lack of earnings, stress and insecurity have now begun to take their toll. A recent study, for example, has found an increase in depression, strain, sleep loss and unhappiness during the 1990s among Britain's six million public service workers, whose job satisfaction has now fallen dramatically.[4]

All this suggests that rather than hanker after technical fix solutions that might keep the 'work and spend' economy on course (and these, in any case, seem very unlikely to be forthcoming), we would be better off in Britain, and contribute a much needed alternative model of progress and development for the rest of the world, were we to break with current ways of thinking about our well-being and prosperity and to open ourselves to the possibility of a steady-state or very low growth economy and the pleasures of its 'alternative hedonist' way of living.

Everything at present, of course, conspires against any such rethinking of the 'good life'. Companies, with little restraint from government, continue to pressurise us into ever more self-destructive and environmentally vandalising forms of consumption, and they are constantly expanding the outlets for their merchandising activities. The infiltration of the child's world by branding gurus and marketing experts is highly ingenious and particularly blatant.[5] Indeed it amounts to a corruption and theft of youth that would be regarded as sinisterly totalitarian were it to occur in any other context but that of the market. Magazines such as *Bliss, Sugar, CosmoGirl* and *ElleGirl* are specifically designed to co-opt pre-teen girls into a life of beauty-product buying, while the consumer research agency Mintel has recently recommended, on the basis of a report on this age range, that cosmetic vending machines be placed in secondary schools to further encourage consumption.[6] Pets, too, have begun to figure as a vast potential new market. In Tesco one can now buy silver-packaged gourmet meals for one's dog. Should it become too obese, there is a Fit-fur-Life dog tread-mill for indoors exercise, on the market at £700, or treatments are available in the heated hydrotherapy pool at the Triple A Pet Resort near Newcastle upon Tyne. And for the delectation of the better off adult humans, there are always new bling items, new luxuries, new adventures to be had, or at the very least more flying to be done. Burberry's was reported in May 2008 as doing a fast trade in crocodile skin handbags at £11,000 each. Virgin has recently appointed European agents for its commercial space travel, Galactic Service, and, like many other airlines, is also pressing ahead with Business Class only transatlantic flights. To help things along, the then Transport Secretary, Ruth Kelly, set out plans in November 2007 for a third runway and Sixth Terminal at Heathrow airport. She, and others who argued that the airport might otherwise lose its global clout, are hoping, one presumes, that as memories over the fiasco of the opening of Terminal Five fade, it will encourage a doubling or trebling by the wealthier of their annual shopping trips to New York or other consumer meccas. And if amassing the necessary funds to enjoy all this jetting between shopping malls leaves these people a little time impover-ished, they can always invest in one of those holiday breaks that promise to make good the loss. As the brochure for one such holiday provider puts it:

> For those of us with huge overdrafts at the Bank of Hours-in-the-Day, the real luxury is time. Time with the kids, phone switched off. Or time for yourself, to read and relax in peace. Luxury is a long lunch recovering the person you love, or a gourmet dinner with friends, cooked to order and served by your own private pool. It's me-time. Family time. The elusive holy grail of modern life.[7]

It is, of course, all too easy, as the planet heats, to be ironic about the waste, absurdity and decadence of 'late' capitalism's modes of consumption. But the irony can also help to point up the very real and serious paradox at the heart of contemporary consumerism, namely, that even as it offers its extensive range of psychic and physical pleasures, its prevailing tendency is to deflect the unmet needs of the spirit towards material comforts and more tangible consolations, or to promote material goods as means of meeting more spiritual desires – and this applies in respect of both carnal and non-carnal appetites and pleasures. Even where it is a question of meeting the needs of the flesh (of satisfying hunger, for example), the tendency of the consumer society is very often to whittle away or downgrade the more distinctively ritualised (spiritual and aesthetic) dimensions of this. Food, for example, is fast food, eaten on the run, and very often consumed in solitary mode and while doing something else such as watching television. What has gone missing from it is the sense of the meal as a prepared, shared, convivial event having its own intrinsic value in structuring time, fostering human exchange, and providing food for thought as well as bodily renewal.

It will be pointed out, maybe, that more people in Britain are now visiting restaurants and spending 'quality' time within them than ever before. But this only goes to prove the point that the primary momentum of consumerist culture is to reduce and drive out this form of time expenditure from a more ordinary, immediate, commonly shared and everyday experience. And if the need for it nonetheless persists, as is suggested in the increase in restaurant eating (and in the growth of the Slow Food movement and the huge popularity of heritage and other cookery TV programmes), then that is no surprise. It is one manifestation of an 'alternative hedonist' dialectic, through which the satisfaction denied or marginalised at one level returns to claim attention in some other mode. It can then, in turn, provide new opportunities for commercialisation. In other words, the return of the repressed desire (for conviviality, more free time, better health, a less stressed existence, etc) is readily caught up in what one may term the 'satisfaction at second remove' imposed by the consumerist dynamic: by a dynamic that tends to the elimination of certain forms of relatively straightforward and inexpensive gratification, only then to further profit through the provision of more expensive (and therefore often more socially exclusionary) compensatory modes of consumption. (The luxury holidays that sell you back 'quality' time; the extra you often now have to pay for dealing with a person rather than a machine; the speed dating and Wife Selecting agencies that promise to make up for your loss of the arts of loving and relating; the multiplication of gyms to which people drive in order to do treadmill running in cities where – largely because of the consequences of extensive car use in urban space – they no longer find it pleasant or safe to walk or run).

The tendency, then, of consumer culture is both to 'ultra-mate-rialise' the sources of satisfaction of the more materially oriented and sensual needs, and to materialise the ways in which we meet the more intangible and spiritual needs (and this often also comes at the cost of reducing the time and space for other, less resource-intensive and commercialised, means of meeting those needs). It is as if in consumerism we do indeed have an attempt to accommo-date all the more irreducibly symbolic and affective dimensions of human needing, whether for the more sensual or the more cere-bral satisfactions, by treating them on the model of physiological need: as if they were, indeed, mere extensions or complications of such need, and could be met, for the most part, through the provi-sion of tangible objects.

The consumer society, one may therefore argue, is now becoming increasingly dependent for its continued flourishing on our collective preparedness to spend the money we earn by working too hard and too long on the goods which help to satisfy, if only 'at second remove', the 'goods' we have increasingly sacri-ficed through over-work and over-production. What is more, it would appear very likely that if we are incapable of springing this trap, and reverting to a more rational economic order, we are destined for ecological collapse and all the social horrors that will entail. Now, therefore, more than ever before, we need to chal-lenge the seemingly ever more tenacious hold of the work ethic on the British way of life, and to campaign for a socio-economic order of the kind developed in the argument of André Gorz and others, in which work and income are more fairly distributed, co-parenting and part-time work become the norm, and everyone has the means and time for sustainable forms of activity and life-enhancement that are not subject to, or co-optable by, market forces or values.[8] In Gorz' argument:

> We have to see the guarantee of a basic social income and the expansion of disposable time not as something which would reduce activity, but as a way of increasing it. Their purpose is not to exempt people from doing anything at all, but to open up possibilities for everyone to engage in a whole host of individual or collective, private or public activities – activities which no longer need to be profitable in order to flourish.[9]

Any move in that direction would, of course, require that as a society we had come to give much greater attention to other measures of prosperity than GDP. It would mean that education had come to be seen as an as an intrinsically valuable preparation for life rather than merely as an adjunct of industry, and that the care of mind had come to command something of the same attention that is currently devoted to the body. It would also, as I have argued at greater length elsewhere, be dependent upon the emergence of a radically different response to material culture – an 'aesthetic revisioning', whereby goods currently viewed as enticingly glamorous lose their appeal in virtue of their association with unsustainable resource use, noise, toxicity or their legacy of unrecyclable waste.[10] And it will need – though I recognise how controversial this will sound – a more courageous challenge to the 'political incorrectness' of excessive and nonchalant consumers. It is still very difficult to criticise the environmental squandering involved in people's consumption habits – and there is much embarrassment all round if ever one does. But faced with the catastrophic effects of the climatic impact of first world affluence on other, more deprived, areas of the globe, and on all future generations, it is no longer clear why highly wasteful and polluting forms of personal consumption should remain 'off limits' and exempt from the kinds of criticism that we now expect to be brought against racist or sexist or blatantly undemocratic attitudes and modes of behaviour. If Britain is to feel less bad in the future, then its people will certainly need to go through a cultural revolution in attitudes to work, consumption, pleasure and self-realisation. And such a revolution will surely be comparable in the forms of personal epiphany and transformation it will demand to those brought about through the feminist, anti-racist and anti-colonialist movements of recent history.

REFERENCES

1. George Monbiot, 'Ethical Shopping Is Just Another Way of Showing How Rich You Are', *Guardian*, 24 July 2007, p27.
2. For evidence on this, see for example A.T. Durning, *How Much is Enough?*, Earthscan, London 1992; R.A. Easterlin, 'Income and Happiness: Towards a Unified Theory', *Economic Journal*, 111, 2001, pp465-494; Richard Layard, *Happiness: Lessons from a New Science*, Allen Lane, London 2005; New Economics Foundation, *Happy Planet Index*, at www.happyplanetindex.org/index.htm; R. Levett, *A Better Choice of Choice: Quality of Life, Consumption and Economic Growth*, Fabian Society, London 2003.
3. New Economics Foundation, *Manifesto on Well-Being*, 28 September 2004, at: www.neweconomics.org.
4. For evidence on this, see for example responses to the BBC programme 'Do We Work Too Hard?', www.news.bbc.co.uk/1/hi/talking_point/626333.stm; Madeleine Bunting, *Willing Slaves: How the Overwork Culture is Ruling our Lives*, Harper Collins, London 2004; Andrew Oswald and Jonathan Gardner, study reported in, 'Job Satisfaction Falls for Public Workers', *Guardian*, 22 March 2001.
5. Cf Zoe Williams, 'The Commercialisation of Childhood', Compass, February 2008, at: www.compassonline.org/publications.
6. Cf Owen Boycott, 'Make-up and Marketing – Welcome to the World of 10 Year Old Girls', *Guardian*, 8 September 2004.
7. Coastline Holidays, at: www.coastline.co.uk.
8. See André Gorz, *Paths to Paradise: On the Liberation of Work*, trans. Malcolm Imrie, Pluto, London 1985; André Gorz, *Critique of Economic Reason*, Verso, London 1989; André Gorz, *Reclaiming Work: Beyond the Wage-Based Society*, trans. Chris Turner, Polity, Cambridge 1999; David Purdy, 'Human Happiness and the Stationary State', *Soundings* 31, 2005, pp133-146; David Purdy, 'Citizens' Income: Sowing the Seeds of Change', *Soundings* 35, 2007, pp54-65.
9. Gorz 1999, op cit, p100.
10. Kate Soper, 'Alternative Hedonism, Cultural Theory and the Role

of Aesthetic Revisioning', *Cultural Studies*, Vol 22, 5, September
2008, pp567-587; Kate Soper and Lyn Thomas, 'Alternative
Hedonism and the Critique of Consumerism', Working Paper 31
in the Cultures of Consumption Programme, London 2007.

5. Can British democracy be revived?

David Beetham

The condition of British democracy under New Labour is marked by an acute paradox. On the one hand the government has presided over an unprecedented programme of constitutional reform, of a kind that normally only takes place after revolution or defeat in war. This programme has included: the devolution of power to Scotland, Wales and Northern Ireland; the establishment of the Greater London Authority; the incorporation of the European Convention on Human Rights into UK law through the Human Rights Act; the introduction of a Freedom of Information Act; the abolition of the hereditary element in the House of Lords; the reform of the role of Lord Chancellor and the creation of a new Supreme Court; the establishment of an Electoral Commission; and much more.

Admittedly, these reforms have been carried out under the rubric of 'modernisation' rather than 'democratisation', but they are all measures that democratic reformers have long advocated and campaigned for. Moreover, Gordon Brown was initially keen to give the reform process new momentum, as evidenced by the first published paper of his premiership, *The Governance of Britain* (July 2007), which presaged a number of current legislative proposals – on citizenship, limitation of the royal prerogative, strengthening parliament, and so on.[1] By any standard this has been an impressive programme, and evidence of more than a fleeting commitment.

On the other hand, these institutional reforms have taken place alongside the acceleration of a secular deformation in the democratic process in Britain, which began under Margaret Thatcher and intensified under New Labour. Aspects of this deformation have already been mentioned in the opening chapter of this book, and it is worth analysing them more systematically here. Three different processes have combined to degrade the quality of public life and decision-making in Britain.

UNRESTRAINED PRESIDENTIALISM

First is the progressive concentration of power in the hands of the prime minister, and the elimination of significant checks on that power. Of course most contemporary democracies are characterised by what Max Weber called 'leadership democracy', in which there is a pervasive concentration on the individual personality of the leader, whether as president or premier.[2] However, two features of the UK's political arrangements have given the prime minister an unusual degree of individual power. One is the electoral system, which virtually guarantees single party rule on a minority of the popular vote, and with it secure control by the executive over parliament. Second has been the elimination of the institutional constraints which have traditionally served to temper that power. Members of the cabinet no longer enjoy a power base of their own independently of the prime minister, to whom they owe their appointment and continuation in office. One reason for that has been the parallel decline in inner-party democracy, as party policy and candidate selection are increasingly concentrated at the centre. Parliament is largely subservient to the executive, through the tight control exercised by the whips and the potent incentives and sanctions available to them. Civil service independence as a source of unwelcome truths to ministers has been compromised by a promotions system that emphasises a 'can do' approach and support for government policies. In addition, local government, in England at least, has been neutered as a source of alternative policies, through ever tighter control from the centre.

One consequence of this unique concentration of power in the hands of the party leader and prime minister is a proneness to policy disasters, of which Mrs. Thatcher's poll tax and Tony Blair's war on Iraq are only the most egregious examples.[3] The typical disaster course is that a policy fashioned in the leader's head is fleshed out by a special unit in Downing Street, ignoring departmental and external expertise, and is only presented to the cabinet and parliament at a point where rejection would fatally damage the position of the prime minister and possibly the survival of the government. In Mrs Thatcher's case the policy led to by-election disaster, her removal from office and the subsequent reversal of the policy under a new leader. With Tony Blair the erosion of authority and removal from office was much longer drawn out, and the damaging consequences of the policy remain with us, and the Iraqi people, to this day. In any case, removal of a premier from office after the event is no substitute for a system of checks on power which might prevent the disasters in the first place, and save the leader from his or her own worst mistakes.

Arguably of much longer term significance for the quality of democratic politics has been the way recent prime ministers have used their unchecked power to recast whole political parties in their own image. Mrs Thatcher turned a 'broad church' Tory Party into an ideologically driven and ideologically riven organisation, which gradually fell apart once she was removed from office and subsequently became unelectable for a generation. Tony Blair turned the Labour Party into another right-wing party, subservient to business and finance capital at home and to US interests abroad, and always on the lookout for wrong-footing the Tory opposition by appropriating their policy clothes. The ideological bankruptcy of this position has been cruelly exposed by the leader's resignation and the change in the economic climate, probably making the Labour Party in turn unelectable for another generation.

The consequences of the resulting weakness of the opposition parties have been profound. For most of the past thirty years governments have not had to fear a credible alternative government in waiting as a potential constraint on their power. From the citizens' point of view, there has been a significant narrowing of effective electoral choice, and a corresponding long-term decline in electoral turnout. One of the quirks of the first-past-the-post electoral system under New Labour has been that, as a considerable electoral space has opened up on the left with the party's shift rightwards, the Liberal Democrats have been unable to take consistent advantage of it, as most of their winnable seats happen to have been in Tory-held constituencies. Nor have other parties been able to establish themselves to take advantage of the vacuum created. As a result large sections of political opinion have been effectively disenfranchised.

No account of executive and prime-ministerial supremacy would be complete without acknowledging two potential checks on that power – one informal, one institutional – which have been evident since New Labour came to office. Britain's longstanding tradition of civic activism has produced numerous protest movements against government policies, on issues ranging from the global to the local, which have proved capable of mobilising widespread popular support.[4] Mostly, however, these have been reactive, rather than proactive, and when ignored, as the Iraq protests were, have only intensified disillusionment with the democratic process.

The main institutional check on the executive over the past decade has been the judiciary, which time after time has ruled against the government for breaches of due process, of individual rights and of the rule of law. No doubt the government's own Human Rights Act has encouraged the judges to moderate their traditional 'executive mindedness', and show much greater independence. Yet they remain vulnerable to populist campaigns by both media and government against their unelected status; and the Human Rights Act itself, never given popular endorsement through a referendum, is threatened with erosion if not outright repeal at the hands of a future Conservative government.

In conclusion, while the popular mobilisations of civil society and the rights-protection afforded by an independent judiciary are both necessary components of a democratic polity, neither can serve as a substitute for a parliamentary system that is both fully representative of political opinion in the country and able to provide effective oversight over the executive, within a pluralism of checks and balances on prime ministerial supremacy. Instead of representative democracy, in sum, we have what Jack Straw himself has termed 'executive democracy', albeit more executive than democratic.

MARKETISATION OF THE PUBLIC SPHERE

The second trend damaging to the quality of democracy and public life in Britain that was begun by Mrs Thatcher and intensified under New Labour has been the systematic exposure of the public sphere to market forces and values. Other chapters in this book trace its impact on particular public services, and the financial burdens and distortions placed on them into the distant future as a result. Here the more general effects of marketisation on the quality of the public sphere will be explored.

The general point to make is that the public sphere in a democratic society possesses distinctive qualities which differentiate it from the market: it serves a public rather than a private interest, and one determined by open discussion and debate rather than market signals; it provides and protects public goods which cannot be reduced to the sum of individual goods; it is based upon the principle of equal citizenship rather than ability to pay; and it is characterised by collective and public-service orientations, rather than the maximisation of individual or corporate reward. Together these features characterise a distinct public domain whose integrity depends on being protected from erosion by or subordination to market imperatives. As David Marquand has well put it in his book *Decline of the Public*, echoing Karl Polanyi:

> The great work of the Victorian era was to carve out from the encircling market and private domains a distinct, self-conscious and vigorous public domain governed by non-market and non-private norms, and to erect barriers protecting it from incursions by its market and private neighbours.[5]

As Marquand's account shows, this public domain had a distinctly elitist complexion, which was at best only moderated in the course of the twentieth century, and which rendered it vulnerable to discrediting by governments from Mrs Thatcher onwards, and to a deliberate process of deconstruction. Three different aspects of that deconstruction can be identified. First has been the privatisation of public services and the subjection of those remaining in public hands to competition, proxy markets and management on a private sector model, under the explicit rubric: 'private sector good, public sector bad'. Although the perverse effects have played out differently in the core public services of health, education and transport, a common feature has been the cherry-picking of profitable activities by private companies, which diminishes the quality of basic provision and compromises equality between differently placed citizens. The decline of the universal postal service and network of post offices is a classic example of a public good being sacrificed to market imperatives.

A second aspect of the market invasion of the public sphere is the reconfiguration of the public as consumers rather than as citizens. Here we need to be more precise about these terms than is sometimes the case. Citizens in a democratic polity should expect prompt and effective service at the hands of government officials and public services, and there is nothing wrong with incorporating good practice methods from the best of the private sector in a publicly run service. What is damaging, however, is the attempt to construct the citizen in receipt of a public service as a consumer in the market place, with a choice between competing goods and services, and the ability to 'exit' if not satisfied. What people have shown they want from the public services is a good quality of service, rather than choice, which has all kinds of perverse effects and is far from the only way to improve the quality of provision. To use Hirschman's distinction, the method appropriate to the public sphere is 'voice' rather than 'exit', and this includes forms of collective voice to influence the policy and priorities of service provision *ex ante*, as well as mechanisms for complaint and redress *ex post*.[6]

A third distorting aspect of the subordination of the public sphere to market imperatives and models has been the erosion of a professional and public service ethic, as activities at all levels have been subjected to centrally imposed targets, performance indicators, league tables, and so on. What began as an attack by Mrs Thatcher on feather-bedding and a producer-oriented culture in the public sector has become a way of life, in which working to centrally directed targets has replaced professionally determined priorities. Indeed, the concept of a profession itself, with the independence that comes from the internalisation of norms of good practice alongside training in relevant skills, has been eroded by the market-driven assumption that effective performance can only be secured by externally structured incentives and sanctions.[7]

It would be mistaken to suggest that the old public sector model did not have its own weaknesses, or to imagine that the shift towards a more individualist, consumer-oriented culture could be easily resisted in public life. Nevertheless, the deliberate subordination of the public sector to market imperatives by successive governments has not only had the perverse effects outlined here and in other chapters. It has served to erode the distinctiveness and narrow the scope of the public sphere that is necessary to a democratic society, with its opportunities for public discussion and debate on priorities, provision of public as well as private goods, and promotion of collective rather than purely individual values and orientations.

SPINNING TO EXCESS

A final element which has degraded the democratic process and the quality of public life over the past decade or more has been the growth of spin. If 'spin' were simply a concern with public image and good public relations, then this would be nothing new, as it has always been part of the politician's stock in trade. Relatively new, however, are the huge budgets now assigned to government communication and its staffing, the ruthlessness and degree of political coordination employed to ensure that everyone is on message, and the preoccupation with news management and presentation. Governments are now shamelessly 'economical with the truth'; they are practised at creating diversions so as to bury bad news; and they marginalise critical experts and induce others to give opinions favourable to government policy. And public confidence in their credibility and integrity has been damaged as a consequence.[8]

Although these practices were evident under Conservative governments, they have been brought to a new level under New Labour, in response to two pressures. One was the experience of seventeen years in opposition, scarred by a consistently hostile press, and by the latter's treatment of any internal party disagreements as evidence of chronic division or personalised power struggles. A second pressure has been the development of the rolling twenty-four hours' news agenda, creating new stories by the hour which demand immediate response from government. Tony Blair came into office determined to control the news agenda, to coordinate communication across government, and to marginalise anyone in government or party who spoke out of turn. At the same time he vigorously courted the previously hostile tabloid press, especially the *Sun* and the *Daily Mail*, and showed himself acutely responsive to their agendas, as voicing the concerns of Middle England.

Blair's response to these pressures has given New Labour some of its most distinctive characteristics in government: a tendency to confuse the appearance with the substance of policy; a propensity for constant new initiatives and instant legislation; and a practice of going through the motions of extensive consultation when its mind was already made up. As early as the year 2000 Philip Gould, Blair's chief focus-group guru, was complaining that 'the New Labour brand has been badly contaminated ... It has been undermined by a combination of spin, lack of conviction and apparently lack of integrity'.[9] Yet nothing in Labour's first term could equal the lack of integrity demonstrated in the run up to the Iraq war, with the pretence that war had not already been decided on by the summer of 2002, the charade of the UN arms inspection process, the dodgy dossiers, the manipulation of legal advice, the bugging of UN delegations, and more.[10]

Given such a record, it is not surprising that levels of public trust in government, parliament, political parties and politicians generally have shown a consistent decline over the period that New Labour has been in power. This goes deeper than scandals over parliamentary allowances or cash for honours, to the credibility of government itself. Few people are prepared to believe what politicians tell them. While a change of ruling party may bring temporary relief, there is little evidence that the Conservatives under David Cameron will be markedly different, in this or any other of the respects in which the democratic process has been degraded over time.

Can the processes described above, which have combined to diminish the quality of democracy and public life in Britain, be reversed? What would be needed to do so? The last section of the chapter will briefly look at Gordon Brown's latest proposals for constitutional reform, before proceeding to outline an alternative agenda to revive our ailing democratic process.

DEMOCRACY RENEWED

It was always mistaken to expect that Gordon Brown as premier would change New Labour's deeply embedded mode of governing, since as Chancellor he had been implicated in it all along. To be sure the July 2007 Green Paper on *The Governance of Britain* acknowledged the collapse of public trust in government, which a new programme of constitutional reform would seek to remedy. 'Action is now needed across the breadth of the political system', it boldly declared, 'to promote and restore trust in politics and our political institutions'.[11] However, it nowhere asked the obvious question as to why the earlier set of constitutional reforms, important and necessary as they were, had coincided with a decline in public confidence in government, or why anyone should expect a new round of constitutional reform to be any different. And the reforms themselves – to strengthen parliament and its oversight of the executive, improve consultative processes, redefine British identity and values, and add a large dose of citizenship education – offered nothing sufficient to address the deficiencies outlined in the first part of this chapter. In any case, even they were soon watered down to the point where they were described by Lord Falconer as 'trivial' and 'containing nothing of significance'.[12]

So what might an alternative agenda look like? It would have to be one which offered proposals relevant to each of the distortions of democratic process discussed earlier. Suggestions for each one are outlined below.

Re-establishing pluralism in the political process

A healthy democracy requires a pluralism of institutions with which people have an incentive to engage politically. One dimension of that pluralism is territorial. The devolution of power to Scotland and Wales shows what benefits can come from elected governments with the power to decide policy priorities across the board at a lower level than Westminster. Although proposals for regional government in England have proved unpopular, this is partly because people do not identify with the regions as constituted, and partly because the powers offered were so pitiful. The old metropolitan councils of city regions should be revived to start with, along the lines of the Greater London Authority, but with the wide-ranging powers across the board of the Scottish Parliament and Welsh Assembly, within a determined budget distributed from the centre but with additional borrowing powers. At the same time the proliferation of unelected quangos should be brought under the control and oversight of these elected bodies.

The constitutional arrangements for Scotland and Wales show another important dimension of pluralism, which comes from a more proportional electoral system, allowing a greater diversity of political parties and denying any one a parliamentary majority and a monopoly of executive power. Such a measure for Westminster elections would also make proposals to strengthen the central parliament much more effective in practice. Scotland and Wales also show the advantages of fixed-term parliaments of four years, to which should be added a two-term limit of office for any prime minister. A second chamber elected on a different cycle from the Commons would possess more independence from the executive, as well as greater legitimacy than the current House of Lords. Many other ways to pluralise the political process could be suggested, but the principles at issue should be clear: to diminish the enormous concentration of power in the central executive, and make electoral democracy both more diverse and more meaningful.

Reinvigorating the public sphere

The direction which renewal of the public sphere should take is already implicit in the principles outlined earlier in the discussion about the distinctive qualities of the public domain. It involves more than simply reversing processes of privatisation and deregulation in the delivery of public services, and the distortions brought by running the public sector on the model of market institutions. It means also taking seriously the role of citizen voice rather than consumer choice in the planning and delivery of public services. Across the country people have shown their readiness to use their voices in defence of local hospitals, schools and post offices threatened with closure. These are reactive rather than proactive forms of citizen engagement. Much better to have systematic public involvement at an earlier stage, working with the relevant professionals through public consultations, user groups, different modes of user survey, and so on, to help shape services to local needs.

Of course this means decisions over priorities will be taken more locally than Whitehall, along the lines of the pluralism outlined already. And this necessarily leads to a diversity in priorities and modes of provision, as the evidence from Scotland and

Wales already demonstrates. Objections on grounds of the 'post-code lottery', however, can be met if the differing priorities are clearly the result of public debate and electoral endorsement rather than the product of inefficiency or bureaucratic indifference, and conform to nationally agreed standards.

At a wider level there has to be a change in the culture of denigration of the public sphere in comparison with the private, and a reversal of the assumption that there can be individual solutions to all our problems. The limits of this way of thinking have long since been reached and its failings clearly exposed to view – as they were in the first onslaught of ultra-liberalism in the Victorian era. Many of the most serious problems facing society require collective solutions, and governments at every level have to find new ways of involving the public in adult discussion about priorities for solving them. This cannot be done, however, in a culture of spin, of phoney consultation, or of knee-jerk reaction to every latest media scare, which only increase resistance to collectively required solutions.

Restoring integrity to public life

There are no simple solutions to restoring public trust in the integrity of government once it has been as deeply compromised as it has been in Britain over the past two decades. Some benefit would come from reforms to party funding and the system of parliamentary expenses; some also from strengthening the Freedom of Information Act and the independence of the official statistical service from government intervention, both welcome Labour initiatives. Much of the solution, however, lies in the hands of politicians themselves, and in changing a deeply rooted government mind set which regards public opinion as something to be manipulated rather than something to be engaged with in open and honest discussion.

Politicians themselves blame the media for preventing such a discussion, and for offering a distorted image of their role and activities. Nothing has been more shameful in New Labour, however, than its unholy alliance with Rupert Murdoch, and its subservience to the right-wing tabloids, which has only served to increase their power. This subservience has not only encouraged the tendency to instant policy creation or reversal. It has produced an alignment with their own long-term political agenda, of which the prioritisation of the US connection and hostility to the European Union are perhaps the most pronounced features. Yet no issue in British politics calls out more for a full and honest public discussion than the subordination of our policies to US interests, the multiple dependencies which frame it, and its consequences for our role in Europe and relations elsewhere. Breaking the deafening silence on this subject, and initiating the long overdue debate, however controversial, about what sort of country we want to be in this globalised world, would be the hallmark of a truly progressive government or political party.

REFERENCES

1. Ministry of Justice, CM 7170, July 2007.
2. Max Weber, 'Politics as a Vocation', in H.H. Gerth and C. Wright Mills (eds), *From Max Weber*, Routledge and Kegan Paul, London 1948, esp. pp105-14.
3. For the poll tax see David Butler, Andrew Adonis and Tony Travers, *Failure in British Government*, Oxford University Press, Oxford 1994; for the Iraq war see John Kampfner, *Blair's Wars*, Free Press, London 2003, chs. 8-10. For a wider examination of the lack of checks on the executive in foreign policy, see Simon Burall, Brendan Donnelly and Stuart Weir, *Not in Our Name: Democracy and Foreign Policy in the UK*, Politico's, London 2006.
4. A far from complete list under the Blair government is given in David Beetham, Andrew Blick, Helen Margetts and Stuart Weir, *Power and Participation in Modern Britain*, Democratic Audit 2008, pp58-60.
5. David Marquand, *Decline of the Public*, Polity Press, Cambridge 2004, p41.
6. A.O. Hirschman, *Exit, Voice and Loyalty*, Harvard University Press, Cambridge Mass, 1970.
7. See Marquand, op cit, pp110-25.
8. Peter Oborne, *The Rise of Political Lying*, Free Press, London 2005; George Pitcher, *The Death of Spin*, John Wiley, Chichester 2003.
9. Quoted in Pitcher, op cit, p118.
10. John Kampfner was the first to reveal that the key decision by Blair to support Bush's plan to invade Iraq was taken at a meeting at

Crawford, Texas, in April 2002. Documents were later shown to support this: see report in *Independent on Sunday*, 1 May 2005; for Goldsmith's shifting legal advice, see the *Guardian*, 28 and 29 April 2005.

11. Ministry of Justice, op cit, para 123, p40.

12. In evidence given to the joint committee scrutinising the draft constitutional renewal bill, 21 May 2008. See also Democratic Audit, 'Beating the Retreat: The Government's flight from Constitutional Reform', Democratic Audit, London and Essex 2009.

6. A decade of health service reform: from transparency and restructuring to competition and choice

Linda J. Patterson

2008 is the sixtieth anniversary of the founding of the National Health Service. As a tax-financed public service available to all citizens free of charge, the NHS was a great step forward. It allayed fear of the financial consequences of illness, injury and ill health; helped to create a more equal and just society; gave the middle class free access to general practice, previously available only to insured employees (mostly men) and their families; and gave the working class free access to specialist care. Both general and specialist care were expanded, the former under a regulated franchise of GPs, the latter by enlarging the capacity of nationalised hospitals. And all this was achieved amidst post-war austerity and against opposition from the Conservative Party and the medical profession, particularly GPs.

The pioneers of the NHS believed that, as the backlog of untreated disease was dealt with, the demand for healthcare would diminish and the recurrent costs of the service would fall. This was a misapprehension. It took no account of chronic sickness, and failed to anticipate either advances in medical science or the emergence of new illnesses. No one foresaw the burgeoning health needs of an ageing population which, thanks to mass immunisation and reduced infant mortality, was living longer, let alone the way in which growing material affluence and declining social deference would revolutionise public expectations.

Nevertheless, sixty years on, the NHS compares well with services in other developed countries, not least the US, where more than fifty million people have no health insurance and still fear the financial consequences of becoming ill. The NHS retains the affection of the British public and has long enjoyed cross-party support: even Mrs Thatcher left it substantially intact. As a nationwide public service, centrally financed and controlled, the NHS can be developed in a planned and coordinated manner. By the same token, it is cumbersome and slow to change. If it is to meet the needs of the whole population, provide equally for all social groups and all geographical areas, treat patients equitably, use resources efficiently and keep up with medical advances, the service has to be periodically reformed and renewed. The question is how.

TWENTY-FOUR HOURS TO SAVE THE NHS?

During the 1997 general election campaign, the NHS was a key issue. Indeed, on the eve of the election, Labour warned voters that they had 'twenty-four hours to save the NHS'. Even discounting political rhetoric, the new government faced a formidable array of problems. The NHS had been under-funded by a cumulative total of £220 billion over twenty-five years.[1] New building and maintenance had been neglected, while the pay of both professional groups and, more especially, ancillary staff, had fallen relative to comparators.

There was widespread discontent, particularly with hospital care. There were long waiting lists for appointments and operations which, in cases such as hip replacement, could stretch to years. At the same time, although queues for operations were a particular bugbear, the number of people with long-term conditions, such as diabetes and heart disease, was seventeen times the number needing an operation. Access to care was a vexed issue, with complaints about the 'postcode lottery' surfacing whenever patients with the same conditions in different areas received different treatments. A further source of frustration was long waiting times in Accident and Emergency (A&E) departments. Even when someone was admitted to hospital, they could spend many hours lying on a trolley waiting for a bed on the wards.

People had also come to expect more from public services, demanding personalised care at times and locations that suited them. Pressure for more user-friendly provision comes from the middle class, though the major users of the health service are the old and the poor. Nevertheless, all sections of society now want public services to respond to their wishes. The challenge facing the government was not simply to plough more resources into the NHS, but to modernise working practices in the face of opposition from staff, particularly the medical profession, whose professional autonomy was a potential obstacle to change. However, the government controlled the levers of power and had a near monopoly position as an employer; the workforce remained committed to the ethos of public service, though it was often frustrated with healthcare delivery; and the public was committed to the principles of the NHS, though increasingly critical of its performance.

After sticking to Conservative spending plans for two years, in 2000 the government announced its intention to increase spending on the NHS from about six to nine per cent of GDP, the average for Western Europe, and set out a ten-year programme of reform.[2] There were to be more and better-paid staff using new ways of working, together with major investment in hospitals, primary care centres and IT systems. This hike in spending was coupled with plans to create a patient-centred service, a transformation that would require huge changes – in culture, organisation and practice. One New Labour policy that had far-reaching effects on the NHS was devolution, initially in Scotland and Wales, and more recently in Northern Ireland too. As devolved government has bedded in, policy and practice have diverged across the UK. Indeed, it might be said that there are now four national health services, all funded from general taxation and mostly free at the point of use. For reasons of space, the focus here is on England.

Three broad strategies were pursued to a greater or lesser extent in all four devolved services. The first focused on improving operational transparency by developing better measurements of costs and outcomes, by reviewing performance, with an emphasis on quality as well as efficiency, and by sharing more information with the public. The second involved restructuring NHS organisations and management systems so as to make services more responsive to patients' needs. The third strategy stemmed from frustration at the slow pace of change and a determination not to let productivity fall as the NHS took on more staff. By introducing patient choice and market mechanisms, New Labour hoped to accelerate the reform process.

TRANSPARENCY

The new government announced the first ever strategy for improving the quality of NHS healthcare in *A first class service*.[3] Standards of care were to be more explicit, and national frameworks of best practice were set out through the *Cancer Plan* and the *National Frameworks for Coronary heart Disease* [4], *Mental Health*[5] and *Older People*.[6] The Department of Health later published national minimum standards for general care in England.[7] The National Institute of Clinical Excellence, NICE (now the National Institute for Health and Clinical Excellence), was set up to cover England and Wales. Its remit is to identify and disseminate best practice in drug therapy, medical technology and public health.

In reviewing the costs of treatment as well as evidence on efficacy and acceptability, NICE countervails pressure from the pharmaceutical industry. It also seeks to rebut claims that the availability of new drugs, particularly expensive ones, is subject to a 'postcode lottery'. In this it has had some success, but high-profile cases in which NICE has ruled against treatments on clinical or cost grounds have prompted demands that patients should be allowed to make co-payments – topping up the cost of drugs denied to them by NICE (such as the anti-cancer drug Herceptin), rather than paying the whole cost, as at present. Charging for treatment, albeit at patient discretion, violates the principle that health care should be free for all, regardless of ability to pay. Politicians are currently wary of the idea, but it is under active consideration.

Prior to the publication of *A first class service*, the NHS had no statutory duties with regard to quality. In 2000, for the first time, chief executives became accountable for the quality of care in their organisations. Clinical governance was monitored through a new independent inspectorate, the Commission for Health Improvement (CHI), covering England and Wales, and a similar body for Scotland was set up. Other bodies monitored social care and private health care and in 2004 these were all merged with CHI into the Healthcare Commission.[8] Reports on quality in hospitals, primary care and mental health services are now in the public domain. The CHI also published reports of investigations into serious service failure. The new openness has sometimes led to embarrassing press coverage and ministers worry that exposing deficiencies will dent public confidence and cause political ructions. As against this, one can argue that the public will have more confidence in a service that is seen to admit its mistakes and take steps to correct them. The tension remains, and those concerned still attempt to influence the regulator's decisions.

Quality auditing was a revolution for the NHS. There had been voluntary quality accreditation before, but its coverage was patchy. Now, for the first time, the whole service became publicly accountable for the quality of healthcare. At first, the idea of external regulation was unwelcome to most NHS staff, particularly the medical profession. However, it gradually came to be accepted that regulation can improve the quality of service.

Centrally imposed performance targets were also used as tools of reform. A maximum four-hour wait in A&E and a maximum waiting time of six months for elective surgery were early instances. Clinical and financial targets were bundled together, alongside quality reviews, and factored into published star ratings for acute Hospital Trusts, thus creating league tables. Initially, assessment was conducted by the Department of Health, giving rise to suspicions of political interference. Later, ratings were awarded and published by the external regulator. The chief impact fell on providers rather than users, who stayed with local providers regardless of stars. But low ratings did put pressure on managers and clinicians to improve results. Some chief executives were sacked, and in some cases the whole board was replaced by outside management teams. However, punitive sanctions can be intimidating, leading to demoralisation and poorer performance – staff who are bullied and harassed will not give of their best.

Targets have been much criticised, particularly by clinicians. Of course, there is 'gaming', when managers adopt various ruses to ensure compliance rather than striving to improve performance. There are also perverse incentives, as when patients are admitted to hospital wards from A&E departments after four hours, rather than allowing a longer period of observation before an earlier discharge. And if organisations are preoccupied with what is measured, activities that are not measured may be neglected. Even so, waiting times for appointments and admissions do matter to the public, and they have fallen dramatically. In Wales, where targets for access were not used, waiting lists have continued to rise.[9]

RESTRUCTURING

The New Labour government has repeatedly reorganised the NHS. Primary care was first organised into Primary Care Groups, then merged with community services to form Primary Care Trusts. Many of these merged with each other a few years later. The Department of Health's regional outposts in England were reorganised into twenty-eight Strategic Health Authorities. These were later regrouped into nine Strategic Health Authorities. Patient and public involvement bodies were also reorganised several times: Community Health Councils in England were replaced by a new Commission for Patient and Public Involvement, but this in turn is now giving way to a new system of local consultation. Many Hospital Trusts have merged managerially, with subsequent repercussions for clinical services. The regulators have been reorganised at least once and another large reorganisation is due in 2009.

Permanent revolution may have been intended to keep staff on their toes, and is perhaps inherent in a centrally planned organisation whose leaders are constantly striving to reduce the power of middle managers. But for NHS staff, the search for the holy grail of the 'perfect' structure has been immensely wasteful, disruptive, stressful and demoralising.

'MODERNISATION' AND 'REFORM'

To reduce waiting times and improve access, much work has been done on systems of flow, applying quality improvement methodology from other sectors and other countries. The Modernisation Agency was formed, to provide training and share expertise, and was then subsumed into the NHS Institute for Innovation and Improvement – another reorganisation. New forms of service provision, such as one-stop clinics and day surgery, have been introduced, though their spread is uneven and depends on the enthusiasm and engagement of local managers and clinicians.

More medical and nursing staff have been appointed and more places for medical students created. Pay has been raised and linked to changes in working practices. Hospital consultants received a twenty per cent pay rise in return for agreeing to be more accountable for the use of their time. However, this pledge was hard to enforce and it is doubtful if any improvement has occurred. Similarly, GPs were allowed to opt out of out-of-hours cover, with responsibility for providing cover passed to Primary Care Trusts, at great expense to the public purse. The new GP contract also rewarded GPs for meeting quality standards. But specifications were slack and payments ballooned. Whilst professionals should be adequately paid, it is debatable whether the public has derived any benefit from these expensive contracts. Indeed, there is public disquiet about GP opening hours, yet government attempts to extend opening times have been resisted by GPs and their representatives.

Investment in IT systems has also been beset by problems. The aim is to make clinical data accessible throughout the NHS, so that records accompany patients as they move from one part of the system to another. But with concerns about confidentiality, spiralling costs and the difficulty of managing complex, large-scale projects centrally, the scheme is well over budget and far behind schedule.

To meet targets for shorter waiting times, the NHS needed more staff and buildings. Contracts were agreed with private providers to supply extra operating capacity and outpatients' clinics and extra staff were recruited on a short-term basis from outside the NHS, often from overseas. Recourse to the private sector was initially seen as a temporary expedient, until the NHS had enlarged its own capacity. Unfortunately, the NHS has little expertise in setting and monitoring contracts: quality regulation is *post hoc* and inadequate. Moreover, responsibility for detail was devolved to local level, where expertise was even thinner. Contracts were awarded on favourable terms, and sometimes contractors were paid without having met their quotas. Nor did the government differentiate between 'not for profit' enterprises and 'for profit' companies. Nevertheless, in the end extra capacity was delivered.

In keeping with New Labour's ideology that business and markets know best, the building of new hospitals and primary care centres was only permitted under the private finance initiative (PFI). To keep the capital cost off the public accounts, buildings constructed by private contractors were leased to local Trusts on a long-term basis. Given that 20-25 per cent of PFI projects overrun on cost and completion date, compared with 70-75 per cent of public projects, in theory PFI offers better value for money.[10] But contracts for public sector projects are complex and transaction costs high, the allocation of risk is unclear and competition to provide finance weak. Hence, the costs of PFI to the taxpayer are higher than those of public procurement.[11] Moreover, PFI ties the NHS into recurrent payments for up to thirty years, when flexibility may be needed to adapt to changing patterns of care. Thus, any short-term gains must be weighed against long-term commitments.[12] This said, given the government's self-imposed financial rules, there was no other way of renovating the fabric of the NHS.

ACCELERATING REFORM

Impatient with the slow pace of progress towards a more patient-centred system and disappointed at the returns from increased spending and structural reorganisation, the centre set out to speed up the process of reform by devolving operational control, extending patient choice and promoting competition.[13] Henceforth, having set policy and standards, the centre would allow providers, public or private, more freedom to respond to local needs, improve services and launch new initiatives.

So far the new approach has been applied mainly to the hospital sector, though the intention is to extend it to the mental health and community health sectors as well. Hospitals that meet predetermined standards become Foundation Trusts, which have more autonomy and are separately regulated. There is meant to be more public involvement in their governance, but this has yet to materialise. Foundation Trusts compete for contracts offered by Primary Care Trusts. Their income depends on the number of contracts they win and whether they manage to keep costs below tariff. Since tariffs are fixed, competition is on quality and efficiency, not price. At present, Trusts remain part of the NHS, but it would not be a big step for private companies to buy them out, legislation permitting.

The government has also promoted patient choice as a means of making the NHS more responsive to individual wants. Thus, patients needing hospital treatment have a choice of five providers who, in turn, compete on quality, with money following the patient. The value of this arrangement is questionable. The amount of information on hospitals currently available to the public is limited and people typically seek guidance from GPs.[14] Surveys suggest that what most patients want, especially those with chronic conditions, is good, accessible local services.[15] Moreover, extending 'consumer choice' adds to bureaucracy, fragments services and erodes the social solidarity which both sustains and is sustained by the NHS.

The use of market mechanisms has now come full circle. In 1992, the Conservatives introduced a limited internal market by offering GPs the chance to become 'fund-holders', with a devolved budget to purchase elective care on behalf of their patients. In theory, patients could switch provider – say, from the local hospital service to another public sector provider offering faster access or better service. In fact, there was very little switching, though some power did shift from providers to purchasers, as intended. Responses to the scheme were patchy: some practices used it to develop new services for patients, others to swell their profits. There were also disparities of treatment among patients living in the same area, but registered with different practices: some might enjoy better access to physiotherapy or be seen more quickly at an additional outpatient clinic, while others waited for the normal NHS service. The system did, however, force hospitals to think about how to retain GP goodwill and 'custom'.

In its 1997 election manifesto, Labour declared: 'Our fundamental purpose is simple, but hugely important: to restore the NHS as a public service, working co-operatively for patients, not a commercial service driven by competition.' By its third term, the government had embraced the market model as its primary tool of reform. To be sure, prices are set centrally at levels designed to keep all providers in business. But in NHS England the risk of privatisation has never been greater. GPs have always been independent, profit-making contractors, not NHS employees. Now taxpayers' money is used to commission services from either public or private providers. In time, the NHS could become little more than a commissioning agent, and even this task could be outsourced to the private sector. The centre has put pressure on Primary Care Trusts to award contracts to private sector providers, and multinational healthcare companies from the US, Europe and South Africa are anxious to further their stake in the NHS. Some GP practices in Derbyshire have already been taken over by United Healthcare, a for-profit American company.

The turn to the market has never been explicitly debated as an option: it represents a policy slide in line with New Labour ideology. But as the logic of the policy unfolds, the distinctive ethos of the NHS will be irretrievably lost. Competing, privately owned companies under scrutiny from shareholders are bound to focus on profits, and as they penetrate the NHS the attitudes of both healthcare workers and the general public towards the service will change. Competition will lead to a greater fragmentation and individuals will find it harder to navigate through the system. Whether private provision will be more responsive to patients' desires – for example, for longer opening hours – remains to be seen. The planned introduction of 'polyclinics', bringing together GP services, outpatients, diagnostics and possibly minor surgery in one location may well see contracts awarded to private providers.[16] But NHS commissioners who lack the expertise required to negotiate and monitor complex contracts may well be outclassed by private healthcare companies and their legal teams.

RESULTS AND PROSPECTS

Over the past decade, New Labour has made strenuous efforts to reform the NHS. There is general agreement that the service should continue to be financed out of taxation, rather than moving to an insurance-based system, though these arguments are revisited from time to time.[17] But there is no comparable consensus about how healthcare should be provided. The government sought to make the service more patient-centred and after trying a number of different strategies, it plumped for competition and choice.

On many indicators, the NHS has improved. In England, waiting lists and waiting times have fallen, for both outpatients and inpatients, including A&E departments. There are better outcomes for coronary artery disease and for cancer, while quality and patient safety have improved. A recent national patient survey of 76,000 users of the NHS hospital services in England showed that 92 per cent thought their care had been either good or excellent.[18]

Yet the benefits of increased expenditure on the NHS have not been as great as might have been expected,[19] and major deficiencies remain. Provision for dentistry has deteriorated. A new contract for dentists meant that many dentists opted out of providing NHS services and many people have experienced difficulty accessing dental treatment, unless they are willing to pay or take out private insurance. The gap in life expectancy between England as a whole and its most deprived areas is wider now than in the mid-1990s.[20] And public health issues – notably, rising obesity and excess alcohol consumption – are causing concern. Of course, it must also be recognised that health inequalities and public health problems cannot be tackled by the NHS alone: they require integrated strategies aimed at eradicating poverty, widening educational opportunity, improving social amenities and strengthening social cohesion.

Eight years after the NHS Plan, the government has produced another long-term strategy for the NHS in England.[21] This emphasises quality, dignity, compassion and more personalised care for all, to be pursued by means of competition and choice, rather than centrally imposed targets. More specialised hospital centres will be developed, alongside GP-led community centres hosting services such as diagnostics, which will have longer opening hours and will be accessible to all, registered or not. Services will be reconfigured, with the closure of smaller hospital units leading inevitably to public protests. The development of polyclinics is bound to disturb established patterns of general practice, and the new centres themselves are likely to be run by private companies. Private sector management is also being invited to bid to take over commissioning. Integrated care organisations will be encouraged, similar to Health Maintenance Organisations in the USA, bringing together community services, some general practice, possibly social services and some specialist provision.

New Labour has made more use of market mechanisms and created more scope for privatising clinical care than any previous government. Large injections of money into the NHS have been conditional on centrally directed, market-based 'modernisation'. What began as a pragmatic expedient intended to speed up reform is now received wisdom among both ministers and senior managers, who are promoting competition and choice in an increasingly aggressive way. Without a change in policy direction, the NHS, if it survives at all, will look very different in another sixty years.

I wish to acknowledge Steve Iliffe for valuable discussion and comments on this chapter.

REFERENCES

1. Derek Wanless, *Securing Our Future Health: Taking a Long-Term View Final Report*, April 2002, http://www.hm-treasury.gov.uk.
2. Department of Health, *The NHS Plan: a plan for investment, a plan for reform*, July 2000, http://www.dh.gov.uk.
3. Department of Health, *A first class service: Quality in the new NHS*, July 1998, http://www.dh.gov.uk.
4. Department of Health, *Coronary heart disease: national service framework for coronary heart disease - modern standards and service models*, March 2000, http://www.dh.gov.uk.
5. Department of Health, *National service framework for mental health: modern standards and service models*, September 1999, http://www.dh.gov.uk.
6. Department of Health, *National service framework for older people*, May 2001, http://www.dh.gov.uk.
7. Department of Health, *Standards for Better Health*, July 2004, http://www.dh.gov.uk.

8. Healthcare Commission, *Home page*, http://www.healthcare-commission.org.uk.

9. G. Bevan & C. Hood, *'Have targets improved performance in the English NHS?'*, *BMJ* 2006 Feb 18; 332 (7538): 419-22.

10. P. Grout and M. Stevens, 'The Assessment: Financing & Managing Public Services', *Oxford Review of Public Policy*, 2003:19(2), pp215-234.

11. T. Jenkinson, 'Private Finance', *Oxford Review of Economic Policy*, 2003:19(2), pp323-334.

12. A. Glynn, *Capitalism Unleashed*, Oxford University Press, Oxford 2006, pp43-44; Allyson Pollock, *NHS plc: The Privatisation of Our Health Care*, Verso, London 2005.

13. Department of Health, *Shifting the balance of power within the NHS: Securing delivery*, July 2001, http://www.dh.gov.uk.

14. Martin Marshall and Tim Wilson, 'The NHS revolution: health care in the market place. Competition in general practice', *BMJ*, 2005: 331, pp1196-1199.

15. Peter Burge, Nancy Devlin, John Appleby et al, *Understanding patients' choices at the point of referral*, Rand Corporation 2006, http://www.rand.org; Rebecca Rosen, Natasha Curry and Dominique Florin, *Public Views on Choices in Health and Health Care*, King's Fund 2005, http://www.kingsfund.org.uk.

16. NHS Confederation, *Ideas from Darzi: polyclinics*, 2008, http://www.nhsconfed.org.

17. Nick Bosanquet, Henry de Zoete and Andrew Haldenby, *NHS reform: the empire strikes back*, Reform 2007, http://www.reform.co.uk.

18. Healthcare Commission, *Patient survey, 2007*, http://www.healthcarecommission.org.uk.

19. Office of National Statistics, *Public Service Productivity – health summary*, January 2008, http://www.statistics.gov.uk; Derek Wanless, John Appleby and Anthony Harrison, *Our Future Health Secured? A review of NHS funding and performance*, 2007, http://www.kingsfund.org.uk; King's Fund, *Health and ten years of Labour government*, April 2007, http://www.kingsfund.org.uk; Sheila Leatherman, Kim Sutherland, *The Quest for Quality in the NHS: Refining the NHS Reforms*, Nuffield Trust, 2008, http://www.nuffieldtrust.org.uk.

20. Department of Health, *Tackling health inequalities: 2007 Status report on the Programme for Action*, March 2008, http://www.dh.gov.uk.

21. Lord Darzi, *High quality care for all: NHS Next Stage Review final report*, June 2008, http://www.dh.gov.uk.

7. What has gone wrong with education in England and how to start putting it right

Patrick Ainley and Martin Allen

There is a crisis of purpose in education, which has not been resolved by the official focus on employment. New Labour emphasised the link between education and employment, but many of those working in schools, colleges and universities have not been convinced, despite the additional money that has been spent, feeling that the culture of education is not just changing but declining. Paradoxically, but not coincidentally, allegations of what is incorrectly referred to as 'dumbing down' have accompanied reports of rising standards in schools. Similarly, as more people than ever have entered post-compulsory education and progressed to higher education, social mobility has decreased. From primary to post-graduate, education at all levels seems to have turned into its opposite. Instead of aspiring to emancipate the minds of future generations, it increasingly forecloses their possibilities. This chapter will explore these contradictions by explaining what has gone wrong in England's schools, colleges and universities, and how it can begin to be addressed by those who study, teach and research in them.

EDUCATION IN A RIGHT STATE

In the 1980s Mrs Thatcher imposed a centralised 'new market-state'.[1] This new state form replaced the post-war welfare state compromise between public and private sectors. In education and training, where the new state formation was pioneered, its consequences are perhaps clearer than in any other area of public policy.

The 1988 Education Act replaced the national system of locally administered state education that had existed since 1944, by a national system, nationally administered. In this new regime, power was concentrated in the centre, despite responsibility for delivery being devolved to local agents. Responsibility was also placed on individuals, who had only themselves to blame if they did not take advantage of the new learning opportunities 'enabled' by the new state.

This process began with the end of post-war full employment and the raising of the school leaving age in 1972. A series of make-work Youth Training Schemes (YTSs), introduced by the Manpower Services Commission (MSC), marked the transition from 'lifelong earning' (for men at least) to today's 'lifelong learning'. The MSC was modelled on the advice that the then Prime Minister Edward Heath received from his Businessman Team in 1971, to make the civil service more like the private sector by responding flexibly to consumer demand. Democratically accountable local authorities were bypassed by the MSC, which gave money on a per capita basis to local training agents in return for enrolling unemployed school-leavers on a succession of schemes. These were intensely unpopular and did not prevent social unrest in response to Thatcher's abandonment of the Keynesian commitment to full employment.

Young people voted with their feet and stayed on in new school sixth forms or migrated to further education (FE) colleges. These were removed from local authority control and followed the polytechnics in competing for students funded per capita by centralised funding councils. The polytechnics joined the universities under the Higher Education (HE) Funding Council for England, while, following bi-partisan agreement in 1997 to end free public service higher education, students paid fees to top up their central unit cost. Eventually all schools could follow the universities and colleges into what is already a competitive market for school places. Indeed, Tony Blair proposed that all schools become independent Foundations – not just the state-funded but privately sponsored Academies. Now David Cameron echoes him, returning to Keith Joseph's idea of school vouchers as an entitlement to basic state provision that could then be used, topped up by those who could afford it, in the private sector. Free nursery school hours entitlement, tax-free child care vouchers and Gordon Brown's 'baby bond' have already laid the ground for such state-subsidisation of the private sector.

Funding schools, colleges and now universities according to the number of students allows 'popular' institutions to expand, and threatens others with closure. Even without vouchers or privately paid fees, this has created a quasi-market in which, just like in any other market, there can only be winners if there are also losers. As in business, failure to meet production targets can result in the merger or closure of the enterprise. So 'setting schools free from local authority bureaucrats', as the *Daily Mail* would have it, actually subjects them to an oppressive new bureaucracy. The new form of centralised state administration sets quantifiable targets, requiring armies of auditors and inspectors to check whether they are being met. 'Schools plc' is run like a corporation, with thousands of outlets inspected and policed by the Office for Standards in Education (OfSTED), as Her Majesty's Inspectors have become, which is in turn are regulated by the Department for Children, Schools and Families (DCSF), perhaps more appositely known as the Department for Counting, Spelling and Fonics.

Although funding for FE colleges is to be returned to Local Authorities on a formula basis, the content of their courses is dictated by the employer-run Sector Skills Councils, and courses are delivered by colleges in competition with private providers. HE could soon go the same way, with mergers if not yet closures of universities already happening, as is now common with colleges. The New Labour government has been integral to sustaining and developing this new market-state of education and training.

AFTER TEN YEARS OF NEW LABOUR

In his first major speech on education as prime minister, Gordon Brown, like Blair before him, renewed the emphasis on raising standards and argued that the global technical and economic revolution provided unbounded opportunities for social mobility and individual advancement: 'There is virtually unlimited global demand for new talent. Unskilled jobs are disappearing'

(Greenwich University, 1 November 2007). In so far as this is true, it is primarily because, as employers ruthlessly apply new technology to automate, deskill and outsource labour, those in employment have to train and retrain just to keep their jobs, while new entrants to the labour market face rising qualification hurdles to secure employment.

Meanwhile, the ongoing independent review of primary schooling by Professor Robin Alexander has suggested that reading standards have not improved since the 1950s, pointing to the 'persistence of a yawning gap between high and low attaining pupils – bigger than in most comparable countries' (*TES*, 2 November 2007). OfSTED reported in 2008 that 20 per cent of children leave primary school functionally illiterate. Additional resources spent since 1997 on increasing the 'diversity' of secondary schools had failed to improve results significantly.[2] According to the OECD, Britain has fallen from seventh to seventeenth place in reading, and from eighth to twenty fourth in maths (reported in the *Independent*, 5 December 2007).

The Children's Plan, published six months into Brown's leadership, set itself the task of making Britain the 'best place in the world to grow up'.[3] It identified some of the problems blighting the lives of many children – relentless commercialism, screen-based entertainment instead of outside play, fast-food and growing obesity – and it promised more facilities in inner-city areas. Yet, its repeated reference to the need to improve the educational performance of the lowest achievers revealed that for New Labour 'world class children' could only be those who did well in SATs and GCSEs. The Plan addressed parenting and early-years, but with the costs of full-time nursery places at around £8000 a year, and those of out of school clubs increasing at more than six times the rate of inflation, its funding proposals were paltry. Moreover, the Plan lacked detail, being often no more than a series of aspirations.

Nor has there been any let up in the creation of state-funded private Academies, although New Labour has been forced to rethink their sponsorship. As Francis Beckett has argued, the turn towards elite universities and the involvement of Local Authorities as junior partners in sponsoring Academies was the result of the refusal of leading British businesses to volunteer to run a service that many of them considered should be provided by the state;[4] and 'second order' sponsors have tended to seek political influence and peerages. Worse, some of the initial Academy sponsors were such a ragbag of second-hand car-dealers, creationists and other adherents of fringe religions that they alienated parents and aroused hostility from backbench MPs. New sponsors now include FE colleges and universities, along with the trade union AMICUS and the Steiner Foundation.

However, the reality remains far from the TUC's call for reintegration of Academies into local authority frameworks for schools.[5] The new Academy prospectus prevents LAs from sponsoring Academies, and the intention seems to be for Children's Services Departments, as Local Education Authorities have now become, to provide little more than a brokerage service in handing over schools to private investors. Academies are springing up anywhere sponsors can be found, though Ed Balls's threat in June 2008 to replace 'failing schools' with Academies (even though some of them are Academies already!) would necessarily mean that many of them would be in deprived and inner-city areas, or secondary moderns in the remaining selective local authority areas, such as Kent. Academies continue to represent an extension of the new market-state, through the transfer of public assets away from local authorities in a process of state-subsidised privatisation. Their governing bodies have an in-built majority nominated by the sponsors, allowing minimal influence for teachers and parents.

DESPERATE DIPLOMACY

As to curricular and qualifications reform, Ed Balls's announcement of three new 'subject based', rather than just 'vocational', Diplomas for 14-18 year-olds should not be seen as a return to the Tomlinson proposals for reform of A-levels that were rejected by Blair in 2005. Balls was merely attempting to shore up an ailing programme that has failed to convince parents, employers or head teachers. The initial uptake for the first batch of Diplomas in September 2008 will not meet government targets. Who among the thousands of existing A-level candidates will risk untried Diplomas in subject areas already well provided for? With an incredible ineptness that confirmed everyone's low opinion of 'the Dips', the fast food giant McDonalds got backing from Gordon

Brown for their own McDips, which count as GCSE and A-level equivalents!

New Labour education policy really seemed to have lost any connection with reality. However, although there is little connection between the content of vocational qualifications and the demands of the 'new' workplace, the role of vocational training in the social control of youth should be recognised. This applies also to the new apprenticeships that have been announced, along with the raising of the school leaving age to eighteen. In place of the traditional educational divisions, learners have been divided into 'pathways' – the vocational being a 'middle track,' between the academic royal road above, and the 'work-based' route below. As a result, the Diploma syllabuses have become less practically orientated and more academic, as was the case with the previous academic drift of General National Vocational Qualifications into 'Applied A-levels'. If there is a prolonged recession, Dips provided in FE could become the end-qualification for apprenticeships, as the new YTS, leading only exceptionally to employment but more commonly to two-year Foundation 'degrees' in former-polytechnics.

Apart from these broader concerns, the Diploma remains fraught with logistical problems, particularly, as Martin Allen has noted, in relation to the operation of local partnerships.[6] Ironically, the employers who are supposed to benefit have played only a minor role in drawing up the syllabuses, which were rushed out by the Qualification and Curriculum Authority to meet the 2008 pilot deadline. The consequence of the persistent failure of vocationalism has been that young people continue to sign-up for A-levels as the only show in town, resulting in a situation where a qualification designed in 1951 for a small post-war elite of less than 5 per cent now attracts well over 800,000 individual entries. The increased recognition of the importance of qualifications for labour market placement has inevitably led to grade inflation – one in four A-level candidates now obtains an A grade.

Private and the 'better' state schools have lost confidence in A-levels as the 'gold standard' qualification. For this group, despite the introduction of an additional A* grade from 2010 onwards, modularised A-levels have become 'too easy'. The argument is that modules encourage a fragmented approach, with assessment concentrated on data handling instead of reflecting candidates' academic subject knowledge. Rather than Brown and Balls abandoning A-levels, it would appear that the private sector is doing it for them. Some private schools are signing up for the International Baccalaureate, but it is the new Cambridge Pre-U that is most favoured as an A-level substitute. The Pre-U is a return to a traditional linear approach, re-emphasising the importance of literary presentation. The Headmaster of Eton told *The Times* (27 November 2007) that Pre-U exams offered pupils more stimulation and tested creativity and lateral thinking, while the Head of Dulwich College said the Pre-U represented a return to traditional A-levels as university entrance qualifications.

The Pre-U lobby is disingenuous. According to the Headmaster of Harrow, reported in the same *Times* article, A-levels are flawed because too many pupils get top grades. In other words, the private sector can no longer ensure what the parents are paying for – that their pupils are first in the queue for top universities. The Pre-U gives them a new gold standard. It is unlikely to feature in many state schools, being designed to restore the positional advantage of top private schools. Needless to say, the Pre-U quickly received backing from the Russell Group of elite universities, and syllabuses in up to nineteen subjects are expected to be available from September 2008, the same time that new A* A-levels begin. This contrasts with the Russell Group's attitude to the new Diplomas: according to the *Telegraph* (23 November 2007), their admissions tutors are 'not likely' or 'not at all likely' to consider students with Diplomas, despite Balls introducing an 'extended' Diploma worth four and a half A-levels in University and Colleges Admissions Service entry points.

TERTIARY TRIPARTISM

The proportion of children being privately educated continues to edge up from the 7 of 1944, having reached more than 15 per cent in Inner London, over 10 per cent across the South-East as a whole, and 20 per cent in Bristol, compared with just 4 per cent in the North-East (*Education Guardian*, 29 January 2008). The latest figures from the Independent Schools Council suggest that pupils at its schools are five times more likely than the national average to gain a place at a Russell Group university (*The Times*, 27 November 2007).

For the really rich, qualifications have always been less important than other aspects of social capital in guaranteeing the future earning power of their inheritors. This is not to say they won't happily spend £25,000-plus annually to secure a place at a leading private school. This compares with the £9000 average across the private sector as a whole, with its ubiquitous cut-price crammers, private tutors and on-line courses of variable quality. In such a competitive market the personal connections between those who teach in the top private schools and their old Oxbridge colleges are highly valued. If, as a result of the 2009 review of university fees, the twenty-strong Russell Group of elite universities raise their fees closer to the market levels already obtaining for overseas students, then, notwithstanding increasingly frequent references to bursaries for the poor, the ability to pay will be at least as important an entry qualification as A*s or Pre-Us.

Whether or not undergraduate fees rise after 2010, HE is increasingly divided into three tiers: the selective research universities recruiting internationally, represented by the Russell Group, and wanting to decide their own tuition fees; the mainly teaching universities recruiting nationally, represented by the 94Group of campus-based universities; and finally, the local/sub-regional former polytechnic training universities, which systematically have desperate recourse to clearing, represented by the Million+ Group, so called because its members have the majority of undergraduates, full- and part-time. In many of this third group, it is an open secret that widening participation on a reduced unit of resource has already turned large parts of 'higher' into *de facto* further education.

This emerging tertiary tripartism reproduces exactly the post-war 11-plus secondary tripartism of private and grammar, technical, and secondary modern state schools, actually a binary divide between the privates plus grammars and the rest, just as the binary line is today redrawn in higher education between former-polytechnics and the rest.[7]

Meanwhile, raising the school leaving age to seventeen in 2013, and then to eighteen in 2015, is aimed at the 10 per cent of young people estimated by OfSTED to be 'Not in Employment, Education or Training' (NEET). Proposals to raise the school leaving age (ROSLA2) aim to reintegrate the NEETs, a group clearly identified with an emerging so-called 'underclass', most visible on inner-city estates. However, a more likely outcome, notwithstanding a willingness by government to use an array of Draconian sanctions, is that many NEETs will be street-wise enough to avoid what is, in effect, a return to a form of national conscription.

'EDUCATION (STILL) MAKE YOU FICK, INNIT?'

This was the response by one FE student asked why he was not 'aiming higher', for university. Disillusion is also widespread even amongst those with a professional self-interest in providing 'learning services' in schools, colleges and universities. Brown and Balls initially attempted to placate school teachers by announcing a pay award 0.5 per cent above the 2 per cent public sector ceiling, on the grounds that 'our world class teachers' were a special case. Not only did this upset other public-sector workers, who had also been told they were special, but it was met by the first one-day national strike by teachers in twenty-one years!

If teachers and lecturers increasingly feel bad, it is also true that many students only consider the 'exchange value' of their qualifications. Rather than being judged in terms of its intellectual benefits, succeeding in education has become an obstacle course. Instead of producing a learning culture, a 'culture of instrumentalism' prevails, in which students from primary to post-graduate schools only learn what they need, when they need it. Worse, the pressures of league tables, which now apply to universities and departments within them, as well as to schools, mean teachers only teach what they need to do to score well. For example, a *TES* front page declared, 'No need to read books' (13 October 2006), as English teachers provided 'extracts' for GCSE courses.

Under pressure to 'Go to College or Die!', as Stanley Aronowitz[8] says of the strikingly similar situation in the USA, the mass of 18+ students and trainees working their way through this certification system get less and less for more debt and more effort. Working up to twenty hours a week in McJobs, students pay more for lower quality courses reduced to bite-sized chunks of 'education'. Further and higher education students move from one module to another, without established peer groups, sensing that no one cares about them in increasingly chaotic and over-crowded institutions where they sink or swim. They have little time and space for generalised reflection or dialogue with their teachers, who are in any case too busy with administration or trying to find time and money for research to teach them. Even on the most traditionally academic courses in elite universities, students churn out essays and other exercises as a mark of quality over competitors. Most are well aware that the standard formats do not require any thought on their part, but are rather a matter of acquired technique.

A multi-million pound internet industry enables students to purchase finished essays and assignments written for them by 'specialists', often other students. The repeated accusations of plagiarism and cheating – from primary head teachers fiddling their SATs returns, to students buying and selling GCSE, A-level, undergraduate and postgraduate coursework – is further confirmation that many students no longer consider it necessary to learn at all, while teachers are too busy assessing to teach. As a result, the government has culled coursework, long regarded as a cornerstone of progressive education, from GCSE in order to stop 'internet cheats', and urged a return to traditional examinations at all levels, like the Pre-U. However, it is unlikely that this will prevent students, their parents, or even some of their teachers, from ensuring somehow that they, their children, their schools, and their courses, stay on the standards juggernaut.

Parents are increasingly prepared to use all means necessary to get their children into what they consider 'good schools' – private coaching, moving house, even regularly attending church for a year or two! Yet at the same time they show little desire to become involved in day-to-day decision-making, for example by being school governors, or even attending school AGMs. For many teachers, meanwhile, 'teaching' continues to be a daily grind, restricted in schools by 'behaviour problems', and made worse by endless administration, as is also the case in colleges and universities. And everywhere there is relentless pressure to meet new market-state targets which only set them up to fail.

Does it have to be this way? Unlike academic traditionalists who seek to limit participation by increasing selection, we see the need for popular and democratic alternatives and argue that grounds for optimism persist. In particular, we argue that the draining of meaning from the official learning system contradicts its purpose of supposed enlightenment. Unless people really can be seduced into thinking that their 'skills' represent new capabilities, and their 'knowledge' adequately comprehends reality, then a critical space remains within public education for discussion and debate.

ALTERNATIVES

There are some clear long-term goals that most reformers would agree on. The aim must be to reverse the trend towards privatisation and instead move education towards the democratic control of civil society. This requires an end to Academies: parents want good local schools, not competition between supposedly 'specialist' schools. OfSTED needs to be reformed or abolished and exam boards brought under democratic control. Charitable status and other state subsidies for private schools have to go. Student fees must be abolished so that free public service higher education is restored, as in Scotland, where there are no fees for Scottish students, although most Scottish students borrow from the Student Loan Fund and, as in England, a high proportion have part-time jobs.

On other issues, however, we need more discussion. For example, without an alternative conception of 'standards', how can we engage with the upsurge in opposition to testing, which has seen the National Association of Headteachers threaten a boycott, and even a Parliamentary Select Committee call for the abolition of SATs in primaries, anticipating their scrapping in secondaries? As well as developing an inclusive curriculum, there is a need for new forms of accountability and democracy within schools, colleges and universities that go beyond the crude performance indicators reflected in league tables. We need to bring educational institutions together in new ways at local and (sub)-regional levels, rather than just going back to the democratic control of local authorities, because these too have changed. Research needs to be undertaken both in dedicated national research centres and also in the activities of scholarship, scientific investigation and artistic creation of teachers and students at all levels of learning. We need to reform assessment with a multi-level general diploma at eighteen that entitles students to a range of learning experiences. Beyond that, Platonic divisions of first, second and third class degrees should be replaced by a continuous grading system, together with a report on students' experience throughout the whole of their undergraduate course. First degrees should be lengthened to four years, as in Scotland, followed by two years at Masters level.

There is also a need for new types of campaigning alliances between teachers, students and local communities. While recognising the central importance of education, trade unions, particularly the NUT and UCU, need to use their resources and organising power in new ways, transcending their narrow 'professionalist' perspective on teaching and learning and turning outwards to become social movements, able to engage in real discussion about programmes for education. Organised teachers need to challenge academic selectivity and competition across the board, along with particular inanities like Diplomas and apprenticeships without jobs. This is as important as building workplace militancy over pay and conditions.

To achieve the changes necessary to transform schools, colleges and universities from credential mills, where the curriculum is dominated by standardised tests, into sites of genuine education, we need a national conversation concerning the nature and purpose of education. This would be 'a movement' for the political construction of 'a national popular collective', such as Stanley Aronowitz, drawing upon Gramsci, has suggested in the USA. It is not, he says, a question of abandoning state educational institutions but rather of rendering them benign, by removing them as much as possible from the tightening grip of the new market-state.

REFERENCES

1. P. Bobbitt, *The Shield of Achilles, War, Peace and the Course of History*, Allen Lane, London 2002.
2. Office for Standards in Education, *Integration of the Inspections of Welfare and Education from September 2008 Consultation*, OfSTED, London 2008.
3. Department for Children, Families and Schools, *The Children's Plan*, DCFS, London 2007.
4. F. Beckett, *The Great City Academy Fraud*, Continuum, London 2007.
5. TUC, *A New Direction – A Review of the School Academies Programme*, TUC, London 2007.

6. M. Allen, 'Learning for Labour: Specialist Diplomas and 14-19 Education', *Forum* 49:3, 2007.

7. See P. Ainley and M. Weyers, 'The Variety of Student Experience', in J. Canaan and W. Shumar (eds), *Structure and Agency in the Neo-liberal University*, Routledge, London 2008.

8. S. Aronowitz, *Against Schooling, For an Education that Matters*, Paradigm, Boulder 2008.

8. Tackling climate change

Pat Devine

The chair of the Intergovernmental Panel on Climate Change (IPCC), Rajendra Pachauri, has argued that 2007 'marked a watershed in awareness of environmental issues, and in particular the challenge of climate change'.[1] A Guardian/ICM Poll in July 2008 reported that a majority of voters think 'taking action against climate change matters more than tackling the global economic downturn'.[2] The scientific evidence is now overwhelming that greenhouse gas emissions due to human activity are contributing to global warming and climate change at an accelerating rate. It is also clear that, as the Stern Review noted, the consequences of increasing water scarcity, aridity, agricultural failure, disease, mass migration, and a greater frequency of extreme weather conditions, will be felt most acutely by the poor.[3] The 2007 UN Annual Human Development Report estimated that in 1980-84 in developing countries about eighty million people annually were affected by some kind of weather related disaster, which had increased to 260 million people by 2000-04 – about one in nineteen people in developing countries, compared with only one in 1500 people in wealthy countries.[4]

There is now almost complete agreement in Britain across the political spectrum that greenhouse gas emissions must be reduced by at least 80 per cent, probably 90 per cent, by 2050, with New Labour, Conservatives and Liberal Democrats vying with one another to appear the most green. There is also widespread recognition of the problem by business and the unions. This consensus was institutionalised in 2008 in the Climate Change Act, which places the government under a legal obligation to reduce emissions by 80 per cent by 2050. Yet the unchallenged conventional wisdom, shared by all except some green organisations, is that the major changes that are needed can – and can only – be achieved using a variety of market mechanisms to promote technical change and modifications in consumer behaviour. The principal mechanism envisaged is carbon trading, supplemented by carbon capture and storage, green subsidies, and to a lesser extent green taxes.

The message is that while there is a serious problem, it can be dealt with through conventional measure on the basis of business as usual, with only minor changes in socio-economic organisation and consumerist lifestyles, and no interruption to unending, but now allegedly sustainable, growth. The UK's Department of Environment has argued that business will benefit from these changes, which will pay for themselves in a short period through lower costs, thus 'saving business money, and enabling green growth.'[5] This is in keeping with the Stern Review's estimate that future damage of up to 20 per cent of global GDP per annum could be avoided by measures to reduce greenhouse gas emissions costing only 1 per cent of GDP per annum if embarked on soon enough, although Stern has more recently revised his estimate of the cost upwards to 2 per cent, in the light of new scientific findings that emissions are rising faster and absorptive capacity is lower that previously thought.[6]

SOME STATISTICS

Although there is general agreement on the scale of the problem, optimism over the ability of market-based measures to deal with it is not supported by the government's record. Figure 1 shows the trend in British greenhouse gas (GHG) emissions since 1990, the baseline date from which Kyoto treaty obligations are measured. While the UK is on track to meet its obligations, it is evident that nearly all the decline occurred under the previous Conservative government, prior to the election of New Labour in 1997. This was because the first part of the 1990s saw a massive change from coal to gas, mainly in power generation. More recently, however, as gas prices have risen, coal has made a partial comeback, primarily in the form of imports rather than domestic production, with the government now supporting new coal-fired power stations without any guarantee of carbon capture. Since 1997, the year Kyoto was signed, virtually nothing has been done to combat climate change, despite all the talk and targets.

Britain is not alone. The rest of Western Europe also has a dismal record with respect to greenhouse gases. As Figure 2 shows, EU15

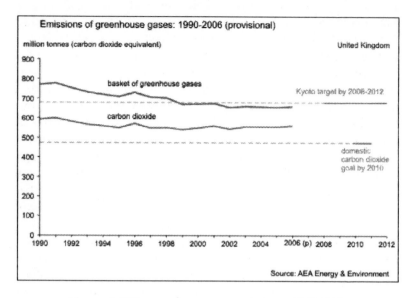

Figure 1 UK greenhouse gas emissions, 1990-2005

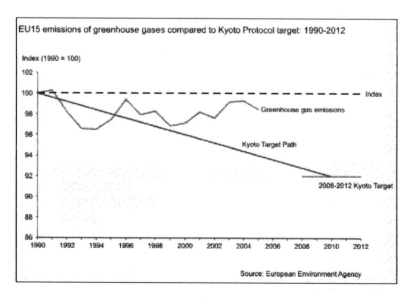

Figure 1 UK greenhouse gas emissions, 1990-2005

emissions in 2005 were virtually the same as in 1990. However, if the whole of the Europe is considered, the picture seems at first sight more promising. This is because the 1990 baseline for measurement of Kyoto reductions is the last year before the economies of the ex-communist countries collapsed and their industrial production and fuel consumption declined dramatically. As a result, these countries, which all have mandatory emissions reduction targets under Kyoto, are easily meeting their targets.

Russia and Ukraine, in particular, have Kyoto surpluses which exceed the combined deficits of all other countries with mandatory targets, and which will be available for deficit countries to buy from 2008-12, the period for which Kyoto targets are legally binding. Not surprisingly, some people in the carbon trading business are unhappy about this:

> For Kyoto to achieve anything there must be a shortage of allowances such that their traded price is high enough to incentivise change ... Kyoto looks to have fallen at the first fence in this objective. The surplus of allowances in the hands of Russia and Ukraine during the period is vastly greater than the shortages of all other capped countries put together ... This suggests that the price of carbon may be so low in the period 2008-2012 that there will be no incentive to cut emissions.[7]

It is important to realise that the reduction in emissions in both the UK, due to the switch from coal to gas, and in the ex-communist countries, due to the collapse of their economies, has been at a high social cost. This has been evident in the devastated mining communities in the UK and the years of economic decline and stagnation in Eastern Europe, with the cost, of course, being borne by the poor, so achieving the market's apotheosis – the monetisation of social pain and its packaging into neat units for international sale. Seen in this light, Kyoto can hardly be regarded as a success, not to mention the refusal by the USA and other developed countries to ratify it.

The rich countries have done nothing positive since 1997 to reduce carbon emissions, while China and India, together with some other developing countries, have been growing rapidly, largely based on coal-powered energy. It is the failure of the rich countries to reduce their emissions that has made it so difficult to agree on post-Kyoto reduction targets that allow for the growth of the poorer countries that is necessary if they are to catch up with the developed world. Recent UN figures show that between 2000 and 2006 emissions in the developing countries rose by only 2.3 per cent, while those in the developed countries rose by 10 per cent, and emissions have also been rising in the ex-communist countries since 2000.[8]

SOCIALLY BASED ACTION

The New Labour government under Blair did nothing effective to stop climate change. Figure 1 shows that CO_2 emissions if anything increased over this period, and the situation is no better when looked at in detail. Britain has the worst record of any major EU country for installing renewable energy sources, which in 2006 contributed only 1.5 per cent of total energy. This compares with the target of 15 per cent by 2020 which the UK has agreed with the EU as its contribution to the overall EU target of 20 per cent. Yet despite the urgent tone of the Stern Review, nothing has been done since it appeared in 2006 to implement its recommendations. The Brown administration produced its *Renewable Energy Strategy: Consultation Document* in June 2008, with the aim of publishing the final strategy in spring 2009, a further nine months' delay. Subsequently, in December 2008, its Climate Change Committee's report, *Building a Low Carbon Economy: The UK's Contribution to Tackling Climate Change* appeared.[9] Both documents estimate that to achieve the target of 15 per cent of total energy consumption from renewables by 2020, the proportion of electricity generated from renewable sources will have to be increased from the 5 per cent expected on the basis of policies currently in place, to 30-35 per cent, a step change that will require a major discontinuity in policy and funding.

Yet the underlying policy approach makes it highly unlikely that this target will be achieved. All the major parties – New Labour, Conservative and Liberal Democrat – are totally committed to market-based policies, which are not only ineffectual but can be actually counterproductive. Thus, the *Strategy Consultation Document* states: 'Underpinning this strategy is our belief that independently regulated, competitive markets are the most cost-effective way of delivering our objectives'; and 'Our main policy for achieving carbon reductions involves putting a price on carbon, notably via the EU Emissions Trading Scheme …'.

There are essentially two reasons why market-based policies are not the way forward.

First, in many situations direct state intervention is clearly more effective than any market-based alternative. As has already been noted, the European emissions trading scheme has so far been largely ineffective. But it is now almost universally accepted that 'feed-in tariff' (FIT) schemes, in which the government guarantees prices to producers of electricity from renewable sources, work better than market-based trading schemes. Even the Stern Review, which generally favoured market-based solutions, concluded that 'comparisons between deployment support through tradable quotas and feed-in tariff price support suggest that feed-in mechanisms achieve larger deployment at lower costs'.[10] Yet even when, as a result of growing pressure, the government in 2008 announced its intention to introduce feed-in tariffs, it restricted them to small-scale renewable energy production, initially up to three megawatts, then increased to five. It resisted the inclusion of larger scale renewable production in order to avoid spoiling the market for tradable quotas.

However, the second, and most compelling, reason for not relying on market-based policies is that an 80-90 per cent reduction in GHG emissions by 2050 can only be achieved by altering the social basis, the structure and fabric, of our lives; and such a massive shift can only be brought about by developing a social consensus around the non-marginal changes needed, and the collective action required to achieve them. These necessary changes run counter to the pressures of a market-based, consumer society, premised on endless growth, which is why policy has to be socially led, rather than based on modifying business and consumer behaviour through altering the incentive structure to which people respond in terms of their pursuit of profit or positional consumption.

In the following sections, I look at socially based policies in three sectors – household energy use, transport, and electricity generation. The data on energy use show that reduction of carbon emissions comes down to three big problems: how to get gas out of households; oil out of transport; and coal and gas out of electricity generation.

HOUSEHOLD ENERGY USE

Household energy use is central to any programme to reduce GHG emissions. It is also very complex and very dependent on social habits. In the late 1970s a grant was made available towards the cost of loft insulation. A subsequent audit showed that in most households loft insulation did not result in lower fuel use, because previously unheated bedrooms became warmer as gas-fired central heating was installed. A household group which eats home-cooked meals together will use energy very differently from one which eats separately, uses a lot of ready prepared food, and often eats out. Household impact on GHG emissions will also depend upon how the energy supply is sourced. It is conventional wisdom that turning off electrical appliances rather than leaving them on standby saves energy. However, in a household which has switched to 'green' electricity and is heated by gas, leaving appliances on standby in the heating season will reduce emissions, because a carbon-based fuel is being displaced, indirectly, by the heat from a green electrical appliance.

Heating houses accounts for around 26 per cent of total energy use, with a further 3 per cent going to appliances and other uses. There are roughly twenty five million dwellings in the UK, which might cost on average £10,000 to modify in the ways needed to achieve the 80-90 per cent reduction in GHG emissions required, amounting to £12.5 billion annually if spread over twenty years – a small and surely affordable amount compared with total annual government expenditure of around £400 billion. Household energy use, of course, also occurs indirectly in the form of the energy used to produce consumer goods and services, and if this indirect energy consumption is taken into account, households are responsible for well over half the energy used in the UK, as well as that used in the production of imported consumer goods. In the longer run, leading up to 2050, more far reaching changes will be needed, as discussed in the next section on transport.[11]

TRANSPORT

A reduction in carbon emissions on the scale required means fewer road journeys, in vehicles driven primarily by green electricity. The implications of this for our way of life are enormous. On the one hand, we need a huge expansion of public transport – rail for necessary long distance and commuter journeys, bus and bicycle for local journeys. On the other hand, we must also travel less. There is much to learn from the examples of vehicle-free urban areas in continental Europe and, to an increasing extent, in the UK, as the 'slow' and 'transition' towns and regions movement gathers pace, and people rediscover the joy of physical movement. Planned communities which enable people to work locally, with easy access to essential services and amenities, would allow most journeys to be made by walking or cycling.

This approach to transport and urban planning intersects with the argument for a change in the work-life ratio discussed in chapter two. A more caring, convivial and creative life requires time. The Slow Food movement has reminded us of the joys of cooking and social eating. It is not just that the quality of the food itself would be better; re-learning the art of cooking, taking enjoyment from it, convivial meals with family and friends, would also greatly improve the quality of life. And, of course, to reduce unnecessary journeys we will need to source our food, preferably organic, as locally as possible – with the added implication that we need to rely more on seasonal produce, rather than expecting everything and anything to be constantly and immediately available. Local sourcing reduces the number of food miles, including of course sea and air miles.

Yet, although GHG emissions from air travel are increasing more rapidly than from any other source, the government continues to plan for airport expansion, making the same mistake as it has in relation to road building – seeking to meet projected increases in demand for air freight and cut-price holidays rather than restricting demand through limiting capacity, green taxes and seeking to convince public opinion. Instead, we need to travel less and slow down, to enjoy the real benefits and pleasures to be had from a more relaxed and sensuous approach to life.[12] However, the attractions and benefits of seeing the world must also be recognised. There needs to be a public debate about how the joys of travel can be experienced by all over a lifetime in a context in which the total amount of travel is severely limited by the carrying capacity of the ecosystem.

ELECTRICITY GENERATION

If we are to move rapidly away from non-renewable, carbon-based energy sources there is an urgent need to develop renewable sources of energy. Future energy use must rely primarily on sustainable, low-carbon electricity generation, which will involve long term planning and huge investment. Nuclear power is not sustainable in the long run, yet the government seems determined to stick to its usual short-termism, despite the uncertainties surrounding security, decommissioning and waste storage, not to mention cost. Bio-fuels are being taken up in a big way but have proved controversial, as in some cases they have been at the expense of rain forest and food crops. That leaves wind, wave, hydro and solar power, all subject to technological uncertainties and in many cases surrounded by controversy over their environmental effects.

There are no easy answers. Wind farms can add to noise pollution in urban areas and are regarded by some as unsightly, yet if located in remote rural areas can have very damaging effects on the landscape. One possibility is for offshore wind farms, but these may interfere with marine life and shipping. Wave technology is still at an early stage of development and wave farms may also have adverse effects on wild life, as in the case of the proposed Severn Estuary project. Hydro- and solar power possibilities are not evenly distributed geographically, and they too may have adverse environmental consequences. And yet, the need to move away from carbon-based energy is paramount, with the most suitable combination of the various sources of renewable energy likely to depend on geographic location, topography, climate and aesthetics.

In the long run, the objective must be to reduce demand for electricity to the level that can be produced from renewable sources. The immediate question is whether we can reduce demand and increase renewable supply quickly enough to the extent needed if an 80-90 per cent reduction in GHG emissions by 2050 is to be achieved. Some ecologists, notably James Lovelock, argue that with the best will in the world the expansion of renewables is not going to be sufficient to bridge the gap between plausible projections of electricity demand and supply, and that there is, therefore, a defensible case for increasing reliance on nuclear power as a transitional, stop-gap measure. The danger with this line of argument, of course, is that it risks sowing the illusion that nuclear power can at best be anything more than a temporary expedient solution; and it is likely to detract from efforts to promote the energy-saving changes in lifestyle which are required in the long run, and will eventually necessitate wholesale changes in the way in which our economy is organised. Again, as with transport, what is needed is an informed public debate, involving the principal stakeholders, to negotiate an acceptable way forward given the best available scientific and technical evidence.

SOCIAL JUSTICE AND ECOLOGICAL SUSTAINABILITY

Although global warming is the most pressing ecological problem, it is by no means the only one. More generally, human use of non-human nature as sites for habitation, resources for production, and sinks for waste, including GHGs, greatly exceeds the carrying capacity of the earth. One way of measuring this is our 'ecological footprint', the amount of land, sea and air needed to produce the resources we use and absorb the wastes we produce. A recent WWF report estimates the global average footprint as 2.2 hectares (5.4 acres) per head, with Britain on 5.6 hectares (nearly 14 acres). If everyone in the world had the same ecological footprint as the British average, three planets would be needed to accommodate this.[13]

The only vision compatible with social justice and ecological sustainability is that of an equal global per capita ecological footprint, including an equal carbon emission allowance, at a level that when aggregated is equal to the best estimate of sustainable global carrying capacity. Given the grossly unequal distribution of resource use across countries and within countries, major redistribution is unavoidable. In poorer countries a larger average ecological footprint is essential if decent living standards are to be achieved for all; in richer countries a smaller footprint will be needed, involving major changes in the way we live. And the same holds true for people within each country.

The extent of the socio-economic, life-style, and cultural changes required for this kind of shift is enormous. Changes of this magnitude will not be easy and will take time, although time is getting very short. They will require a combination of strong government intervention and equally strong social support for the required changes in life-style. For such changes to carry legitimacy and be effectively implemented they will need to have popular support, and this can best – perhaps only – be achieved through popular participation in decision-making. Ecological economics, which studies the relationship between economic activity and non-human nature, emphasises that urgent action is required now, even though there is considerable uncertainty surrounding the scientific issues involved. In this situation, decisions cannot be made on the basis of scientific evidence alone. To be effective and carry legitimacy they must be made through a deliberative democratic process involving all those with a significant interest in the outcome. How else, for example, could a decision be made about what weight should be given to the precautionary principle, as against the alleged benefits of action or non-action now?[14]

This can be illustrated by the way in which future generations are brought into the decision-making process. Orthodox economists, including Stern, apply a discount rate to the future. The argument is that somehow income and consumption matter less in the future than in the present, so that, when assessing different policies, future levels of income and consumption count for less, and have to be reduced by a certain percentage – the discount rate. This can be thought of as the opposite of the interest rate, a reduction rather than an addition. Yet it is by no means obvious what the discount rate should be. Is next year's income or consumption 1 per cent, or 5 per cent, or ten per cent less important that this year's? Simply postulating some 'pure' rate of time preference – simple preference for today over tomorrow, is subjective, lacks credibility, and is undemocratic. In any case, even a low discount rate, by reducing each successive year's lower level by the same percentage, effectively removes the future from consideration beyond the next thirty to forty years, whereas the effects of climate change will be felt for hundreds of thousands of years.

The alternative is to discuss inter-temporal ethical judgments (e.g. how to weigh the future against the present) explicitly, something to which orthodox economists are strongly averse. This is a particular example of a general reluctance to accept that the most important economic and social decisions raise ethical questions that cannot be discussed at all if values are reduced to a single monetary expression of today's 'tastes and preferences'. And of course, if one is to avoid the charge of elitist paternalism, ethical debate needs to be conceived as a part of an ongoing and inclusive process involving the whole human community.

CONCLUSION

Although I have argued that market-based solutions cannot achieve the huge reductions in GHG emissions required to avert climate change, it is not suggested that all market instruments should be rejected. There is a strong case, for instance, for raising the price of transport fuels to reflect the real external damage caused by GHGs, not to mention the other external costs involved in road and air transport. However, exhortations to alter our individual behaviour, market manipulation, and technological change, cannot by themselves bring about the 80-90 per cent reduction that is urgently needed. They all presuppose the possibility of business as usual, 'green growth', thus diverting attention away from the fundamental social and structural changes without which the inexorable increase in global GHG emissions will not be halted. In his 2008 Pre-Budget Report Chancellor Darling made passing reference to proposed measures to tackle climate change in the future, but these fell so far short of the Green New Deal proposed by the New Economics Foundation earlier in 2008 as to be almost insignificant.[15]

In the end, the fundamental changes needed are incompatible with global capitalism, whose dynamic is limitless growth, albeit punctuated by periodic crises, as we are currently experiencing. The terms 'green' or 'sustainable' growth are a form of greenwash, suggesting that continuous growth is possible, subject only to minor changes in technology and consumption patterns. As has been argued above, this does not mean opposition to economic growth in the less developed world. Rather it means that the rich capitalist countries must move slowly but surely to a zero-growth economy, made possible by an end to capitalism and the democratisation of economic activity to bring it under social control. It is the unwillingness to recognise this that gives impetus to the endless variations around the theme of green or sustainable growth. As Fredric Jameson has reminded us, someone once said: 'it is easier to imagine the end of the world than to imagine the end of capitalism'.[16]

However, as has also been argued, the changes in lifestyle that are needed in the rich countries, far from resulting in a reduction in human welfare and the quality of life, would enable us to transcend our present identities as isolated consumers in an unequal society and rediscover the joys, pleasures and satisfactions of living a more equal, more convivial, slower, and more sensuous life. And by extension, the possibility exists for the poorer countries to learn from our mistakes and pursue growth and increases in living standards in ways that do not destroy the environment and the ecological basis of human existence. In this way, policies for a low-carbon, sustainable future become part of a global project both to resist climate change and to raise living standards in the poorer parts of the world. Utopian? Well, it is worth noting that these twin projects already command active and widespread political enthusiasm. What is now needed is for this enthusiasm to engage with the political and socio-economic transformations that are needed to make them possible. Our individual and collective actions today need to be informed by such a vision of a good life in a better possible tomorrow.

I should like to thank Mike Prior for his contribution to earlier versions of parts of this chapter, and David Purdy for helpful suggestions on nuclear power and discounting the future.

REFERENCES

1. Rajendra Pachauri, 'The world's will to tackle climate change is irresistible', *Guardian*, 30 June 2008.
2. 'Climate more urgent than economy, say voters', *Guardian*, 2 July 2008. This was true of all social classes except the top AB group. However, when asked if they would be prepared to pay more for environmentally friendly products, a majority said no. The poll was taken before the autumn 2008 financial crash and developing economic depression.

3. N. Stern, *The Economics of Climate Change: The Stern Review*, CUP, Cambridge 2007.

4. UNDP, *Annual Human Development Report*, Palgrave Macmillan, New York 2007, p76.

5. As reported by the Scottish government, *The Carbon Reduction Commitment*, 2007, http://www.scotland.gov.uk/Topics/Environment/ClimateChange/16327/EnergyPerComm/Introsumm.

6. 'I underestimated the threat, says Stern', *Guardian*, 18 April 2008.

7. L. Bossley, Director, CEAG energy market consultancy, *Oxford Energy Forum*, November 2007, p26.

8. *New Scientist*, 22-28 November 2008.

9. Department for Business, Enterprise & Regulatory Reform, *Renewable Energy Strategy: Consultation Document*, 2008, http:/renewableconsultation.berr.gov.uk; Climate Change Committee, *Building a Low Carbon Economy: The UK's Contribution to Tackling Climate Change*, http://www.theccc.org.uk/reports.

10. Stern, 2007, op cit.

11. The figures in this paragraph are mainly derived from: *Consultation Document*, op cit, 2008; and Department for Business, Enterprise & Regulatory Reform *Meeting the Challenge: A White Paper on Energy*, Cm 7124, 2007, http:/www.berr.gov.uk/energy/whitepaper/page38534.html.

12. This argument is developed further by Kate Soper in Chapter 4.

13. WWF, 'The UK Needs 3 Planets to Support It', 2006, http://www.wwf.org.uk/news/n_0000003149.asp.

14. On ecological economics, see B. Ozkaynak, P. Devine and D. Rigby: 'Whither Ecological Economics?', *International Journal of Environment and Pollution*, 2002; and 'Operationalising Strong Sustainability: Definitions, Methodologies and Outcomes', *Environmental Values*, 2004.

15. *A Green New Deal: Joined-up Policies to Solve the Triple Crunch of the Credit Crisis, Climate Change and High Oil Prices*, New Economics Foundation, London 2008.

16. Fredric Jameson, 'Future City', *New Left Review* 21, May-June, 2003.

9. Gramsci now

Andrew Pearmain

The British left has had very little to say of positive interest or lasting impact since the mid-1970s, when the neoliberal project of market-utopian 'globalisation' took shape in obscure right-wing think tanks and the stuffier corners of academia, and found local British expression in the ideological movement of 'authoritarian populism' and 'regressive modernisation' that we came to know as Thatcherism. In response, most of the British left retreated into the comfortable certainties of trade union 'wage militancy' on the one hand, and the ineffectual posturing of parliamentary and municipal Labourism on the other. The hyperactivism of the far left and the media glitz of New Labour – in surprising respects (especially their elitism) two sides of the same sectarian coin – have supplied a noisy, occasionally diverting soundtrack to this dismal story of defeat and withdrawal. But compared to the immediate postwar period, or the cultural and social convulsions of the 1960s, the organised left now has very little presence or meaning in most people's lives. In the meantime, capitalism and the political right have been given free rein to dictate the terms on which those lives are led, with all the destructive and divisive consequences we have tried to portray in chapter one.

It didn't have to be like this. At the risk of being accused of 'wishful rethinking', it is worth looking back to a time when all four authors of the original *Feelbad Britain* essay and many others were part of a very different, more positive and constructive political project. This was the first phase of what became known as 'Eurocommunism' in the mid-1970s. To begin with, it was simply an attempt to respond to capitalist crisis with more than 'mindless militancy', to find ways to use the residual strength of the working class and labour movement to address the social needs of more than just a relatively well paid and organised few. But we were also looking for ways to relate 'class politics' to the struggles and perspectives of the 'new social forces' which had emerged in the 1960s, most obviously but not only the women's liberation, gay rights and anti-racist movements. Taking on the lessons and experiences of communists elsewhere, especially in Italy, we sought ways of working in the liberal democratic societies of the west that would win mass, popular support for fundamental social and cultural change, and that did not ultimately depend on heavy-handed and always compromised 'statism'. The theoretical underpinning for this democratic, mass-based 'Eurocommunism' was the writings of Antonio Gramsci, which were translated and rapidly disseminated in Britain following publication of his *Selections from Prison Notebooks* in 1971.[1]

The 'discovery' of Gramsci in the 1960s and 1970s was central to the temporary, partial revival of the political left in Britain, and to a new, more open and creative form of Marxism that broke out of the dogmatic impasses of Stalinism, Trotskyism and the remnants of Second International social democracy. In particular, Gramsci helped to explain the complexity of our western liberal democracies and the need to intervene in every sphere and level to persuade people of the need for democratic socialism. With the onset of Thatcherism and the decline of the left, interest in Gramsci waned. For the last thirty years or so, Gramscism in Britain has been largely confined to the increasingly obscure and arid terrain of 'cultural studies', robbed of its political and historical charge. However, there are signs now of a revival of interest and of a distinctive, more historically based and textually secure 'neo-Gramscism'. Amongst many other aspects of the modern world, Gramsci offers us a way of understanding the continuing stranglehold of Thatcherism and the false dawn of New Labour, and a way out of the isolation and fragmentation of whatever remains of the 'democratic left'. So who was Gramsci, what did he have to say, and what does it mean to us now?

GRAMSCI'S LIFE AND DEATH

Antonio Gramsci (1891-1937) was born and brought up on the (then) remote Italian island of Sardinia. His family was cast into dire poverty by the imprisonment (on probably trumped-up charges) of their father Francesco when Antonio himself was still small. Disabled from infancy by curvature of the spine, Antonio excelled at his studies and eventually won a scholarship to Turin University in 1911. He began writing articles soon after for socialist journals and newspapers, and in 1916 left university to work as a journalist for the Socialist Party newspaper *Avanti!* Gramsci was swept up in debate and agitation over the First World War, then the insurrectionary upheaval that peaked in the Soviet Revolution. The highpoint of the 'Red Years' in Italy was the wave of factory occupations in 1919. The biggest and best organised were in Turin, where Gramsci helped to found the weekly *Ordine Nuovo* to direct and coordinate the factory council movement. In the wake of the movement's defeat by the employers' organisations, and amid bitter recrimination, the Italian Socialist Party split in 1921. Gramsci, already a convinced and committed Marxist, joined the newly founded Communist Party.

Soon after, he became a member of the Communist International Executive and spent much of 1922/23 in Moscow, where he met his wife Giulia. Back in Italy, the ex-socialist Mussolini and the Fascists seized power and began harassing the Communist Party and arresting its leaders. Gramsci returned to Rome in 1924 as party leader and elected MP with parliamentary immunity, leaving his wife and two sons in Moscow. Two years later, after much agonised debate on the left about whether its response to fascism should be democratic or revolutionary, Mussolini established an effective and lasting dictatorship. Gramsci and other communist leaders were arrested or forced into exile. Gramsci spent the remaining ten years of his life in various fascist prisons, often in ill health and appalling conditions. In that time, he wrote thirty-three tightly packed notebooks of reflections on the history of Italy, Europe, the USA and the Soviet Union, on Marxist and liberal philosophy, and much else besides. He was, for obvious reasons, preoccupied with the defeat of proletarian revolution in Western Europe and with the ways in which the ruling classes had managed to restore or maintain their rule. He also sustained regular, insightful, and often deeply moving correspondence with his wife, sister-in-law, sons and other relatives and friends, though he never saw his wife and children again (his younger son was born after Gramsci's imprisonment, and never met his father).

The notebooks were smuggled out of Italy on Gramsci's death in 1937, and published in Italy in 1948-51. The Italian Communist Party (PCI) had emerged from the war a mass party, with enormous influence and prestige, and a commitment (partly based on Gramsci's analyses) to democratic majority rule and struggle on every front – not just economic or industrial, but cultural and political, and at every level of society. Within the international communist movement this was a highly unusual approach, leading towards an explicit anti-Stalinism and scepticism about the 'Soviet model'. The PCI was able to survive the Cold War and remained through the 1960s and 1970s a major force in Italy, coming close to national government on several occasions. Gramsci's legacy survives, despite Berlusconi and the various modern incarnations of fascism and reaction, in the rich political culture of the Italian left.

GRAMSCI IN BRITAIN

There has been more interest in Gramsci in Britain than in any other country outside Italy, partly because of the strong historical parallels between the two countries, most obviously their partial 'bourgeois revolutions', which left them with sizeable aristocracies incorporated into their ruling 'historic blocs' (the French just chopped their heads off). The first English translations of Gramsci appeared in the 1950s, but interest in Gramsci really took off in the 1970s, with the publication of *Selections from the Prison Notebooks*, brilliantly translated, edited and introduced by Quintin Hoare and Geoffrey Nowell Smith.[2] In the aftermath of '1968 and all that', there was an appetite for the kind of open-minded, libertarian Marxism Gramsci seemed to offer. He was untainted by Stalinism and Trotskyism (ironically because of his imprisonment by Mussolini early in the tormented life of the Communist International), and insistent upon the importance of cultural, social, political, ethical and ideological 'superstructures' alongside the classical Marxist economic 'base'. Gramsci was consistently 'anti-positivist', which in a Marxist context set him against any notion of the 'historic inevitability' of socialism. He insisted on the primacy of political action – this was Gramsci's most obvious common ground with Lenin, though Gramsci was plainly uncomfortable with Bolshevik vanguardism. He also consistently criticised the 'economism' and 'corporatism' of exclusively trade union or industrial action, and the idea that 'wage struggle' was somehow inherently revolutionary or even progressive. He did, however, retain a deeply humanist commitment to the idea of historical progress, and insisted that all political regimes (even fascism) necessarily embodied some progressive, constructive impulses.

Two 'centres' of Gramsci studies emerged in the 1970s in Britain, around *New Left Review* and the 'Eurocommunist' wing of the Communist Party, offering quite different and sometimes conflicting interpretations of Gramsci's writings. The *Prison Notebooks* in particular can be cryptic and internally contradictory, largely because of the circumstances of their composition, but also because Gramsci was unusually open to other, non-Marxist traditions and prepared to change his mind. Certain key Gramscian concepts have proved especially resonant in Britain, though they're not always properly understood and deployed. Gramsci is more often bandied about than read in the original, even by people purporting to be 'Gramscian' (Marx suffered a similar fate). In particular, the term 'hegemony' is far richer than simply electoral defeat of your opponents or (as often applied to US foreign policy) military attack or threat, but represents a whole system of domination and collaboration which reaches into every aspect of life and society (in fact, US militarism represents a retreat from the moral and cultural hegemony America once enjoyed across much of the post-war world). Crucially, hegemony relies on the consent as well as coercion of subordinate or 'subaltern' groups, and through a subtle blend of encouragement and intimidation, constructs a 'common sense' about the way the world is, and how it can and cannot be changed. Custom, tradition and culture are central elements of this hegemonic common sense, which assembles a dominant 'historic bloc' of social and political forces to support the ruling order. The leading British Gramscian Stuart Hall made much use of the term 'national-popular', to demonstrate how such successful historic blocs invariably connect to patriotism.[3] For the left, the central task is to identify those elements of prevailing ideology that embody 'good sense', and can be assembled into a new, progressive, national-popular historic bloc or alliance.

The role of intellectuals is crucial to the process of hegemony: both 'traditional' intellectuals undertaking formal intellectual functions in education, the law, religion and so on, and 'organic' intellectuals, who take upon themselves responsibility for organising change, and provide a crucial point of contact between ruling elites and the masses. Periods of history are characterised either by 'war of movement' – where change occurs rapidly and at particular points in society (the Soviet revolution was Gramsci's most obvious example; Britain in the mid-1980s came close to it) – or by 'war of position', where change is much slower, broader and deeper, and less dramatic. This is the more typical situation in the west, with its relatively developed and established (less 'gelatinous') economic, political and cultural systems. Finally, 'optimism of the will, pessimism of the intellect' became a kind of Gramscian watchword or motto in the 1970s, and has helped to see more than a few of us through dark times. In fact, the phrase was coined by the French author Romain Rolland, and appreciatively appropriated by Gramsci, helping him not just to endure imprisonment, but to keep working whenever he was physically and mentally capable. We could do with some of his endurance and determination, ruthless honesty and reasoned hope, right now in these, our ever less certain, times.

WHY GRAMSCI? WHY NOW?

Gramsci, over all other left wing theoreticians, helps to explain the political defeat of popular forces and the restoration and maintenance of ruling class 'hegemony', especially in advanced, democratic, complex capitalist societies like our own. What changes and what remains effectively the same? What is truly significant ('epochal') and what is relatively trivial ('conjunctural')? How can new social alliances be constructed, and what can be done to broaden and strengthen them? What action is best conducted through 'civil society', and what should be done to or by the state?

Gramsci has, I am aware, been cited by some of its luminaries as an inspiration for New Labour. His name and ideas pop up in the strangest places, from Radio 4 profiles of government ministers, the briefly communist John Reid, to published memoirs – Philip Gould makes pivotal use of the term 'Conservative hegemony' in his seminal New Labour text *The Unfinished Revolution*.[4] There is a tenuous thematic connection between Gramsci and New Labour, via the latter-day *Marxism Today* and the 'New Times' analysis of 'post-Fordism': the argument that new times required the construction of new hegemonic alliances was interpreted as necessitating an obsessive concern with being 'modern' and a shift to the centre right. But I would argue that Gramsci offers a means of making sense *of* rather than *for* New Labour.

In particular, Gramsci helps us see the historical continuities of Labourism, the ruptures wrought by Thatcherism, and New Labour's curious (if often unacknowledged) relationship with both – and for that matter with the past in general, which in part the New Labour 'project' harks back to nostalgically, and in part likes to pretend never happened. These historical themes run far deeper than the daily doings of parliamentarians and journalists – what passes for the stuff of contemporary politics in the 'Westminster village'. Crucially, they also condition what politicians can and cannot achieve in any particular time or circumstance. For us, now, they help to explain why New Labour has turned out to be such a major disappointment and, arguably, missed historic opportunity. It is an object rather than an agent of history, forced to operate on terrain chosen and shaped by others. Of course, as Marx observed, all human endeavour takes place in a real historical and material context, but New Labour has proved peculiarly inept, with its utterly vacuous 'Third Way', at making any kind of permanent mark of its own. Ministers may recite formulaic mantras – 'a lot done, a lot still to do', 'for the many, not the few', 'hard-working families' – and endless lists of government 'achievements', but few people are fooled. Political 'business' is no substitute for strategic purpose.

Labour and Tory basically the same? How can this be? Don't they say they hate each other? Is this some kind of variant on the old anarchist cliché 'whoever you vote for, the government always gets in'? Not at all. It is rather an observation of the tendency towards convergence of electoral politics onto the sacred 'middle ground'. A broader analytical view reveals deep ideological and social currents at work alongside the more easily detected and documented daily rumblings of the economy and the political system. Stuart Hall and other prominent Gramscians have argued a consistent and (I find) compelling narrative.[5] The post-war social democratic consensus of Keynesian economics and welfare statism was broken in Britain in the 1970s, because the trade-off between capitalism and the welfare state was no longer sustainable. Thatcherism set about its dynamic, destructive/creative project of 'regressive modernisation', producing an entirely different political and economic, and above all ideological, climate, characterised by the celebration of certain values – primarily self-reliance and self-interest – and the demonisation of others, especially anything that smacks of the social and the collective. This culminated in the domination of neoliberal capitalism and its associated 'politico-ethical' framework in Britain (and in much of the rest of the world, where other pro-market political formations existed, articulated in different ways to the resurgence of capitalism after the 1970s).

Along the way, 'national-popular' support was won for a whole range of measures, which would have previously been anathema, such as the sale of council housing, privatisation of utilities, cutbacks in public services and benefits, and limitations on trade union power. This approach has been characterised as 'authoritarian populism'. Certain key events served as intimidatory/educative jolts to public feeling (recalling Gramsci's pivotal couplet of coercion/consent in the exercise of hegemony), such as the Falklands War and the 1984/5 miners strike, or the late-1980s 'big bang' of financial deregulation. Fundamental shifts took place in our social ethos – from the collective to the individual, from the public to the private, from society to family, from we to I, from production to consumption – and congealed into a new, all-embracing and almost incontrovertible (i.e. hegemonic) 'common sense'.

New Labour explicitly accepted this new settlement, and set itself the task of reshaping the people to suit the needs of the new global market economy, thus inverting the logic of orthodox social democracy in the service of capitalist reconstruction. From privatisation and deregulation, mass redundancy and unemployment, it was but a short step to welfare-to-work and the minimum-wage service-economy, via the popular folk-devil of the 'scrounger' and the politer terms 'underclass' and 'dependency culture' – and now the darker-hued bogey of the 'asylum seeker'. As such, New Labour represented a 'transformist' or 'molecular' adaptation of the continuing Thatcherite 'passive revolution' (radical change imposed from above), to use particularly resonant and apposite Gramscian terms.

It remains to be seen what comes next. The financial crisis that started in 2007 is developing into a fully-fledged economic recession, perhaps heralding the return of 'boom and bust'. The original New Labour project of Blair and Brown became deeply unpopular and has remained so under the new Brown administration. The renaissance of the Tories under Cameron, while rhetorically ditching the legacy of Thatcher herself, has nevertheless stayed faithful to the underlying ideological core of Thatcherism. We are clearly due another transformist stage in what Gramsci always insisted was the dynamic, constantly adaptable *process* of hegemony. It will be especially interesting to see whether the electoral 'winners' pursue Thatcherism's more authoritarian or libertarian impulses (right now, weirdly, Brown represents the former and Cameron the latter); or whether they will forge some new national-popular combination (as the 'high' Thatcherism of strong state/free market so effectively did). In the meantime, the democratic left could do a lot worse than take a close, hard look at our own recent history, see where we went wrong, and, as Gramsci would insist, take full responsibility for our own (generally inglorious) failures. In the meantime, dig out your dusty old copy of *Prison Notebooks* and have another look. Every reading of Gramsci yields some new insight. Here's one of my current favourites, written about early twentieth century Italy but so readily applicable to our own tired public realm and inward-looking society:

> Hence, squalor of cultural life and wretched inadequacy of high culture. Instead of political history, bloodless erudition; instead of religion, superstition; instead of books and great reviews, daily papers and broadsheets; instead of serious politics, ephemeral quarrels and personal clashes.[6]

Let's take each of these and see how they might apply to contemporary Britain. Gramsci began his writing career as a theatre critic and for the rest of his life took a close interest in culture and art. He was an early and enthusiastic fan of modernism, in the theatre of Pirandello and the poetry and art of Futurism, with its joyous celebration of the mass and the mechanised, the industrial and the urban. He wrote a number of ground-breaking studies on the history of language and popular literature in Europe, and the folk cultures of Sardinia and the Italian south, with their function as an expression of 'subaltern' grievance and sentiment. He was fascinated by the interplay of mass taste and feeling and artistic creativity and innovation, and the possibilities it offered for moral, ideological and ultimately (without falling into any kind of crass 'agitprop' trap) political change. He was always ready to appreciate art on its own terms, without subjecting it to some kind of predetermined test of political correctness, as in Stalinist 'social realism'. But there is in all his writing a recurring question posed of any cultural or political phenomena. Do they deepen or subvert bourgeois hegemony? Do they assist 'the mass of people' to understand, explain and take greater control over their own lives? Are they artistically progressive, truly democratic, in both form and content? We could usefully pose the same questions of the product of our own 'creative industries'.

What of academia and our public discourse? Well, there are plenty of contemporary examples of 'bloodless erudition', much of it driven by the Research Assessment Exercise and other attempts to regulate the 'output' of our universities, which reward ever more obscure, insular and essentially private intellectual work amongst proliferating bands of ghettoised, jargon-trading, nitpicking boffins, while serving up an increasingly arid, formulaic and uncritical education to our student hordes. On the other hand – something Gramsci anticipated elsewhere in his critiques of the intellectual functionaries of fascism – we see the passing parades of media-friendly 'public intellectuals' and professional controversialists, people paid to disagree with us and each other in supposedly eye-catching, briefly provocative columns and declamations of opinion. Their broader, longer-term effect on public debate is disorientation and confusion, a rising babble of shouted outrage, the pretence of difference and insight which fails to change or even much interest people's minds.

For a Marxist, Gramsci was unusually appreciative of the historical role of the Catholic church, especially its Jesuit 'shock-troops', who played a key role in propagating its precepts and enforcing its strictures. At its best, religion supplied a popular, comprehensive and common rationality to industrial development and social progress, and above all, to scientific discovery and invention. When he rails against 'superstition', he is attacking popular morality which is not based on reason and requires an unthinking, infantilising 'faith' in a set of notions that might have some symbolic force but lack any basis in common material reality. In our own time, with the rapid decline (at least in the west) of older forms of institutionalised religion, we see the emergence of quite new forms of 'superstition', from astrology and other variations of 'New Age' nonsense to the explicitly 'political' (i.e. reactionary) forms of militant Islam or the Christian right. In the absence of rational religious (and political) value and belief systems, people are turning to whatever quackery (even, in more intellectual circles, to what the historian Raphael Samuel called 'splashing around in the shallows of postmodernism') that seems to offer some brief comfort, consolation or explanation for their various sadnesses, confusions and disaffections.

Gramsci was himself a journalist, but he would surely struggle to recognise his own professional values in our debased national media – its sensationalism, its abusive brutality and simple falsehoods, its superficiality and tittle-tattle, its fixed narratives of fear, crime and insecurity. Above all, it has served to desiccate and sideline our political process, and to reduce it to endless and ultimately boring 'ephemeral quarrels and personal clashes'. No wonder most people have lost all interest. This brings us to the final question a contemporary re-reading of Gramsci raises: what can we do about it all? In more formal terms, what kind of 'political agency' is available to us? The prospects for progressive politics in Britain are probably bleaker than at any time since the 1880s. The 'mass party of the working class', Labour, has lost any sense of its historic purpose and is now at an all-time low in membership, morale and presence in real communities. New Labour is plainly a last gasp rather than any kind of revival of Labourism. The far left remains noisy but utterly ineffectual.

Our own political tradition, democratic communism, has lacked any formal vehicle since the Communist Party disbanded in 1991 and left a great gaping hole where a thoughtful, constructive, Gramscian-Marxist organisation should be. There is interest in politics, especially among the aware and engaged young, but they have nowhere to go to bring their various concerns together into a coherent movement capable of deep, permanent change.

Antonio Gramsci regarded his own Communist Party as 'the modern prince', the equivalent to Machiavelli's decisive, skilful leader, and spent much of his time in prison considering and debating how it should conduct itself in resisting fascism and constructing socialism. Eventually, long after his death, the PCI went some way towards justifying his confidence. The British left may just be at a similar stage in our own recent, generally miserable history. 'Imprisoned' in our own marginal if generally comfortable enclaves and in our vague feelings of historical redundancy, we at least have plenty of spare time to figure out what to do. Gramsci can help us ask the right questions, even if we still need to find our own answers.[7]

REFERENCES

1. Antonio Gramsci, *Selections from the Prison Notebooks*, edited by Quintin Hoare and Geoffrey Nowell Smith, Lawrence & Wishart, London 1971.
2. Gramsci, op cit.
3. Stuart Hall, *The Hard Road to Renewal*, Verso, London 1989.
4. Philip Gould, *The Unfinished Revolution*, Abacus, London 1998.
5. Hall, op cit; see also his 'New Labour's double shuffle', *Soundings* 24, autumn 2003.
6. Gramsci, op cit, p228.
7. For further reading on Gramsci, see: David Forgacs (ed.), *The Antonio Gramsci Reader*, Lawrence & Wishart, London 1988; G. Fiori, *Antonio Gramsci – Life of a Revolutionary*, translated by Tom Nairn, New Left Books, London 1970; Antonio Gramsci, *Prison Letters*, translated by Hamish Hamilton, Pluto, London 1996; and Hall, op cit.

10. Whatever happened to feminism? Young womanhood under new management

Angela McRobbie

This chapter looks at the processes of feminism being undone, through the high levels of intervention and attention that are currently being directed towards young women, whose significance in terms of wage-earning capacity cannot today be overlooked.

My argument is that there is a new sexual contract (a cultural rather than legal phenomenon) currently being made available to young women, primarily in the West: to come forward and make good use of the opportunity to work, to gain qualifications, to control fertility, and to earn enough money to participate in the consumer culture. This is likely to become a defining feature of contemporary modes of feminine citizenship.

What are we to make of the decisive re-positioning of young women? The transformations that have taken place tend to be seen as positive: across the spectrum, from left to right, the apparent gains made by young women are taken to be signs of the existence of a democracy in good health. But my argument is that there is a need to be alert to the dangers which arise when a particular selection of feminist values and ideals are inscribed within a profound and determined attempt to re-shape notions of womanhood so that they fit with new or emerging (neo-liberalised) social and economic arrangements.

The girl emerges or comes forward across a range of social and cultural spaces, as a subject truly worthy of investment. In New Labour Britain, the girl who has benefited from the equal opportunities now available to her can be mobilised as the embodiment of the values of the new meritocracy. (This term has become an abbreviation for the more individualistic and competitive values promoted by New Labour, particularly within education.) Nowadays young women's success seems to promise economic prosperity on the basis of their enthusiasm for work and having a career. The attribution of freedom and success to young women takes different forms across the boundaries of class, ethnicity and sexuality, however, producing a range of configurations of youthful femininity, entangled in many different ways with race and class. Once assumed to be headed towards marriage, mother-hood and limited economic participation, the girl is now endowed with economic capacity. Young, increasingly well-educated women, of different ethnic and social backgrounds, now find themselves charged with the requirement that they perform as economically active female citizens. They are invited to recognise themselves as privileged subjects of social change. The pleasing, lively, capable and becoming young woman, black, white or Asian, is now an attractive harbinger of social change.

In this chapter I consider this new standing of young women through four key configurations, each of which operates to sustain and re-vitalise the 'heterosexual matrix'[1] (while also re-instating and confirming norms of racial hierarchy as well as re-configured class divisions – which now take on a more autonomously gendered dimension). The first of these is the fashion and beauty complex, from within which has emerged a post-feminist 'masquerade', a distinctive new form of feminine agency. The second is education and employment, within which is found the figure of the working girl. The third figure emerges from within the hyper-visible space of sexuality, fertility and reproduction – the phallic girl. Fourthly, through the production of commercial femininities, there emerges the figure of the global girl in the developing world.

SHINING IN THE LIGHT: THE POST-FEMINIST MASQUERADE

Young women have been hyper-actively positioned in the context of a wide range of social, political and economic changes, of which they themselves appear to be the privileged subjects. We might now imagine the young woman as a highly efficient assemblage for productivity. (This too marks a shift: women now figure in governmental discourse as much for their productive as reproductive capacities.) She can be seen as an intensively managed subject of biopolitical practices (gender-aware but post-feminist), within new forms of governmentality.

It is perhaps helpful here to think about young women as being invited to come forward through a range of social and cultural practices that combine a sense of movement with a putting of the young female subject under a spotlight. The young woman thus becomes visible in a certain kind of way – and here Deleuze's concept of 'luminosity' is a useful one.[2] Writing about what Foucault meant by visibilities, Deleuze suggests that these are not forms of objects, or even forms that show up under light: they are 'forms of luminosity which are created by the light itself and allow a thing or object to exist only as a flash, sparkle or shimmer'.[3] This captures something of the way in which young women might be understood as currently becoming visible. The power they seem to be collectively in possession of is 'created by the light itself'. In some ways the idea of a moving spotlight reflects Foucault's concept of the panopticon, but this is not so much a question of surveillance – what is apparent here, rather, is a theatrical or cinematic effect.[4] These 'luminosities' are suggestive of post-feminist equality, while also serving to define and circumscribe the conditions of such a status. They are clouds of light that give young women a shimmering presence, but in so doing mark out the terrain of the consummately and reassuringly feminine. Through the illusion of movement and agency, it seems as though young women are coming forward through choice, and because all obstacles have been removed. The light simply picks up and traces these movements, while bestowing on them a spectacular cinematic effect.

One can see these new configurations as an adjustment made in response to feminist challenges to old patriarchal symbolic settlements. Both feminism and neoliberalism challenge old forms of representation and the symbolic order. And in a world that remains patriarchal – though its forms are constantly remade and rearticulated – the symbolic is faced with the problem of how to retain the dominance of phallocentrism at a time when the logic of global capitalism is to loosen women from their prescribed roles and grant them degrees of economic independence.

There is, then, a double threat to the symbolic order – first from a now-outmoded and hence only spectral feminism, and second from the aggressive re-positioning of women through these economic processes of female individualisation. One form of defence against these challenges is to discharge (or maybe franchise) certain symbolic duties to the commercial domain (beauty, fashion, magazines, body culture, etc), which now becomes the source of authority and judgement for young women. Because the commercial domain is now so dominant – as social institutions are reduced in their sphere of influence – we can detect an intensification in such disciplinary requirements; and we can also perceive new dynamics of aggression, violence and self-punishment. A key containment strategy on the part of the symbolic is to delegate a good deal of its power to the fashion and beauty complex, where – as a 'grand luminosity' – a post-feminist 'masquerade' emerges as a new cultural dominant.[5] The masquerade has re-appeared, as a highly self-conscious means whereby young women are encouraged to collude with the re-stabilisation of gender norms, so as to undo the gains of feminism and dissociate themselves from this now discredited political identity. As a psychoanalyst Riviere was interested in how women who wished for masculinity might 'put on a mask of womanliness to avert anxiety and the retribution feared from men'. She understood womanliness and masquerade to be indistinguishable: there is no naturally feminine woman lurking underneath the mask. We can see the post-feminist masquerade as a re-ordering of the heterosexual matrix in order to secure, once again, the existence of patriarchal law and masculine hegemony.

There is a useful slippage in Riviere's account between the actuality of the masquerade as a recognisable phenomenon – one which she can perceive in her female patients and their encounters – and images of femininity found in the cultural realm. There is an intersection between the styles of femininity Riviere observes in everyday life and those portrayed in feminine popular culture. I would argue that we can now see the post-feminist masquerade as a mode of feminine inscription across the whole surface of the female body, and as an interpellative device at work and highly visible in the commercial domain – as a familiar (even nostalgic or 'retro'), light-hearted (unserious) refrain of femininity. Post-feminist masquerade has recently been re-instated into the repertoire of femininity, ironically. This signals that the hyper-femininity of the masquerade, which would seemingly re-locate women back inside the terms of traditional gender hierarchies – having them wear spindly stilettos and 'pencil' skirts, for example – does not in fact mean entrapment (as feminists would once have seen it): it is now a matter of choice rather than obligation.

This new masquerade constantly refers to its own artifice: its adoption by women is undertaken as a statement. The woman in masquerade is making the point that this is a freely chosen look. The post-feminist masquerade does not fear male retribution. Instead it is the reprimanding structure of the fashion and beauty system that acts as an authoritative regime. (Hence the seeming disregard for male approval, especially if the outfit and look is widely admired by those within the fashion milieu.[6]) The masquerade rescues women from the threat posed by these figures by triumphantly re-instating the spectacle of excessive femininity (on the basis of the independently earned wage), while also shoring up hegemonic masculinity by endorsing a public femininity that appears to undermine, or at least unsettle, the new power accruing to women on the basis of their economic capacity. There are many variants of the post-feminist masquerade, but in essence it comprises a re-ordering of femininity so that old-fashioned styles (rules about hats, bags, shoes, etc), which signal submission to some invisible authority, or to an opaque set of instructions, are re-instated (e.g., Bridget Jones's short skirt and flirty presence in the workplace and her 'oh silly me' self-reprimands). The post-feminist masquerade comes to the young women's rescue, a throwback from the past, and she adopts this style (for example assuming the air of being 'foolish and bewildered'[7]) in order to help her navigate the terrain of hegemonic masculinity without jeopardising her sexual identity. For now that she is actually and legitimately inside the institutional world of work, from which she was once barred, this can become a site of vulnerability. Alternatively, she simply fears being considered aggressively unfeminine in her coming forward as a powerful woman, and so adopts the air of being girlishly distracted, weighed down with bags, bracelets and other decorative items, all of which need to be constantly attended to. The silly hat and the too-high heels are once again a means of emphasising female vulnerability and fragility, and anxiety about the forfeiting of male desire, as they were in classic Hollywood comedies.

Both Riviere and Butler refer to the sublimated aggression directed towards male dominance in the form of the masquerade. Riviere uses words like 'triumph', 'supremacy' and 'hostility' to describe the female anger which underpins the façade of excessive feminine adornment. She pinpoints the fury of the professional woman who perceives her own subjugation in the behaviour of her male peers. All of this gets transmogrified into the mask of make-up and the crafting of a highly styled look. This strategy re-appears today in very different circumstances. Women now routinely inhabit these masculine spheres. They find themselves in competition with men on a daily basis. They take their place alongside men thanks to the existence of non-discriminatory policies and, more recently, to systems of meritocratic reward as advocated by New Labour. The woman in masquerade wishes to have a position as a 'subject in language' (i.e. to participate in public life), rather than to exist merely as 'woman as sign'.[8] But precisely because women are now able to function as subjects in language, a new masquerade exists to manage the field of sexual antagonisms – and to re-instate women as sign. The masquerade functions to re-assure male structures of power by defusing the presence and competitive actions of women as they come to inhabit positions of authority. It re-stabilises gender relations and the heterosexual matrix by repeatedly and ritualistically interpellating women into the knowing and self-reflexive terms of highly stylised femininity. The post-feminist masquerade works pre-emptively, in the light of the possible disruptions posed by the new gender regime. It operates with a double movement: its voluntaristic structure works to conceal that patriarchy is still in place, while the requirements of the fashion and beauty system ensure that women remain as fearful subjects, driven by the need for 'complete perfection'.[9]

EDUCATION AND EMPLOYMENT AS SITES OF CAPACITY: THE VISIBILITY OF THE WELL-EDUCATED WORKING GIRL

The post-feminist masquerade, and the clouds of light bestowed on the figure of the young women by the fashion and beauty system, are matched – if not surpassed – by (and frequently inter-sect with) the visibilities which produce the well-educated young woman and the working girl. Enormous governmental activity is put into making young women ready for work, and this require-ment takes the form of urging them towards agency across the whole range of talents and abilities.[10] The young woman comes to be widely understood as a potential bearer of qualifications. She is an active and aspirational subject of the education system, and she embodies the success of the new meritocratic values which New Labour has sought to implement in schools. This re-positioning is a decisive factor in the new sexual contract. And it means that the acquisition (or not) of qualifications comes to function as a mark of a new gender divide. Young women are ranked according to their ability to gain qualifications that provide them with an iden-tity as female subjects of capacity. (They can become obsessed with grades.) The young woman comes forward as someone able to transcend the barriers of sex, race and class. She will step forward as an exemplary black or Asian young woman on the basis of her enthusiasm for learning, taste for hard work, and desire to pursue material reward. Meanwhile young women under-achievers, and those who do not have the requisite degrees of motivation and ambition to improve themselves, become more emphatically condemned than would have been the case in the past for their lack of status, and other failings.

There is, however, a decisive shift in the transition to work for young women, as their movement forward finds itself coming up against the idea of social compromise: the new sexual contract operates in the workplace to set limits on patterns of participation and gender equality. This is particularly the case for women who are also mothers, and who are repositioned in the labour market on return to work after the birth of children.[11] For these women there is an implicit abandonment of any critique of masculine hegemony, in favour of compromise. Young working mothers, it appears, draw back from entertaining any idea of debate on inequality in the household, instead finding ways, with help from government, to manage their dual responsibility. As with the post-feminist masquerade, this is a strategy of undoing, a re-configuring of normative femininity, this time incorporating motherhood so as to accommodate with masculine hegemony. This social compromise is a further process of gender re-stabilisation.

Crompton points to the significant rates of retention in employment or return to work shortly after having children among UK women. This corresponds with government's focus on women's employability, and the transition to lifelong work for women as an alternative to traditional economic dependence on a male breadwinner. The compromise requires that woman play a dual role, active in the workplace and also primarily responsible for children and domestic life. Instead of challenging the traditional expectation that women take primary responsibility in the home, there is a shift towards an abandonment of the critique of patriarchy, and to a heroic attempt to 'do it all' – while also looking to government for support in this Herculean endeavour. This transition comes into existence by means of a series of luminosities (the glamorous working mother, the 'yummy mummy', the high-flyer who is also a mother, etc); and these images and texts are supplemented by popular genres of fiction, including best-selling novels such as *I Don't Know How She Does It*.[12]

The UK government substitutes for the feminist, displaces her vocabulary, and intervenes to assist working mothers – and thereby averts the possibility of critique of women's double responsibilities, and any possible crisis within the heterosexual matrix. Government thus acts to protect masculine hegemony by supporting women in their double role, while the media and popular culture endeavour to re-glamorise working wives and mothers through post-feminist styles of self-improvement, hyper-sexuality and capacity.

This feature of the new sexual contract requires compromise in work as well as within the home. Despite the rhetoric of heroism in combining primary responsibility for children with maintaining a career, in practice the various agencies whose subject of attention is the young working women tend to emphasise the scaling down of ambition, in favour of a discourse of managing following the onset of motherhood. In the light of these new responsibilities, the young woman is counselled to request flexibility of her employer. Government is certainly not encouraging women back into the home after having children. Instead, the new sexual contract offers support and guidance, so that the return to employment (often part-time) is facilitated in the form of a 'work-life balance'. There is an implicit trade-off. What the working mother now wants or needs from her employer is recognition of her dual role, and some degree of accommodation in this respect. The work-life balance for women is now underpinned by better safeguards in law for part-time workers, and also pension rights. The state thus makes it possible through these provisions for the husband to pursue his working life without female complaint. A decade ago Nancy Fraser argued that men must again become more accountable to gender inequities in the household.[13] What I have attempted to demonstrate here are the forces which prevail against this kind of expectation re-emerging as a possibility. Fraser also argued that the Universal Breadwinner Model is increasingly taking precedence over the Caregiver Model associated with the older welfare regime, which took into account women's role as care-givers, and the limits that role put on possibilities for economic activity. But in the current social compromise the Universal Breadwinner Model requires of women a joint responsibility, and thus more or less guarantees subordinate status in terms of wage-earning capacity in the realm of work and employment over a lifetime. At the same time, the coming forward of women into work offers government an excellent opportunity to cut the long-term costs of welfare.

PHALLIC GIRLS: RECREATIONAL SEX, REPRODUCTIVE SEX

Judith Butler sees the 'phallic lesbian' as a political figure who wrestles some power from the almighty symbolic; and when asked if heterosexual women might also be able to pick up the phallus in this way she responded that this might be an important thing to do.[14] But the Symbolic has reacted swiftly to the antagonism presented not just by feminism but by Butler's lesbian phallus and queer theory per se: it has pre-emptively endowed young women with the capacity to become phallus-bearers as a kind of licensed mimicry of their male counterparts. A 'pretence' of equality permits spectacles of aggression and unfeminine behaviour on the part of young women, without apparently invoking the usual kinds of punishment. The phallic girl gives the impression of having won equality with men by becoming like her male counterparts. But in this adoption of the phallus, there is no critique of masculine hegemony, no radical re-arrangement of gender hierarchy.

The ladette is a young woman for whom the freedoms associated with masculine sexual pleasures are not only made available: they are also encouraged and celebrated. She is asked to concur with a definition of sex as light-hearted pleasure, recreational activity, hedonism, sport, reward and status. Luminosity falls upon the girl who adopts the habits of masculinity – heavy drinking, swearing, smoking, getting into fights, having casual sex, getting arrested by the police, consuming pornography, enjoying lap-dancing clubs – without relinquishing her own desirability to men; indeed such seeming masculinity enhances her desirability within the visual economy of heterosexuality.

Female phallicism is a more assertive alternative to masquerade, but it does the same kind of work of re-stabilising gender relations in face of the threat posed to dominant heterosexuality by the loosening of the ties of dependency through access to work and employment. The apparently taboo-breaking phallic girl emerges as a challenge not only to the repudiated feminist but also to the repudiated lesbian. By being able to take up some of the accoutrements of masculinity, the drunken and leering young woman – who is not averse to having sex with other girls – demonstrates that all things are possible within the presiding realm of symbolic authority. Consumer culture, the tabloid press, girls', women's and lads' magazines, as well as downmarket television, all encourage young women, as though in the name of sexual equality, to overturn the old double standard and emulate the assertive and hedonistic styles of sexuality associated with young men. And this assumption of phallicism also provides new dimensions of moral panic, titillation and voyeuristic excitement.

But beneath the pretence of equality promoted by consumer culture, such female phallicism is in fact a provocation to feminism, a triumphant gesture on the part of resurgent patriarchy. The violence which underpins the granting of freedom to the phallic girl warrants more detailed analysis. In coming forward and showing herself to be, in common parlance, 'up for it', the phallic girl as a luminosity permits certain modes of 'rollback' of what has become established as feminist common-sense – and this is now made open to revision. Thus her unfeminine behaviour permits the re-visiting of debates on sexual violence and rape – for example if the girl in question has drunk so much she has no idea exactly what has happened, or if she has agreed to have sex with a number of men but has not expected to be treated with violence. By endorsing norms of male conduct in the field of sexuality she removes any obligation on the part of men to reflect on their own behaviour and their treatment of women. Equally, the phallic girl who is perhaps now ageing – for example the glamour model – is expected to bear the brunt of masculine hostility when she is no longer as desirable. Young men's hostility to women re-appears without rebuke, particularly in comedy and in popular culture.

THE GLOBAL GIRL

There are patterns of racialised retrenchment embedded within these re-configured spaces of femininity. The post-feminist masquerade extols the virtues of dissembled feminine weakness and fragility, playing with old traditions and adopting a style of femininity which invites once again a display of masculine chivalry, gallantry, power, and control. In so doing it resurrects norms of white heterosexuality from which black women and men have historically been violently excluded. As a cultural strategy for re-stabilising gender relations within the heterosexual matrix, the post-feminist masquerade produces a new interface between working life and sexuality that is implicitly white, and which assumes kinship norms associated with the western nuclear family. In line with the new ethos of assimilation and integration – as opposed to the apparently 'failed multiculturalism' of the 1980s and 1990s – aspirant young black women are invited, as readers of magazines like *Grazia*, or viewers of television programmes like *Friends*, or films like *Bridget Jones's Diary*, to emulate this model, to write themselves into these scripts – without modification, and without the option of challenge or contestation.

The 'global girl' now also comes forward, as seen in the advertising images of fashion companies like Benetton, but also through the different editions of global fashion magazines like *Elle, Marie Claire, Vogue* and *Grazia*; these are customised from one country to the next, as emblematic of the power and success of corporate multiculturalism. They envisage young women from third world countries as enthusiastic about membership of, and belonging to, a kind of global femininity. The modernity of the global girl today is expressed in her newfound freedoms, her wage-earning capacity, her enjoyment of and immersion in beauty culture and popular culture. She is pleasing and becoming and she does not wear her femininity with the irony of her post-feminist masquerading western counterparts; nor does she display the aggression and sexual bravado of the phallic girls. Global girls are the fantasy constructs of threatened Western masculinity. They combine the natural and authentic with a properly feminine love of self-adornment; and the playfully seductive with the innocent – so as to suggest a sexuality which is youthful, latent and waiting to be unleashed. There is little novelty in this racial fantasy, but these young women are now also envisaged as more active than passive.

This marks out a subtle re-positioning, a re-making of racial hierarchy within the field of normative femininity. The idea of a sexual contract that spans a range of bodily activities, and permits modes of coming forward on condition that any residue of sexual politics fades away, is a western formulation, addressed to those who are assumed to have full citizenship and the right to remain in the country of abode. In this contract economic activity is fore-grounded and politics reduced to the margins, in favour of consumer citizenship. But women who are excluded from this privileged model of freedom – based on the state provision of education, followed by participation in training and in the labour market – are the subjects of different forms of concern, prompting the deployment of more conventional technologies of surveillance. The new figure of global girlhood is expected her to buy into western styles of spectacular femininity as a means of enhancing her position in the international division of labour, and thus show herself to be eager to succeed, uncritical and 'bearing-no-grudges'. We could say that the young unmarried woman from an impoverished part of the world has been re-designated (by means of what Gayatri Spivak calls 'gender planning'[15]) as having even more capacity for work and labour than has been the case in the past. And for this reason there is increasing attention to her education and training, which (as Spivak also points out) now entails various versions of US influenced neo-liberal pedagogy based round entrepreneurship. Spivak suggests that feminists look now at the values underpinning this new curriculum in the third world, which is preparing young women for mobility and living apart from family and community. These dislocations for the poor and the not so poor are giving rise to new forms of diasporic femininity.[16]

CONCLUSION

The feminist critique of masculine hegemony is currently being undermined by a new sexual contract issued to young women. This encourages young women to come forward in various roles or luminosities, but excludes the political. The post-feminist masquerade, the well-educated working girl, the phallic girl, the global girl – all present young women as empowered. And yet there is a gender re-stabilisation and re-instatement of sexual hierarchies in this orchestration of luminosities. Young women are permitted to come forward, but only on condition that feminist politics fades away.

REFERENCES

1. For the concept of heterosexual matrix see J. Butler, *Antigone's Claim: Kinship Between Life and Death*, Columbia University Press, New York 2000.
2. See G. Deleuze, *Foucault*, University of Minnesota Press, Minneapolis 1986.
3. Deleuze, *Foucault*, p52.
4. See P. Rabinow (ed.), *The Foucault Reader*, Penguin, London 1984.
5. The idea of masquerade was first defined in a famous essay by Joan Riviere in 1929, and returned to by Judith Butler in 1990/1999. See J. Riviere, 'Womanliness as a Masquerade', in V. Burgin, J. Donald and C. Kaplan (eds), *Formations of Fantasy*, Methuen, London 1929/1986, p35; and J. Butler, *Gender Trouble: Feminism and the Subversion of Identity*, Routledge, London and New York 1990/1999, p655.
6. This is a regular theme in *Sex in the City*: Carrie's date may not care for her silly hat, which she knows only fashion experts would appreciate. Thus the wearing or not of the hat provokes much self reflexivity. Should she or shouldn't she? Carrie tends to cling onto these seemingly ridiculous items as a mark of her own independent identity. But we (the audience) know that in the end these items work to the advantage of her femininity. They actually make her more endearing to men. Their excessive quality shows her vulner-

ability and her child-like enjoyment of dressing up. If she gets it wrong and she looks a little foolish, it is because she is still a girl, unsure of herself as she takes on the mantle of womanliness. Indeed getting it wrong is a mark of her girlishness and this failing makes her all the more desirable to men.

7. Riviere, op cit, p29.
8. Butler, op cit, 1990/1999.
9. Riviere, op cit, p42.
10. N. Rose, 'Inventiveness in Politics', *Economy and Society* 1999 (28:3), pp467-493.
11. Rosemary Crompton has written interestingly on this phenomenon. See her 'Employment, Flexible Working and the Family', *British Journal of Sociology*, 2002 (53:4), pp537-558.
12. A. Pearson, *I Don't Know How She Does It*, Vintage, London 2003.
13. N. Fraser, *Justice Interruptus*, Routledge, London 1997.
14. J. Butler, 'Gender as Performative' An Interview with Judith Butler by Peter Osborn and Lynne Segal, *Radical Philosophy*, 1994 (67), pp32- 39.
15. G. Spivak, *A Critique of Postcolonial Reason*, Harvard University Press, Cambridge MA 1999.
16. These are analysed in depth in the work of border theorists and others; see, for example, C. Mohanty, 'Under Western Eyes Revisited: Feminist Solidarity Through Anti-Capitalist Struggles', in 'Signs: A Journal of Women', *Culture and Society* 2002 (2), pp499-535.

11. The environmental wedge: neoliberalism, democracy and the prospects for a new British Left

Noel Castree

This chapter's principal argument is that the 'environmental agenda' ought to be a prime vehicle for moving British society in a more progressive direction, yet is currently failing to realise its considerable political potential. My objectives are to explain this troubling situation and to consider what might realistically be done to change it.

NEOLIBERALISM, BRITISH STYLE

As many commentators have observed, the New Labour project has been neoliberal to the marrow. Blair and his successor Gordon Brown have operated within the political economic and cultural parameters established by the Conservative governments of the Thatcher-Major years. The core features of the neoliberal project have all been promoted or, if not, at least respected. New Labour has been committed to extending the reach of the market, to minimising state 'interference' in economic affairs, to making remaining state functions as market-like as possible, to encouraging the growth of 'flanking organisations' in civil society, and to engendering an ethic of self-sufficiency over and against an ethic of solidarity. In his authoritative analysis, Andrew Glyn regards neoliberalism as 'capitalism unleashed' – and so it is, in its pure form.[1] But Blair and Brown intentionally softened its harder edges by offering child tax credits, putting record investment in the National Health Service, instituting Sure Start and the minimum wage, and presenting a raft of other measures designed to suggest that while 'new' they were still nonetheless recognisably Labour.

Over a decade after Blair first entered 10 Downing Street, the wheels of the New Labour bandwagon seem to have fallen off. Gordon Brown has proved himself to be an ineffective leader, and is as unpopular in his way as Blair was at the end of his premiership. Those on the left who hoped that Brown would define a new agenda for Labour and the country – like the Compass group – have been exasperated by his serial equivocation and blundering. His message, like his actions, has been contradictory and out-of-focus so far as his own party and the public are concerned. As one well-known *Guardian* columnist put it, 'those of us who hoped that the man had hidden depths have had to conclude that he's a man of hidden shallows ... on the whole, we're not impressed'.[2] At the time of writing (August 2008), Brown's credibility is in tatters.

Progressives who are left of New Labour ought to be ambivalent about this state of affairs. On the one hand they can feel vindicated: despite its best (some would say token) efforts, New Labour has ultimately been unable to tame the excesses of neoliberal capitalism at home. Authoritative studies reveal record levels of income inequality, no relative increase in people's sense of well-being, unprecedented numbers of mentally ill, depressed and imprisoned individuals, and a near-obsessive quest by all social groups to keep-up-with-the-Joneses. On the other hand, any return to power by the Tories would clearly be a cause for great concern. The Cameron Tories undoubtedly continue to accept the terms and conditions of the neoliberal compact: they would in no sense represent a paradigm shift in the political-economic or cultural senses.

It wasn't supposed to be like this. In his classic analysis of British economy and society during the long era of 'liberal capitalism' (which came crashing to an end with the Great Depression and the second world war), Karl Polanyi showed why the 'free market' is ultimately destructive of the very things upon which its survival depends.[3] Nearly sixty years later, it is worth considering the contemporary relevance of two of Polanyi's key ideas. The first is the concept of a 'fictitious' or 'pseudo-commodity'. This refers to any good whose social value or ecological functions cannot be fully captured by their market price. The fictitious commodities that preoccupied Polanyi were human beings (as wage labourers), money and the biophysical world (as both a source of raw materials and a sink for waste products). The second concept is that of the 'double movement'. Efforts to extend the frontiers of the market, so Polanyi showed, led in Victorian Britain to concerted resistance, as society sought to save itself (and the natural environment) from the excesses of *laissez faire*.

If Polanyi's historical analysis has any predictive value, then we might expect to see three things today. The first is a raft of social and environmental problems attendant upon neoliberalism's exposure of fictitious commodities to the full force of market rationality. The second is the politicisation of these problems by progressive forces determined to reverse the gains that neoliberals have made this last thirty years. The third is the creation by these forces of a new common sense and, indeed, a new socio-environmental reality, as they assume power over the long-term. It seems to me that while the first of these has come to pass, we clearly have some way to go until the second and especially the third eventuate. This suggests either that the parallels between classical liberalism and neoliberalism in Britain today are weak, or that more time and work are required for a present-day double movement to become evident. Despite the manifest differences between Victorian capitalism and early twenty first century neoliberalism, I believe that Polanyi's analysis has contemporary relevance. As I see it, we are at the start of a by no means inevitable shift away from neoliberalism in Britain. As I will now explain, the recent resurgence of environmental concern is a harbinger in this regard. But it will only feed into a wider post-neoliberal left project if a formidable number of challenges and objectives are met.

NEW ENVIRONMENTAL ANXIETIES

The years 2005 and 2006 saw the unexpected rise of environmental issues to the top of political, public and even business agendas. I say unexpected not because these issues were heretofore marginal. What happened in 2005/6 was a sudden spike in environmental concern, one that Polly Toynbee felt might be 'a psychological tipping point'.[4]

Though it's too soon to tell, this spike may well have morphed into a new plateau of concern in British society. Alongside the credit crunch and its ramified effects, the major domestic issues of 2008 have been environment-related ones, such as rising food prices, rising oil (and thus fuel) prices, renewable energy, the possible return of nuclear power, Britain's fudging of its Kyoto commitments, the meaning of sustainable consumption, energy security, and the relative contribution to atmospheric pollution of air, water and terrestrial travel. These and other environmental challenges are not, of course, the result of neoliberal policies alone. More fundamentally, most of them ultimately arise from the dysfunctions of the wider capitalist system, which for the last thirty years has assumed a particular (neoliberal) form but which has existed for over two centuries (on a progressively larger and now truly global scale). This system's signature characteristic is, of course, the relentless commitment to economic growth – one which, to date, has been enormously materials- and energy-intensive. Few in the political mainstream are prepared to name 'capitalism' as the problem however – it sounds too abstract and grand (even for the otherwise cerebral Brown). Only green activists and lobbyists like Porritt – author of *Capitalism as if the world matters* – are willing use the term unapologetically in place of euphemisms and red-herrings like 'industrialism', 'technology', 'consumerism' and 'over-population'.[5] This is a pity, because this term directs our attention to the *systemic* nature of environmental problems. In neoliberal regimes such as Britain's, these problems have intensified because *laissez faire* policies treat the non-human world as a 'normal' commodity, when it is, in fact, a source of material, moral and spiritual values that can never be properly represented by pounds and pence. Nonetheless, people outside the British environmental movement do at least recognise that there is a 'problem' – or rather a family of problems – and that something non-trivial needs to be done to address them. The question is: how do they frame these problems and, thereby, define the field of possible solutions?

FRAMING ENVIRONMENTAL ISSUES

Seasoned environmental campaigners like George Monbiot (agitating as an 'outsider') and Porritt (now operating as an 'insider') may well be encouraged by the recent outpouring of environmental concern, but they know there is a very long way to go – and for good reason. Mainstream politicians, committed to the continuation of neoliberalism, make rhetorically strong claims about the need for action but, in practice, prefer their environmentalism to be 'lite' rather than strong. Business interests variously resist the environmental challenge altogether (witness British Petroleum's sharp move away from its previous 'beyond petroleum' strategy), favour low-octane market-led regulation, or parade their green credentials only as a public relations ploy. Genuine corporate enthusiasm seems only to be displayed by those firms who can see real profits from 'going green' – like wind turbine companies. Meanwhile, the average British citizen is enjoined to spend their hard-earned income in 'ecofriendly' ways, even as they are simultaneously encouraged to holiday abroad, consume ever more imported commodities, and aspire to the lifestyles of the rich-and-famous.

In short, what had become true of British (indeed Western) environmentalism by the 1990s remains true today: it has been mainstreamed. Intellectually, the radical arguments from the 1970s about the need for major change resonate once more, after successive IPCC reports, Stern and all the rest. But in real terms these translate into problem-and-solution framing that is 'technocentrist' and thoroughly neoliberal. A combination of profit-making 'clean technology' and market-disciplined human behaviour will, so our political masters believe, make 'sustainable development' a reality. New Labour, like its political opponents, is most comfortable with 'environmental economics' as the solution to the environmental problems that 'the market' – that is to say, neoliberal capitalism – has created in the first place.

However, things are not all bad. In the first place, there is now a powerful sense in Britain that a range of environmental issues are *real*, not to be dismissed as the fantasies of a few tousle-haired radicals and dope-smoking hippies. Second, there seems – at long last – to be a widespread recognition that 'the environment' is not a 'special interest' issue. The sense that 'the environment' is, in fact, central to *everything* we do (work, leisure, love ...) seems genuinely to have struck home. Thirdly, there is also now a fairly widespread recognition that environmental issues have a certain 'leakiness' in the spatio-temporal sense: they are seen to be about elsewhere and the future, about distant others and our own children.

Fourthly the recent wave of environmental concern in Britain has recognised the social justice and social welfare aspects of the environmental agenda. This is an important development (evident, for example, in consumers' willingness to pay for Fair Trade coffee and tea), because it challenges the stereotype that 'environmentalists' are only interested in nature's welfare not that of people (even though it's true that a smattering of hard-core environmentalists are thoroughly misanthropic).

AGENTS, STRATEGIES AND TACTICS

Environmental issues, I am arguing, have been (re)politicised in Britain in ways at once depressing and encouraging for those who are well to the left of the current mainstream. How, then, to use the environmental agenda as a vehicle for progressive and radical change in Britain? Who will be driving this agenda forward, and to what ends? Let me take these critical questions in reverse order, and in answering them explore what a new British left and a new kind of democracy might look like.

First, who are the likely agents of progressive change in Britain? Though the values and practices of neoliberalism remain hegemonic (even after the considerable and growing financial market turmoil evident since summer 2007), they are not universally admired. There is plenty of discontent out there, and much of it is politically to the left. There is also a desire to be heard and a willingness to take action. Over the last decade, we have seen many inspiring examples of this, from the formation of Compass to direct action campaigns like Camp for Climate Action.

There is, then, still a thing called 'the left' in Britain – despite many commentators suggesting it's gone the way of the dodo. The problem is that it does not recognise itself as a movement with a programme, because it's currently comprised of myriad constituencies with their own agendas – as the chapter on 'Looking for the Left' in this book rightly points out. The 'old' British left – namely, the labour movement – has all but disappeared. Its remnants are disparate. What's now needed is a grand coalition that brings the three main elements of the current non-mainstream British left together: namely, the social, cultural and environmental elements. Rather as it did in the late nineteenth century, the left has to build itself anew. It must be aspirational, confident yet also realistic, trimming its sails to suit the prevailing political weather even as it charts new waters over time.

The 'social left' is still represented, for the most part, by a reconstituted trade union movement, supplemented by a raft of bodies concerned with welfare issues (like Shelter and The Big Issue) and a rag-tag of other groups from the hard left of the 1970s and 1980s. With a membership no longer comprising white males in manufacturing and heavy industry, the unions now represent an increasingly service-based, bi-gender, multi-ethnic, multi-sexual, and immigrant workforce. They still pay great attention to classic labour issues, such as fair pay, workplace rights, and all the rest. But they do so in a way that's increasingly sensitive to their members' diverse needs and wants – think, for instance, of how some unions are trying to reach out to temporary labour migrants. The 'cultural left', by contrast, is far more fragmented institution- ally and ideologically. Never formally linked to Labour or any other political party (except, perhaps, for parts of its feminist arm), its many constituent elements emerged to push forward identity- and issue-specific agendas from the mid-1970s. Think of Stonewall, among many other examples. Finally, the 'environ- mental left' burst into life during the early 1970s and today enjoys a 'thick' institutional presence and fairly large membership cour- tesy of Greenpeace UK, Friends of the Earth UK, and the left elements of the British Green Party (among many other organisa- tions).

How can a whole greater than the sum of the parts emerge from all this? 'With difficulty' is my immediate answer, but let me try to be positive. Despite their (undeserved) reputation as 'single issue' outfits, most left-wing environmental organisations in this country understand fully the human dimensions of the green agenda. For instance, if one looks at its current manifesto, the UK Green Party is less an 'environmental' organisation and more a social justice party which treats environmental issues with the seriousness they deserve. It's strange that so many on the wider left have for so long seen the greens as a community unto them- selves rather than members of an extended political family. That said, if we look at the social left there are also some hopeful signs. While it's true that the trade unions have never had much to say about environmental issues, their newly diverse membership offers far greater potential for them to connect with the agendas of the cultural left than an older white working-class membership ever did. What's more, there is some evidence that union leaders have given up on New Labour after suffering over a decade of arms-length treatment even as their members pour millions into the party's coffers.

Organisationally, five crucial things are required. First, a new political party should be formed without delay. As the fortunes of Galloway's Respect coalition proves, it is very difficult for any new party to break the stranglehold that the big three have on British politics. Even after thirty years, the UK Green Party has not registered significantly in local, national and European elections – and where it has, in terms of votes cast, this has not translated into seats secured. However, the Green Party has a relatively stable membership, considerable campaign experience, and an income stream. Building on this, the many social ecologists within it should disaffiliate and join with willing partners from the social and cultural lefts. Though this risks alienating many party activists and members, very many UK Greens could be persuaded that their fundamental aims are not inconsistent with a wider left project focused on workplace (class), household (reproductive) and cultural (identity) issues – not least because it would make them far more electable. The conceptual glue that could make this project coherent might be the complementary notions of 'livelihoods', 'lifestyles' and 'quality of life', which together cross-cut economic, environmental and cultural issues, and which sound suitably 'twenty-first century'. Secondly, in the absence of public funding for political parties, the new party would need an income stream from some combination of the trade unions (who would disassociate from New Labour) and the larger NGOs. Otherwise it will be too resource-poor to be effective.

Thirdly, it ought to choose a name judiciously, avoiding the apparent narrowness of a term like 'green', and an older language of 'socialism' (with all its baggage). The word 'left' should also not feature in the party's name, even if it drives its politics – too many Brits regard it as a threatening or out-dated term. The New Democratic Party might be a candidate. In the fourth place, the new party would need one leader (not two 'spokespeople' as the Green Party had for a while) and a charismatic, probably youthful one at that. As the election of Boris Johnson to the London mayoralty suggests, image and personality count for a lot (far too much alas). Currently, the non-parliamentary left has no well recognised individuals except perhaps for Galloway and Ken Livingstone, both of whom have controversial pasts. It is a travesty that someone like BNP leader Nick Griffin is better known than virtually anyone within the cultural and green lefts. Finally, the new party would have to ensure that revolutionary, khaki-wearing, militant types remain firmly on the outside, yet without ignoring them altogether. The value of critics sniping from the margins is that it would keep the party honest and encourage out-of-the-box thinking.

So much for organisational matters. What of intellectual ones? Philosophically, such a big tent left would be clearly *against* neoliberalism and transparently *for* a set of strong countervailing values and objectives. It would be for social equality of opportunity for all Britons; for the social regulation of business in the interests of workers, families and the environment; for a fair tax system whose resources sustain expanded, high quality public service provision; for individual and group liberties but always tempered by a concern for the common good, and especially the well-being of society's least fortunate members; for an ethic of shared responsibility and concern about what happens within these shores, even as respect for cultural differences between communities-of-identity is engendered; and it would be for a broad conception of 'the good life' that included but extended well beyond considerations of income and material gain to consider cultural and environmental matters. In sum, it would be for systemic change in British society – envisaged as taking place over a thirty year period. The party, like the broad left it represents, would have to live with capitalism for a long time, but it would certainly have no truck with the excesses of its neoliberal version. It would begin, in practical terms, with small but symbolically important changes and build, through two to three electoral cycles, towards deeper transformations.

USING THE RESOURCES OF OUR IMPERFECT DEMOCRACY

Of course, none of the above would count for anything unless a new British left could make itself popular. A new historic bloc in the Gramscian sense is the only way forward; there is no prospect of garden-variety coups occurring, or militancy succeeding, in Britain. New Labour has made some moves to democratise decision-making since it first came to office (such as the Scottish Parliament and Welsh Assembly), but in other respects remains content with the highly undemocratic system it inherited (with its enormous centralisation of executive power, numerous quangos, and patently unrepresentative voting system). Its current attempts at constitutional reform are hardly radical, and may well amount to nothing in any case. To a considerable extent this shields government from feeling the full force of discontent in the country as a whole, in its left and right versions. A new British left must reckon with the realities of our less-than-perfect democratic system in the here and now. If we ponder the wider failings of our democratic system we can see just how formidable the barriers to be encountered really are. I discuss these barriers in no particular order.

First, notwithstanding the current economic travails, neoliberalism has delivered one definition of 'the goods' to a large number of Britons. In this sense, economics has displaced politics: consumerism and the long-hours culture that underpins it have inured many people to the fact that working and spending are politics by other means. So long as they can afford to drink coffee at Starbucks or take their children to Pizza Express people appear happy enough to accept the status quo. Any successor project to British neoliberalism would have to tread carefully around economic issues, and it would certainly have to persuade voters that national 'growth' can be sustained albeit in a far less materials-intensive way – entailing a redefinition of what counts as a desirable 'lifestyle'.

Second, and relatedly, the neoliberal ethic of individualism has penetrated deep into the British psyche. Most Brits have a very thin or non-existent sense of belonging and solidarity with others. This is the difficult background against which any new left project to de-neoliberalise Britain would somehow have to unfold. As a nation, we lack the ethnic homogeneity and 'thick' social commitments of, say, the Scandinavian democracies and this poses a governance problem for future administrations intent on making social justice and environmental stewardship a key part of their platform. In Polanyi's terms, we have become a 'market society' fitted to a market economy.

Third, there has been a long-run loss of faith in the formal political process. This is not just because of the centralisation of power already mentioned. It is also because of serial scandals and mishaps in Westminster, such as the David Kelly affair, the BAE systems bribery cover-up and the misuse by some MPs of their allowances. Where once politicians were deemed to be responsible and honourable they are now generally regarded as sleazy. Given this, a new British left party would have to claim the moral high ground and occupy it through example, patiently dispelling public disbelief in the good intentions of elected representatives. Any leader of such a party would need a squeakily 'clean' record.

A fourth barrier to progressive change is the world of info- and entertainment. When not working, studying and socialising, the average Briton spends virtually no time considering political issues and an awful lot of time playing computer games, going to the cinema, watching DVDs or viewing reality-TV shows. Relatedly, serious news reporting only appeals to a small minority of the population if the audience figures for BBC News 24 are anything to go by, or the circulation figures for broadsheets versus tabloids are any indication. As with most contemporary capitalist states, the British news media do not innocently 'report' what happens in the 'first estate' – that is, the realm of party and parliamentary politics. To a large extent, they *occupy* this estate themselves, circumscribing public knowledge of politics at the level of facts, concepts and norms.

Fifth, all this has helped to weaken the British public sphere. True, there remains a highly literate and morally vexed fraction of the national population that takes politics very seriously. This fraction is divided between activists working for various political parties, NGOs, think-tanks, etc, and those ordinary citizens who simply understand that politics cannot be left to the politicians alone. But the sort of weekly agora that is BBC's *Question Time* is now the exception that proves the rule. A few hundred thousand politically literate citizens will not be enough to bring a new left party to power. What is needed is a way of reaching not only the general electorate but, more particularly, that minority of voters in particular constituencies that can tip the results of any national ballot. Finally, the first-past-the-post electoral system will continue to work in favour of the big two political parties, however low the votes for them are. This is why it is so critical for a new red-green left to make itself popular: proportional representation is simply not on the agenda in the near future.

CONCLUSION

Current environmental concern in the population at large, and the broad left agenda of many card-carrying greens, together hold out considerable potential for both unifying and rendering popular a new British left. But I have insisted that for this potential to be realised there are serious intellectual, logistical and practical challenges to be faced. The easiest thing would be for a currently divided left to continue with business-as-usual. The more difficult – but wholly necessary – thing would be to go boldly where the British left hasn't gone for decades and start anew, building on what exists but transcending it to create a new project for the country as a whole. The conjunctural conditions suitable for a new British left to emerge may be in the making; but it will require purposeful and bold action to make good on the potential for change that these conditions provide.

REFERENCES

1. Andrew Glyn, *Capitalism Unleashed*, Oxford University Press, Oxford 2006.
2. Jenny Russell, 'This man of hidden shallows is alienating millions of voters', *Guardian*, 16 April 2008, p29.
3. Karl Polanyi, *The Great Transformation*, Beacon Books, Boston 1944.
4. Polly Toynbee, 'Which would Blair prefer – an ID card or a windmill?', *Guardian*, 29 June 2005, p22.
5. Jonathan Porritt, *Capitalism as if the World Matters*, Earthscan, London 2004.

12. Looking for the left

David Purdy

What do we mean by left and right? Is the distinction between them outmoded? Does the British left still exist? My answer to these questions is in three parts. The first reviews the way the words left and right have been used in European politics since 1789. The second provides a short history of the British left since 1918, focusing on the problems posed for the whole of the left, inside and outside the Labour Party, by Britain's centralised, two-party state – a system that is now dissolving. The third offers a rough guide to what the left stands for today and outlines a modest proposal for raising its profile and causing a stir.

LEFT AND RIGHT: THE FIRST TWO HUNDRED YEARS

The habit of dividing political space into left and right originated during the French Revolution. It is a useful habit, serving to describe or evaluate the two sides in a conflict and to mark shifts in the balance of forces. Left and right are, of course, antithetical terms: one cannot be on both sides at the same time and to commend one is to condemn the other. Yet the difference between them is relative, not absolute: ideas, programmes and parties may be left-wing at one time and right-wing at another. Until the mid-nineteenth century, for example, the European left was primarily concerned with civil freedom, political reform and national liberation. But as liberal demands were achieved without disturbing the prevailing class structure, the mantle of the left passed to socialists and anarchists, hitherto minority sects, who argued that the ideals of 1789 could not be realised within the framework of bourgeois democracy, but would require radical changes in the ownership of property, the organisation of the economy and the distribution of life-chances. Thus, the entire political spectrum shifted to the left. A distinct right and centre continued to exist, but they were now defined by virtue of their opposition to the socialist movement, which rapidly outstripped its anarchist siblings and henceforth formed the core of the left, notwithstanding the later schism between Soviet communism and social democracy.

Political discourse employs temporal as well as spatial metaphors: radical versus conservative, innovative versus traditional, progressive versus reactionary, and so on. Until the 1970s these contrasting pairs were aligned with the left-right axis: the left stood for radical transformation, the reduction of social inequality and progress towards a better world; the right for tradition, order, hierarchy and scepticism about ambitious schemes for social improvement; the centre stood somewhere between these poles and since it claimed to be neither left nor right, its whole *raison d'être* depended on the underlying antithesis.

The rise of neoliberalism changed all that. From the 1970s onwards it was the free-market right that emerged as the radical, dynamic and forward-looking force, particularly in Britain and the US, forcing the left into a conservative, defensive and backward-looking posture. This historic reversal of roles ushered in a period of defeat for the left, which the collapse of communism only intensified, and from which it has not yet recovered. Indeed, it is a commonplace of contemporary commentary that the division between left and right is more or less irrelevant to today's world.

Yet, as Norberto Bobbio argues, the left-right distinction survives, not just in everyday speech, but at a deeper philosophical level.[1] What continues to divide left from right are their respective attitudes towards the origins and consequences of human inequalities and the possibility of overcoming them. Roughly speaking, the left believes that although some inequalities result from natural conditions, most are the product of social arrangements; that the consequences of inequalities, not only for those at the sharp end, but for society as a whole, are mainly harmful; and that while the scope for reducing inequalities is constrained by the need to avoid compromising other values such as liberty and democracy, in general the pursuit of equality is both highly desirable and far more feasible than its opponents allow. On each of these counts, the right takes the opposite view: that inequalities are largely natural, the consequences broadly beneficial, and attempts to overcome them either futile or pernicious.

Besides the horizontal division between left and right, political space also contains a vertical dimension, along which parties and movements can be placed according to their commitment to personal liberty and democratic norms. The resulting cross yields four basic categories: liberal-democratic left and right, and authoritarian left and right. At the authoritarian end of the vertical axis, on either side of the left-right divide, stand communism and fascism. At the liberal-democratic end, ranging from left to right, are social democracy, liberalism and conservatism. The course of political conflict in Europe from the First World War to the collapse of communism falls into three broad phases marked by successive realignments of these formations.

In the aftermath of the Russian revolution, liberals and conservatives were more or less united in seeking to repel the perceived threat of Bolshevism, while social democrats were divided between those who supported the new Soviet republic and were prepared to work with the communists and those who saw them as enemies. In Italy, where the post-war crisis was particularly severe, conservatives threw in their lot with the fascists in a pre-emptive strike against the left, anticipating a realignment that became more general in the 1930s. After the Nazis came to power in Germany, communists made common cause with social democrats and liberals in order to combat the growing threat to democracy itself. This pattern of conflict persisted throughout the Second World War and its immediate aftermath, and only came to an end with the onset of the Cold War. Then, a third phase began in which social democrats, liberals and conservatives united in opposition to communism, while continuing to compete with each other for influence, votes and power.

In Italy and France, where the communists were strong, they were systematically excluded from government. In Eastern Europe, generally weak communist parties came to power on the back of the Red Army and proceeded to eliminate the opposition. Elsewhere in Europe communism remained politically marginal. In an attempt to break out of their ghetto, western communist parties sought to distance themselves from the Soviet Union and to develop 'national-democratic' roads to socialism. By the 1970s, broad left coalitions in which 'Eurocommunist' parties played a prominent role stood on the brink of power in Italy, France and post-Franco Spain.

Meanwhile, a new right was emerging in the Anglo-Saxon states. Unlike the fascist movements of the inter-war years, the radical right proclaimed its commitment to liberty, free markets and democracy, while repudiating the post-war settlement, which its conservative forebears had endorsed and, indeed, helped to shape. The collapse of communism gave added impetus to the market revolution and initiated a general realignment, which has not yet run its course. Communist parties have disbanded, declined or reinvented themselves as technocratic parties of the centre, while ex-fascist parties now pay lip service to democracy and have repositioned themselves on the nationalist or xeno-phobic right. Thus, the authoritarian side of political space currently stands vacant. At the same time, the triumph of neolib-eralism has pulled the entire political spectrum to the right, dragging erstwhile social democrats and liberals with it and leaving a desert on the left populated only by small bands of 'anti-capitalists', green activists and ageing reds, while the mainstream parties cluster around a narrow range of positions in the centre. Thus, although the ethical and philosophical issues that divide left and right have lost none of their significance, the political arena has contracted, creating an unhealthy gulf between the political class and the general public and weakening the culture of democ-racy.

THE LEFT IN BRITAIN AND THE PROBLEM OF THE LABOUR PARTY

In continental Europe, the great convulsions of the twentieth century – the Russian Revolution, the struggle against fascism and the collapse of communism – marked the landscape of the left with living reminders that neither states nor parties are immutable. In Britain, a single party has dominated the left, from 1918 when the Labour Party became a membership organisation to the days of Blair and Brown. This near monopoly resulted from the political upheavals that followed the First World War. Once established, however, it proved impossible to break, owing to the handicap faced by minor parties under first-past-the-post voting. Formed decades after its European counterparts, Labour won only 6.4 per cent of the votes cast at the general election of December 1910. In December 1923, its share leapt to 30.7 per cent, just ahead of the Liberals, who were damaged by the feud between Lloyd George and Asquith. When Liberal MPs decided not to support the Conservatives, who were the largest single party, Labour formed a minority government and promptly lost its earlier interest in electoral reform. Too late, the Liberals, who had hitherto been equivocal, realised that their only hope of parliamentary survival lay in the adoption of some form of proportional representation. Thus, Labour ousted the Liberals as the main opposition to the Conservatives, without disturbing the pattern of two-party politics. Labour also displaced the Liberals as national-popular champion in Scotland and Wales, ensuring that after the Irish settlement in 1922 secessionist versions of nationalism played no part in mainland British politics until the late 1960s.[2]

Labour was never a socialist party in the classic mould of the Second International, even though its 1918 constitution enshrined the famous Clause 4. It inherited the non-conformist conscience from the Liberals, and its leaders owed more to the Webbs than to Kautsky or Bernstein. There was, nevertheless, a strong socialist current among the party's membership, which normally stood to the left of the leadership. For decades, the annual party conference was a battleground, as policies supported by the majority of constituency delegates were regularly defeated by trade union block-votes. Yet despite these repeated collisions, the Labour Party managed to avoid damaging internal splits. The breakaway of the ILP in 1931 and the defection of the SDP in 1981 were the only serious schisms, and neither broke the two-party system, though by fighting the 1983 election in alliance with the Liberals, the SDP came close, winning 25.4 per cent of the votes cast compared with Labour's 27.6 per cent – the only time since 1923 that Labour had fallen below thirty per cent.

Labour's relative immunity to splits was largely due to the electoral system. Under first-past-the-post, breakaway parties whose voters are thinly spread throughout the country stand little chance of winning seats in a general election, however many protest votes they pick up at by-elections. Moreover, even during the dark days of the 'National Government' formed after Labour's ignominious ejection from office in 1931 and dominated by the Tories, Labour retained important bastions in local government and thus kept its finger-tips on state power. These facts of political life, brutally encapsulated in Aneurin Bevan's jibe that the ILP was 'pure, but impotent', were reinforced by class sentiment. In the eyes of many trade unionists, splits in the party of labour were akin to breakaway unions, acts of betrayal that served the class enemy.

Thus, the Labour Party exhibited a curious stand-off: a largely left-wing membership with nowhere else to go confronted a right-wing leadership which relied on trade union block-votes to avoid conference embarrassments, but needed constituency activists to fight elections. The limits of left-right cohabitation were clearly exposed in the impassioned confrontations of the Gaitskell era. After his attempt to remove Clause 4 from the party's constitution was foiled by the left, Gaitskell campaigned against the 1960 conference decision to support unilateral nuclear disarmament, overturning it the following year by getting a couple of unions to change sides.

In a bid to break out of this impasse and broaden its campaign for a socialist alternative to the policies of the Wilson government, the May Day Manifesto group sought to build a new left formation that was less attached to traditional party politics, but after some initial success the movement fell apart in the run-up to the 1970 election. During the 1970s, the left inside the Labour Party set out to take it over: the Trotskyist *Militant* tendency by attempting to build a party within a party, the Campaign for Labour Democracy by means of open networking and dogged committee work. The Communist Party (CP), the main organisation of the left outside the Labour Party, effectively abandoned electoral pretensions in favour of developing broad left alliances in the unions and in student politics.

By the end of the mutinous 1970s, having gained control of both the party conference and the National Executive Committee (NEC), the Labour left proceeded to change the rules of the game. Party members gained a say in the election of the leader and deputy leader, constituency parties gained the power to deselect sitting MPs, and the NEC was charged with ensuring that the party's election manifesto reflected conference policies. Incensed by these reforms, particularly constituency re-selection, twenty-seven MPs on the right of the party resigned the Labour whip and in January 1981 followed the 'Limehouse Four' into the SDP. The chief beneficiaries were the Conservatives. Buoyed by military victory in the Falklands and facing a divided opposition at home, Mrs Thatcher was returned to power at the General Election of 1983 with an overall majority of 144, despite receiving only 42.4 per cent of the votes on a turnout of seventy three per cent.

At this point the British left fell apart. There had been no great dissension on the left in the 1970s. A dissident minority within the CP opposed the strategy of 'militant labourism' – fomenting strikes, especially over wages, and pushing Labour policy to the left via the unions – but was largely ignored. After 1983, however, the left descended into open civil war, while the right sought to regain control over the party machine and restore relations with the unions. Two issues divided the left: Arthur Scargill's suicidal attempt to take on the Thatcher government, and the government's assault on the powers of local authorities. The NUM debacle blew away what remained of the trade union broad left, as even Communist activists demurred at Scargill's tactics. And the introduction of rate-capping and the abolition of the Greater London Council, along with the other metropolitan councils, as part of a general drive to impose monetary and fiscal discipline, raised basic democratic questions about the independence of local government. Councils throughout the country were affected, but the front line was in Liverpool, where the *Militant*-controlled council seemed determined not to set a balanced budget. In the event, *Militant* and the Labour leadership spent more time squaring up to each other than attacking the government, squandering the chance to rally resistance to the neoliberal revolution at a time when public attitudes to it were still malleable.

The main reason for the left's failure to oppose Thatcher more effectively was that it had no hegemonic project of its own. Indeed, it had no political strategy at all beyond the pursuit of 'militant labourism', at root a syndicalist conception of politics, which had already been discredited in the 1970s, when inflation accelerated, tension mounted and profits plunged. Two further, subsidiary factors contributed to the left's decline: the collapse of the CP as rival factions battled for control; and the efforts of the Labour right to 'reclaim the party', a tortuous and clandestine process recently documented by Diane Hayter.[3]

Once Neil Kinnock had embarked on a purge of the *Militant* group, it proved relatively easy to roll back the 1979 reforms, laying the groundwork for the tightly disciplined and centralised party of the New Labour era. Historical amnesia is a besetting weakness of the soft left. Until things fell apart under Gordon Brown, those who had at first supported Blair, but later became disillusioned, drew a sharp distinction between the 'modernising' years from 1983 to the death of John Smith, and the 'Blairite' years from 1994 to the accession of Gordon Brown. In fact, all the elements of the centralised control that became New Labour's stock in trade were put in place during the Kinnock years. The neutering of the party conference and its conversion into a stage-managed spectacle may have gone farther under Blair and Brown than Kinnock intended or foresaw, but the stifling of debate and the cult of the leader began on his watch. Take, for instance, the quiet abandonment of any commitment to social partnership for fear of stirring up memories of the 1970s, or the hubris of the Sheffield election rally three days before the 'shock' defeat of 1992.

Superficially, the Labour Party today resembles that of the mid-1960s: an oligarchic leadership is pursuing policies opposed by most of the membership, while keeping a firm grip on the party machine. But this is misleading. For one thing, Labour Party membership is down to 177,000 and falling, compared with 450,000 in 1997 and 830,000 in 1964. More importantly, the whole political context has been transformed: by the weakness of British trade unions, by the eclipse of the socialist tradition, and by the hollowing out of the British state.

Trade unions used to be central to the politics of the left: as agencies for politicising the working class and as adjuncts of the Labour Party. These two roles were usually at odds because, except for the period from 1965 to 1979, union leaders tended to side with the Labour right. But socialists nursed the hope that one day radicalised union members would elect new leaders and shift Labour to the left. No such prospect beckons today. Union membership fell from 55 per cent of the workforce at its peak in 1979 to 26 per cent in 2006, and while the unions can still play a progressive political role – for instance, in mobilising against the BNP – they now focus on servicing their members, not politicising them. There is no role conflict any more because one of the roles has disappeared. All that remains of the historic partnership between unions and party is the unlovely exchange of union funding and votes for sectional concessions on policy.

The ebbing of the socialist tide is subtler in its consequences, yet even more debilitating. Forty years ago, the left could challenge the party leadership and at least hold its own, because socialism was still a potent moral and intellectual force. Today, it holds little attraction for party activists, whether as an ethical ideal or as a model of economic organisation, and no longer has any pull, even of a residual kind, on the Labour leadership, who are thus entirely free to pursue their own designs. Yet what remains of the Labour left seems oblivious to this fact. For them, the problem is still one of recovering lost members and restoring the party to its historic purpose.

The foundations of the old religion have crumbled. In the mid-1960s, Britain was still a centralised, two-party state. To be sure, the Conservatives were the 'natural party of government', but Labour was the only viable alternative and the left could see itself as a government-in-waiting. At the time of writing (July 2008), Labour appears to face a choice between losing the next general election and losing it badly. In Scotland, Labour has allowed the SNP to champion the cause of enhanced devolution, while soft-pedalling 'independence', and to steal the mantle of social democracy, while courting the business classes. When the Scottish Conservatives flouted mainstream Scottish opinion in the 1980s, they lost all their Westminster seats and now vie with the Lib-Dems for third place in the Scottish parliament. The combination of a Cameron government at Westminster and an SNP government at Holyrood could spell the 'strange death of Labour England', especially if electoral meltdown provokes internal party strife.

Short of a Labour collapse, we could see minority or small majority governments like those elected in 1964 and 1974, but with the two main parties each receiving around thirty five per cent of the votes on a turnout of sixty per cent. Inter-party negotiation might then lead to the introduction of some form of PR for Westminster elections along the lines already operating in

Scotland and Wales. This in turn might produce coalition governments in which the 'left' stretches across several of the governing parties. Alternatively, the Labour or Conservative parties might win a working majority with the support of only twenty per cent of the electorate thanks to the quirks of first-past-the-post. Such a manifest failure of the political system could only deepen the current crisis of legitimacy, especially when parties that are little more than professional cliques with media access swing wildly to snatch at power.

One thing is clear, however: for the left, the 'problem' of the Labour Party is the diametrical opposite of what it was forty years ago. The issue then was how to shift Labour to the left. Now it is how to get out from under the party and how to create a coherent and effective political force out of what remains of the left.

OUT OF THE WILDERNESS

Who are the left today and where do they live? On the broadest definition, the left includes everyone who opposes neoliberalism and shares, in some measure, the following beliefs:

- That, in general, economic and social problems are best dealt with by collective rather than individual action;
- That public services should be provided free of charge and shielded from market forces;
- That education, health care, social security, personal social services and some aspects of housing should all be provided as public services;
- That public utilities, commercial banks and major financial institutions should be 'close to the state', routinely monitored, regulated and held to public account;
- That in many areas of economic activity, some form of social ownership – such as co-operative or community enterprise, mutual trusts and stakeholder democracy – is preferable to either nationalisation or private ownership;
- That democracy should not be limited to periodic elections to decide which party or coalition forms the government, but should extend in some practical form to all areas of collective policy- and decision-making – including, notably, the management of business firms and public agencies;

- That egalitarian societies are healthier, happier, friendlier and more cohesive than unequal societies;
- That patient but persistent efforts are required throughout society to overcome divisions of class, gender and race and to take good care of the environment.

This list leaves plenty of room for interpretation and argument of the kind in which the left has traditionally excelled, and could be broadened to international issues. But the general outlook it serves to identify clearly extends well beyond the old socialist left. It is perfectly possible to oppose neoliberalism without rejecting capitalism, to long for an alternative to capitalism without being sure that there is one, or, indeed, to want a better world while refusing to recognise any neat dichotomy between overarching economic systems.

Where is this wider left to be found? Five main groups can be distinguished: the remnants of the Labour left, including some MPs and councillors; left fractions within other political parties, including the Greens, SNP, Plaid Cymru and, yes, the Liberal-Democrats;[4] members of small socialist groups which derive from the Communist and Trotskyist traditions; ex-members of left parties who have become detached from active politics, but retain their old ideals; and people who are active in various non-party movements and causes and regard political parties with scepticism or downright hostility. Just how many individuals could be counted under these headings no one knows. A guess might be around a quarter of a million, with the majority in the last two categories. But for the moment numbers are irrelevant. The first task is to create a network among these disparate groups, so that they can acknowledge each other and engage in debate about political strategy without denigrating the histories that have led to their current location, but with the aim of making some discernible impact on British politics.

This is not a new project. It was tried forty years ago by the May Day Manifesto group and broached again thirty years ago by Sheila Rowbotham, Lynne Segal and Hilary Wainwright, while in the 1990s attempts were made to build a red-green alliance.[5] Why should any new endeavour succeed where these initiatives failed?

The negative answer is that there is really no alternative. If the old left had no hegemonic project, New Labour's project is not of the left, and the non-Labour left is lost in the wilderness. The positive answer is that the structures of British politics are dissolving before our eyes, presenting a once-in-a-generation chance for realignment. There is already a gaping hole where the democratic green left ought to be. If Labour collapses, the hole will resemble an earthquake zone. But even if Labour survives, the programme of a left coalition could still affect the shape of things to come. If some form of PR were adopted in Westminster elections, organised tactical voting based on simple tests of left credentials could help to break down and redraw party boundaries.

How then should the left approach the next general election, probably in 2010? Many people voted against Labour in 2005 on an anti-war basis and some of these will remain outside the Labour fold. Others will return on the age-old grounds of keeping the Tories out. Others will never have deserted Labour, suppressing the smell with the help of a clothes peg. Still others will have formed new allegiances. There is no possibility of finessing these differing judgments into some common voting pattern. But there is a chance of getting people to recognise the electoral dilemma and to work through a common approach constituency by constituency. This is in itself would be major step towards reconciling differences and finding a way out of the wilderness.

I am grateful to Mike Prior for his help with this chapter.

REFERENCES

1. N. Bobbio, *Left and Right: the Significance of a Political Distinction*, Polity Press, Cambridge 1996.
2. British political parties did not, of course, organise in Northern Ireland, which lies outside the scope of this chapter.
3. D. Hayter, *Fightback! Labour's Traditional Right in the 1970s and 1980s*, Manchester University Press, Manchester 2005.
4. In a poll of public attitudes towards key social, political and economic issues, commissioned by *The Economist* (29 March 2008), Liberal Democrats stood to the left of Labour supporters on every broad category except the role of the state.
5. Raymond Williams (ed.), *The May Day Manifesto*, Penguin,

Harmondsworth 1968; Sheila Rowbotham, Lynne Segal and Hilary Wainwright, *Beyond the Fragments: Feminism and the Making of Socialism*, Merlin, London 1979; Red-Green Study Group, *What on Earth is to be Done?*, Cromwell Press, Melksham, Wiltshire 1995.

Notes on Contributors

Patrick Ainley
Patrick Ainley is Professor of Training and Education in the School of Education and Training at the University of Greenwich. Recent publications include: *Twenty Years of Schooling: Student Reflections on Their Educational Journeys* (editor) (Society for Research into Higher Education, 2008); and, with Martin Allen, *A New 14+: Vocational Diplomas and the Future of Schools, Colleges and Universities* (Ealing NUT and Greenwich University UCU, 2008) and *Education Make You Fick, Innit? What Has Gone Wrong in England's Schools, Colleges and Universities and How to Start Putting It Right* (Tufnell Press, London 2007).

Martin Allen
Dr Martin Allen is a part-time teacher in a school sixth form in west London. He has written extensively on 14-19 education, which was the subject of his PhD, and has been active in the National Union of Teachers for 25 years. He is joint author, with Patrick Ainley, of *Education Make You Fick, Innit? What Has Gone Wrong in England's Schools, Colleges and Universities and How to Start Putting It Right* (Tufnell Press, London 2007) and *A New 14+: Vocational Diplomas and the Future of Schools, Colleges and Universities* (Ealing NUT and Greenwich University UCU, 2008), an educational and campaigning pamphlet.

David Beetham
David Beetham is Professor Emeritus, University of Leeds; a Fellow of the Human Rights Centre, University of Essex; and Associate Director of Democratic Audit. Recent publications

include: *Democracy under Blair* (joint author) (Politico's, London 2002); *Democracy, a Beginner's Guide* (Oneworld Publications, Oxford 2005); *Parliament and Democracy in the Twenty-First Century: a Guide to Good Practice* (Inter-Parliamentary Union, Geneva 2006); and *Assessing the Quality of Democracy: a Practical Guide* (joint author) (International IDEA, Stockholm 2008).

Noel Castree

Noel Castree is a Professor in the School of Environment and Development at Manchester University. He is editor of *Antipode: A Journal of Radical Geography*. His principal research interest is in the relationships between capitalism and the biophysical world, using the theoretical resources of Marxian political economy. He is the author of *Nature* (Routledge, London and New York 2005) and co-author of *Spaces of Work: Capitalism and the Geographies of Labour* (Sage, London 2003).

Pat Devine

Pat Devine is an Honorary Research Fellow at the University of Manchester. He is the author of *Democracy and Economic Planning* (Polity Press, Cambridge 1988), joint author of *What On Earth Is To Be Done?* (Red Green Study Group, 1995), and joint editor of *Reciprocity, Distribution and Exchange* (Black Rose Books, Montreal 2001). Recent articles include, 'The 1970s and After', *Soundings* (2006), and 'The Continuing Relevance of Marxism', in S. Moog and R. Stones (eds), *Nature, Social Relations and Human Needs: Essays in Honour of Ted Benton* (Palgrave Macmillan, Basingstoke 2009). He is a founding member of the Red Green Study Group.

Angela McRobbie

Angela McRobbie is Professor of Communication at Goldsmiths, University of London. Her earliest writing on young women, sexuality, and girls' magazines, was while still a student at Birmingham University's Centre for Contemporary Cultural Studies. She is the author of many books and articles on the UK fashion industry, the new cultural economy, and on feminist theory. Her most recent book is *The Aftermath of Feminism: Gender, Culture and Social* Change (Sage, London 2008). She is also a contributor to the *Guardian*, Open Democracy, and various Radio 4 programmes.

Linda Patterson

Dr Linda Patterson OBE is an experienced consultant physician who has worked in the NHS for over thirty years. Her consultant clinical practice has been in East Lancashire, where she is currently developing an innovative post bringing primary and secondary care closer together. She has extensive management and policy experience and was the Medical Director of the Commission for Health Improvement, the first statutory regulator of the NHS in England and Wales.

Andrew Pearmain

Andrew Pearmain is an associate tutor in History at the University of East Anglia, and a manager/consultant in the social care of people with HIV/AIDS. He lives in Norwich, and works in Essex and London.

Michael Prior

Michael Prior is an economic consultant specialising in international energy and environment issues. He has been a member of the Communist and Labour parties and is now settled in the Green Party until he finds something to resign over.

David Purdy

David Purdy is a social economist and former Head (now retired) of the Department of Applied Social Science at the University of Manchester. Politically active since the early 1960s, he is a member of Democratic Left Scotland. Recent publications include: *Eurovision or American Dream? Britain, the Euro and the Future of Europe* (Luath Press, Edinburgh 2003); and 'Is Basic Income Viable?', *Basic Income Studies* (Berkeley Electronic Press, December 2007).

Kate Soper

Kate Soper is Emeritus Professor of Philosophy in the Institute for the Study of European Transformations at London Metropolitan University. She is best known for her writing on the philosophy of nature and as a theorist of need and consumption.

She has recently published *Citizenship and Consumption* (edited with Frank Trentmann) (Palgrave, London 2007) and *The Politics and Pleasures of Consuming Differently* (edited with Lyn Thomas and Martin Ryle) (Palgrave, London 2008).